The Collected Works of

William Howard Taft

David H. Burton, *General Editor*

VOLUME VII

TAFT PAPERS ON LEAGUE OF NATIONS

Edited with Commentary by

Frank X. Gerrity

OHIO UNIVERSITY PRESS

ATHENS

Ohio University Press, Athens, Ohio 45701
© 2003 by Ohio University Press
Printed in the United States of America
All rights reserved

Ohio University Press books are printed on acid-free paper ⊗ ™

12 11 10 09 08 07 06 05 04 03   5 4 3 2 1

Taft Papers on League of Nations, edited by Theodore Marburg and Horace E. Flack, copyright 1920
by The Macmillan Company.

Publication of *The Collected Works of William Howard Taft* has been made possible in part through the
generous support of the Earhart Foundation of Ann Arbor, Michigan, and the Louisa Taft Semple
Foundation of Cincinnati, Ohio.

Photograph of William Howard Taft courtesy of William Howard Taft National Historic Site.

Library of Congress Cataloging-in-Publication Data
(Revised for volume 7)

Taft, William H. (William Howard), 1857–1930.
Taft papers on League of Nations / edited with commentary by
Frank X. Gerrity.—1st ed.
p. cm.—(The collected works of William Howard Taft; v. 7)
Previously published: New York: Macmillan, 1920.
ISBN 0-8214-1518-2 (cloth : alk. paper)
1. League to Enforce Peace (U.S.) 2. League of Nations. 3.
Peace. 1. Gerrity, Frank X., 1923–2001. II. Title. III. Series:
Taft, William H. (William Howard), 1857–1930. Works. 2001; v. 7.
E660 .T11 2001 vol. 7
[KZ4871]
352.23'8'097309041 s—dc22
[341.22]   2003017871

Dedicated to
the Taft family,
for five generations serving
Ohio and the nation

The Collected Works of
William Howard Taft

David H. Burton, General Editor

VOLUME ONE
Four Aspects of Civic Duty and *Present Day Problems*
Edited with commentary by David H. Burton and A. E. Campbell

VOLUME TWO
Political Issues and Outlooks
Edited with commentary by David H. Burton

VOLUME THREE
Presidential Addresses and State Papers
Edited with commentary by David H. Burton

VOLUME FOUR
Presidential Messages to Congress
Edited with commentary by David H. Burton

VOLUME FIVE
Popular Government and *The Anti-trust Act and the Supreme Court*
Edited with commentary by David Potash and Donald F. Anderson

VOLUME SIX
The President and His Powers and *The United States and Peace*
Edited with commentary by W. Carey McWilliams and Frank X. Gerrity

VOLUME SEVEN
Taft Papers on League of Nations
Edited with commentary by Frank X. Gerrity

VOLUME EIGHT
"Liberty under Law" and Selected Supreme Court Opinions
Edited with commentary by Francis Graham Lee
Cumulative Index

Contents

Contents

Taft Papers on League of Nations

Commentary

Frank X. Gerrity

Taft Papers on League of Nations (1920), a 340-page compendium of speeches, newspaper articles (mostly from the *Philadelphia Public Ledger*), and complementary documents edited by Theodore Marburg and Horace E. Flack, reflects Taft's consistent support, first for a league of nations as projected by the League to Enforce the Peace and subsequently for the Covenant of the League of Nations emanating from the Paris Peace Conference of 1919.

President Wilson's effort to convert the congressional election of 1918 into a vote of confidence on his foreign policy politicized the issue of peacemaking, breaching, so his critics alleged, the principle underlying the popular slogan "Politics adjourned!" While Taft had no great personal liking for Wilson, found him difficult to deal with, disagreed with him on issues of substance such as the self-determination of nations, and found the Wilsonian version of a league of nations far inferior to the model proposed by the League to Enforce the Peace, he did not join in the massive Republican assault on the Treaty of Versailles. He approved Wilson's controversial decision to travel to Paris as head of the American peace delegation, but was openly critical of the composition of the group, especially its lack of any member whose record indicated a strong commitment to an effective league of nations. But Taft was also sharply critical of the "irreconcilables" and the "strong reservationists" in his own party. He jousted with his old Republican colleagues Elihu Root, Philander C. Knox, and Henry Cabot Lodge, rebutting their criticisms of the Covenant's tenth article as a surrender of American sovereignty. He counseled Wilson to insert into the treaty a reservation with respect to the Monroe Doctrine and thus win the support of the bulk of the "reservationists," a group whose votes were essential to Senate approval of the treaty. Even though Wilson ignored his advice, Taft was still willing to tour the country, urging support of the League Covenant. All things considered, this born-and-bred Republican played a remarkably nonpartisan role in the fight for the treaty in America. There is no reason to challenge his statement that "had I been a senator I would have voted for the League Covenant just as submitted and also for it with reservations." The obdurate Wilson and the wily Lodge must share responsibility for the failure of the treaty and its League of Nations, but William Howard Taft can be credited with rising above partisanship and petty personal bickering to emerge as the League's most consistent supporter. Even his endorsement of Warren G. Harding in the presidential election of 1920, misguided as it may have been, was directed toward gaining approval for the treaty and the League.

Foreword to the Original Edition

These addresses, articles and editorials were written when the issue was purely on the merits of the League to Enforce Peace plan for a League of Nations, and of the Covenant of the League of Nations as signed by President Wilson in Paris and by him submitted to the Senate. I have nothing to recall in what is said in them. But the present issue over the League is very different from that when these papers were written, and is made so by the very unfortunate attitude of President Wilson in refusing to allow the United States to join the League of Nations because the Senate would not consent to Article X as he had drafted it and put it into the Covenant.

It is conceded that the other members of the League would have accepted us as a member with the modification of Article X insisted on by a sufficient number of senators to prevent ratification. The Democratic party and its platform adopt completely Mr. Wilson's position and, if Governor Cox is elected, the League will be defeated and a deadlock ensue just as before.

Two-thirds of the Republican senators have already voted for the League with reservations and enough Democrats have expressed themselves in the Senate and elsewhere on this matter to ensure a ratification of the League with the Republican reservations if Mr. Harding is elected and submits the German Treaty to the Senate. The doubt on this point is whether Mr. Harding will do so, arising from his failure to say, in his letter of acceptance, that he will do so. My own belief is that, as Mr. Harding has already twice voted for the League with reservations, and will find that a Democratic minority will prevent his putting through a separate treaty with Germany, he will conclude that the only satisfactory solution is a ratification of the League Covenant with reservations.

For these reasons—though had I been a senator I would have voted for the League Covenant just as submitted and also for it with the reservations—I shall vote for Mr. Harding.

William Howard Taft
Pointe au Pic
Province of Quebec, Canada
July 23, 1920

Introduction

Here in the United States the main attack on both the preliminary project and the perfected Covenant of the League of Nations was on the ground that the League would operate as an interference with our sovereignty and with the Monroe Doctrine, that it involved abandonment of our traditional policy against entangling alliances, and that the country lacked the power, under its Constitution, to enter into such a treaty. These objections are fully met by Mr. Taft in the speeches and articles embraced in this volume. Sovereignty is shown to be just so much liberty of action on the part of States as is consistent with their obligation, under international law and morality, to permit of the exercise of equal sovereignty or liberty of action by their sister States. The League Covenant secures all States in their exercise of this sovereignty free from oppression by other States, and he who wants more is really seeking the license selfishly to disregard these obligations—to reject, for example, the just judgments of a properly constituted tribunal—which is the German conception of sovereignty.

The Monroe Doctrine is shown to be strengthened, not impaired, by the Covenant. In its original form the doctrine opposed future colonization on the American continents by European governments and all interference by Europe with the free governments of America. Later on, the United States, under the Polk and under the Taft administrations, voiced its opposition to the transfer of American territory by sale to any European or Asiatic government. The original doctrine is strengthened by the League Covenant in that it is, for the first time, specifically recognized by the nations, and is extended to the world by the provisions of Article X, which preserves "against external aggression the territorial integrity and political independence of all members of the League." Certainly we are not authorized by that, nor, in fact, by any other article of the Covenant, to acquire territory in Europe by conquest or purchase, and similarly European countries are not authorized by the Covenant to do it in this hemisphere.

The attitude both of Secretary Seward and of President Roosevelt is cited to the effect that the Monroe Doctrine does not forbid non-American Powers from justly disciplining American countries provided the action does not extend to the point of interfering with the latter's independence and territorial integrity. Similarly the guaranties of territorial integrity and political independence under Article X of the Paris Covenant will not come into operation until the character of a war, otherwise legally begun, discloses itself as aggressive in this respect. Neither are wars of independence within the legal purview of the League though it will naturally take notice of them and invite friendly settlement.

The sale of American territory to non-American Powers is not specifically forbidden by the League Covenant; but the motive for such attempted action is lessened by the very existence of the League. When the Monroe Doctrine is to be enforced in the western hemisphere, it is natural to expect that a strong American State, close to the seat of trouble, will be selected to execute the mandate of the League. Similar reason would control the action of the League in employing the forces of a nearby State to quell disturbances in other parts of the world; so that, unless the struggle be formidable or unless an international force be needed to allay fear of abuse of power, the forces of the United States will rarely be called upon to act abroad.

The "entangling alliance" argument is met by a whole series of facts and considerations. The detached position of the United States, which obtained in Washington's day, is shown to have disappeared with the spread of dominion and interests since then. From a country limited to a comparatively narrow settlement along the Atlantic seaboard, the United States has extended its empire over the continent to the Pacific, has acquired Alaska, Hawaii, the Philippines, Puerto Rico, and the Panama Canal strip, while a multiplied commerce and social intercourse tie up her fortunes intimately with the fortunes of other peoples. The life that pulses through her veins today is the life of the world and disease in the body politic elsewhere affects her own health. We have seen that we cannot keep out of a general world conflict and we risk less by assuming the obligations of membership in the family of nations and throwing our great influence in the scale for the preservation of peace than if we were to attempt isolation and play the role of onlooker until the conflagration drew us irresistibly in.

Our presence will make the potential strength of the League so overwhelming that the hand of the would-be aggressor will be stayed, making serious assault on the world's peace unlikely. In most instances the need for the actual use of force will be avoided; just as the declared purpose of the United States to maintain the Monroe Doctrine has resulted in its being respected without our being called upon to fire a shot or sacrifice the life of a single soldier in its defense. Accordingly there will be less likelihood of our being called upon to go to war than if we declined the commitments of the League with a view to avoiding war. While the United States, in entering the League, will assume new responsibilities, it will not assume new burdens. The League will prove to be a source of economy rather than of new expense to us; for it should not only enable us to escape the crushing expense of actual warfare, but, in course of time, should likewise relieve us of part of the present burden of armaments.

So much from the standpoint of self-interest. But, irrespective of self-interest, the United States, having become a powerful nation in point of numbers, talent and resources, has a duty to perform in this respect to her sister nations. Modern ingenuity has so multiplied the destructiveness of war that the very preservation of the race is dependent on adequate organization to suppress war. Such organization cannot come about without the participation of the United States. Unless we join, other important countries will remain out and we will witness the world divided once more in hostile groups. Without a League of Nations, the many new States which have come into being, lacking experience and the self-restraint which makes successful self-government possible, will not only be unable to maintain their independence but will be a source of danger to the general peace, by reason of quarrels among themselves and quarrels with the States of which they were formerly a part; for, on the one hand, racial animosity and the memory of the tyranny formerly practiced against them "will prompt them to be impatient and headstrong" in dealing with their former masters, while, on the other hand, the latter will harbor resentment against States whose independent existence will remind them of their own "deserved humiliation." Our experience in Cuba indicates what we may expect of them. After three years of existence as an independent republic, Cuba indulged in a revolution. "Mr. Roosevelt sent me down there to stop it and launch the Republic once more. Well, I could not stop it except by sending for the army and navy of the United States. That step had a wholesome, conciliatory, quieting effect. We were not called upon to fight. We took over the island and held it for two years. We passed a lot of good statutes, among them an election law, held a fair election under it and then turned over the government to those elected. We had launched her once more. If she ever requires it we will do the same thing over again and launch her again, and then again, until she gets strong enough—I hope she is now—to stand alone."

This unpretentious and good-natured recital of the accomplishment of a task which for another might have proved difficult indeed—and lengthy, if not bloody—shows, more clearly than any abstract dissertation possibly could, exactly the patience and fatherly concern which Mr. Taft feels will be required of us in starting the new nations of Europe safely on their way.

Our own sacrifices and the more awful sacrifices of our allies, who were fighting our battle long before we awoke to the fact, were made in order to suppress militarism, to safeguard democracy and to make peace more lasting.

It was the United States, acting through its President, that pointed the way to a league of nations. The hope of it gave new courage to the armies of our allies and to the people that suffered toil and hardship at home; it helped nerve the arm of our own boys and encouraged the masses in the enemy country to revolt against their leaders. Shall we now disappoint their hope? Prove traitor to our professions? Tell the maimed and the mothers of the dead, at home and abroad, that we did not mean what we said? Suffer conditions to grow up which will make similar—nay, far graver—sacrifices necessary in the future? "I say that the men who advocate our staying out of the League by reason of a policy against entangling alliances laid down by Washington for a small nation struggling for existence, whereas today we are one of the most powerful nations in the world—I say deliberately that these men are little Americans and belittle the United States and its people." Now is the time to set up the international organization which for generations thinking men have sought; now, while the dreadful character of war has so impressed itself on nations that they are willing to make the concessions called for.

Should we not, then, say to the nations of Europe: "We realize that the sea no longer separates us but is become a bond of union. We know that if war comes to you, our neighbor, it is apt to come to us, and we are ready to stand with you in order to suppress this scourge of nations. For love of our brother we will do our share as men and women conscious of the responsibility to help along mankind, a responsibility which God has given this nation in giving it great power."

Led, by experience in furthering new measures, to expect violent attack on the proposed League from the side of the Federal Constitution, Mr. Taft took early occasion to deal with that important question. His full and satisfactory treatment of it is among his most valuable contributions to the discussion of the League project.

The United States is a nation, endowed with all the powers, so far as external relations are concerned, that appertain to a sovereign nation. Practice and legal decisions are cited to show that its treaty-making power extends to all subjects usually dealt with in treaties. These include, in practice and in law, the right to agree to submit to arbitration not only existing disputes but likewise disputes which may arise in future. Among the latter, instance the approval, by the United States Senate, of the Hague convention for an international Court of Prize and of the Bryan treaties. Such agreements may apply to extra-legal controversies as well as to justiciable controversies. The latter are defined as matters resolvable by the rules of law and equity. Precedent for instituting an international Court of Justice to pass upon the latter category of questions is found in the Supreme Court of the United States which is called upon at times to apply international law in controversies between the States of the Union. Settlement of extra-legal questions by a tribunal would simply be arbitration as we commonly know it. A long series of agreements of this nature, beginning with the Jay Treaty of 1794, affirms the practice of the country in respect thereto. Submission of an issue to a judge, which this is, is not a delegation of power to an agent.

Nor is the Government exceeding its constitutional powers when it enters into an agreement to go to war under certain conditions. For the complete act, the exercise of two constitutional functions is required. It is the President who, by and with the consent of the Senate, makes a treaty. "For this purpose the President and Senate are the United States." That is one thing. It is the Congress which, observing the requirements of the treaty, takes supplementary action. That is quite another thing.

A treaty calling for a declaration of war under certain conditions can no more be carried out without action on the part of Congress than a treaty calling for the payment of money; because in Congress alone resides the power to declare war just as in Congress alone resides the power to make appropriations of money form the Treasury. The requirements of the Constitution are fulfilled only by this double action. But that fact cannot be interpreted as limiting the constitutional power of the Government to make treaties. The treaty we made with France during the Revolution was of that character. The Senate accepted the principle when it approved the treaties under which we guaranteed the independence of Cuba and Panama. "The obligation was entered into in the constitutional way and is to be performed in the constitutional way."

Neither can the constitutional power of the country to enter into an agreement to limit armaments be questioned. This power was exercised early in the history of the country by the agreement with Canada (1817) to abolish armaments on the Great Lakes and maintain no fortifications along our lengthy common border.

The charge that the League sets up a Super-State likewise falls before an examination of the project. The central organs of the League recommend—they do not command—definite courses of action by the States of the League. When armaments are in question, the limit prescribed for each State is not definitive until that State has agreed to it. For the United States, it is the Congress, acting under the Constitution, which will finally determine what our armaments are to be. When mandates for administering backward regions are assigned, the mandatory is free to accept or reject the mandate. When the use of force is required, each State of the League will decide for itself whether or not it will observe the recommendation of the central organ of the League that force be used. True, among the positive agreements which may not be ignored, are two of major importance, namely, the agreement to institute a boycott against a member of the League which resorts to war in violation of its covenants and the agreement to "afford passage through their territory to the forces" engaged in disciplining the recalcitrant. These provisions abolish neutrality in the case of an aggressive war; but it is a condition which arises not by reason of any command of the central organs of the League but by reason of the act of the recalcitrant itself in waging war illegally.

The power of the League rests, not on a super-government, but on the covenants of the members to cooperate voluntarily by boycott and by the use of force, to punish aggression.

Combatting the views of persons who object to the element of force in the League program, Mr. Taft declares his respect for the motives of the advocates of non-resistance but doubts whether nations are as yet proof against the "temptations to cupidity, cruelty and injustice" manifested in men, and whether, on that account, an international police is not as requisite as the constabulary which "protects the innocent and the just against the criminal and unjust" within the State.

Mr. Bryan, in the written debate with Mr. Taft, urges that the use of force invites violence, and cites the laying aside of weapons by private persons as having made for the peacefulness of society. Mr. Taft replies that the instance is not well chosen, because "men gave up weapons when they could rely on the police, exercising the force of the community, to protect them against violence. . . . Would Mr. Bryan dispense with the police in city, state and nation?" "There is no means of suppressing lawless violence except lawful force."

Mr. Bryan's view that a popular referendum should be taken before a nation may declare war is met by the supposition that the people of one country to a dispute might well vote for war while that of the other country voted against it. "Shall another vote be taken? In which country? Or shall it be in both?" We may add that when the national legislature had gone so far as to submit the question of peace or war by referendum to the people, what likelihood is there that the prospective enemy would await the decision before striking? Picture any of the great European countries referring to popular vote the question of war against a neighbor. How long would the latter delay warlike action? The debate offers an interesting comparison, throughout, of the minds of the two participants.

The assertion, made in certain quarters, that the League plan has little value because nations will disregard the obligations of the pact is met by the admission that nations are sometimes utterly immoral and shamelessly break treaties on the plea of necessity but that we cannot, on that account, abandon treaty-making "any more than we can give up commercial contracts because men sometimes dishonor themselves by breaking them." Moreover, flying in the face of an organized world opinion and combined world power involves very different consequences from those which followed breach of treaty under the old order.

The fear that judgments of an international tribunal will affect adversely the interests of the United States is dismissed in these words: "If the judgment against her is just she ought to obey it. If it is not, why assume that it will be rendered at all, or, that if rendered all nations would join in world war to enforce it? Indeed, may not our imagination, if we let it run riot, as easily conceive such a union of the military forces of the world against the United States without a league and its machinery as with them?" No inconsistency is recognized between intense love of country, which is regarded as helpful and right, and universal brotherhood. "The relation of one to the other should be as love of home and family is to love of country." They strengthen each other.

A league, such as is now planned, is viewed as a necessary and natural outgrowth of the treaty foreshadowed by the demands of the Allies. In fact the proposed treaty is impossible of fulfillment without the aid of some such organization. Even though drawn "by the ablest lawyers who ever drew a contract" its numerous provisions will call for authoritative interpretation. What instrument is there better fitted than a court to interpret a contract authoritatively? Next, there are sure to be conflicts which are not justiciable among the nations. What better institution for settling such questions than a tribunal of inquiry and conciliation? Unruliness on the part of backward countries, or of those children among the nations to whom reference has already been made, will call for the use of force to confine and restrain it. "You do not always have to use the broad hand but it is helpful to have it in the family." That was the third plank in the platform of the League to Enforce Peace. Lastly, we cannot escape the task of developing and defining international law, and that is the fourth plank.

As the discussion proceeded Mr. Taft was led to change, in the direction of enlarging, his view of the length to which nations might be expected to go in conferring powers on a central organization. Of the desirability of sanction for all the pronouncements of the League there was never a question. The problem was to avoid wrecking the project by demanding more than the nations would be willing to concede at this time.

It will be observed, for example, that in the earliest speeches, intention to enforce the judgment of an international court is denied; whereas, later on and with Mr. Taft's approval, the platform of the League to Enforce Peace moved up to that demand. At the same time Mr. Taft has stood, from the beginning, for the power to hale a nation into court. The framers of the Paris Covenant were manifestly unwilling to confer both powers conjointly on an international tribunal. They neglected to confer on the League the power to hale offenders before a tribunal or court in matters suitable for arbitration—justiciable matters are included in the term—but, having once submitted the matter, the disputants are bound to respect the judgment or award. On the other hand, disputants in the field of extra-legal matters, including conflicts of political policy, may be haled before a tribunal—the Council or a committee thereof—while the recommendation arrived at by the tribunal is not enforcible. Mr. Taft is of the opinion that there is still a way, through the instrumentality of the Council, to bring a nation into the Court of International Justice under the Covenant. Certainly it is not unreasonable to expect further development of the powers of its tribunals, as well as of the general powers of the League, as time may disclose the need for them.

So, too, the earlier position that the League should operate only on its own members was abandoned by Mr. Taft and his associates in favor of insistence on resort to inquiry in the hope of peaceful settlement before even nations outside the League were suffered to go to war. This is the attitude of the Paris Covenant. The messages printed at the end of the volume reveal the part played by Mr. Taft in securing modification of the covenant originally reported to the Paris Conference (February 14, 1919). His suggestions were made with a view to meeting the objections raised against the instrument by members of the United States Senate. The attitude of the latter, after the objections voiced had been largely met by these modifications, indicates the true nature of much of the opposition, namely, desire to destroy the Covenant itself—a fearful responsibility in view of future consequences to the welfare of mankind.

In addition to meeting, with his usual touch of kindly humor and convincing reasoning, the arguments advanced against the League project, Mr. Taft discloses in these papers a deep conviction that a League of Nations is necessary and that within it lie boundless possibilities for good.

Someone has said that the man whom we are inclined to regard as wise is the man with whose views we happen to agree. Be that as it may, in reviewing Mr. Taft's utterances one is struck with the extent to which the things he has advocated are the things that have been realized or are still regarded as desirable. His basket of discarded notions—notions discarded for him by the public—is exceptionally small.

Among the speeches in his best vein is that of Montreal (September 26, 1917; chapter 10) analyzing German motive in the light of Prussia's history and reviewing the events which led up inevitably to our own entry into the war. While stamped with his characteristic fairness, it constitutes such a sweeping indictment of Germany, is so eloquent and full of fire, so exact, comprehensive and satisfactory that it should live as a masterpiece in the literature of the war.

It goes without saying that the Papers are replete with new evidence of our honored ex-President's grasp of the guiding legal principles of our government, gathered on the bench and in executive office, and of the attitude of mind which the best thought and feeling of the country heartily accepts as true Americanism.

Theodore Marburg
Baltimore, November 11, 1919

TAFT PAPERS ON
LEAGUE OF NATIONS

1

League to Enforce Peace

The League to Enforce Peace was organized in Independence Hall, Philadelphia, June 17, 1915. Its objects are set forth in the following:

Proposals

We believe it to be desirable for the United States to join a league of nations binding the signatories to the following:

First: All justiciable questions arising between the signatory powers, not settled by negotiation, shall, subject to the limitations of treaties, be submitted to a judicial tribunal for hearing and judgment, both upon the merits and upon any issue as to its jurisdiction of the question.

Second: All other questions arising between the signatories and not settled by negotiation shall be submitted to a council of conciliation for hearing, consideration and recommendation.

Third: The signatory powers shall jointly use forthwith both their economic and military forces against any one of their number that goes to war, or commits acts of hostility, against another of the signatories before any question arising shall be submitted as provided in the foregoing.[1]

Fourth: Conferences between the signatory powers shall be held from time to time to formulate and codify rules of international law, which, unless some signatory shall signify its dissent within a stated period, shall thereafter govern in the decisions of the Judicial Tribunal mentioned in Article One.

Note

1. The following interpretation of Article 3 has been authorized by the Executive Committee:

> The signatory powers shall jointly employ diplomatic and economic pressure against any one of their number that threatens war against a fellow signatory without having first submitted its dispute for international inquiry, conciliation, arbitration or judicial hearing, and awaited a conclusion, or without having in good faith offered so to submit it. They shall follow this forthwith by the joint use of their military forces against that nation if it actually goes to war, or commits acts of hostility, against another of the signatories before any question arising shall be dealt with as provided in the foregoing.

2

Victory Program

Adopted at a meeting of the Executive Committee, held in New York, November 23, 1918, as the official platform of the League to Enforce Peace, superseding the proposals adopted at the organization of the League in Philadelphia, June 17, 1915.

The war now happily brought to a close has been above all a war to end war, but in order to ensure the fruits of victory and to prevent the recurrence of such a catastrophe there should be formed a League of Free Nations, as universal as possible, based upon treaty and pledged that the security of each state shall rest upon the strength of the whole. The initiating nucleus of the membership of the League should be the nations associated as belligerents in winning the war.

The League should aim at promoting the liberty, progress, and fair economic opportunity of all nations, and the orderly development of the world.

It should ensure peace by eliminating causes of dissension, by deciding controversies by peaceable means, and by uniting the potential force of all the members as a standing menace against any nation that seeks to upset the peace of the world.

The advantages of membership in the League, both economically and from the point of view of security, should be so clear that all nations will desire to be members of it. For this purpose it is necessary to create—

1. For the decision of justiciable questions, an impartial tribunal whose jurisdiction shall not depend upon the assent of the parties to the controversy; provision to be made for enforcing its decisions.

2. For questions that are not justiciable in their character, a Council of Conciliation, as mediator, which shall hear, consider, and make recommendations; and failing acquiescence by the parties concerned, the League shall determine what action, if any, shall be taken.

3. An administrative organization for the conduct of affairs of common interest, the protection and care of backward regions and internationalized places, and such matters as have been jointly administered before and during the war. We hold that this object must be attained by methods and through machinery that will ensure both stability and progress; preventing, on the one hand, any crystallization of the *status quo* that will defeat the forces of healthy growth and changes, and providing, on the other hand, a way by which progress can be secured and necessary change effected without recourse to war.

4. A representative Congress to formulate and codify rules of international law, to inspect the work of the administrative bodies and to consider any matter affecting the tranquility of the world or the progress or betterment of human relations. Its deliberations should be public.

5. An Executive Body, able to speak with authority in the name of the nations represented, and to act in case the peace of the world is endangered.

The representation of the different nations in the organs of the League should be in proportion to the responsibilities and obligations they assume. The rules of international law should not be defeated for lack of unanimity.

3

The Paris Covenant for a League of Nations 1

[Similar provisions of the two drafts paralleled for comparison]

The Paris Covenant for a League of Nations I

[Similar provisions of the two drafts paralleled for comparison]

Text of the Plan Adopted by the Paris Peace Conference
April 28, 1919

Preamble

In order to promote international cooperation and to achieve international peace and security, by the acceptance of obligations not to resort to war, by the prescription of open, just and honorable relations between nations, by the firm establishment of the understandings of international law as the actual rule of conduct among Governments, and by the maintenance of justice and a scrupulous respect for all treaty obligations in the dealings of organized peoples with one another, the high contracting parties agree to this covenant of the League of Nations.

Article I

The original members of the League of Nations shall be those of the signatories which are named in the annex to this covenant and also such

Text of the Plan Presented at the Paris Peace Conference
February 14, 1919

Preamble

In order to promote international cooperation and to secure international peace and security by the acceptance of obligations not to resort to war, by the prescription of open, just and honorable relations between nations, by the firm establishment of the understandings of international law as the actual rule of conduct among governments; and by the maintenance of justice and a scrupulous respect for all treaty obligations in the dealings of organized people with one another, the powers signatory to this covenant adopt this constitution of the League of Nations:

Article VII

Admission to the League of States, not signatories to the covenant and not named in the protocol hereto as States to be invited to adhere to of those other states named in the annex as shall accede without reservation to this covenant. Such accessions shall be effected by a declaration deposited with the Secretariat within two months of the coming into force of the covenant. Notice thereof shall be sent to all other members of the League.

Any fully self-governing state, dominion or colony not named in the annex may become a member of the League if its admission is agreed to by two-thirds of the Assembly, provided that it shall give effective guarantees of its sincere intention to observe its international obligations and shall accept such regulations as may be prescribed by the League in regard to its military, naval and air forces and armaments.

Any member of the League may, after two years' notice of its intention so to do, withdraw from the League, provided that all its international obligations and all its obligations under this covenant shall have been fulfilled at the time of its withdrawal.

Article II

The action of the League under this covenant shall be effected through the instrumentality of an Assembly and of a Council, with a permanent Secretariat.

Article III

The Assembly shall consist of representatives of the members of the League.

The Assembly shall meet at stated intervals, and from time to time as occasion may require, at the seat of the League, or at such other place as may be decided upon.

The Assembly may deal at its meetings with any matter within the sphere of action of the League or affecting the peace of the world.

At meetings of the Assembly each member of the League shall have one vote, and may have not more than three representatives.

the covenant, requires the assent of not less than two-thirds of the States represented in the body of delegates, and shall be limited to fully self-governing countries, including dominions and colonies.

No State shall be admitted to the League unless it is able to give effective guarantees of its sincere intention to observe its international obligations and unless it shall conform to such principles as may be pre-scribed by the League in regard to its naval and military forces and armaments.

Article I

The action of the high contracting parties under the terms of this covenant shall be effected through the instrumentality of meetings of a body of delegates representing the high contracting parties, of meetings at more frequent intervals of an Executive Council, and of a permanent international secretariat to be established at the seat of the League.

Article II

Meetings of the body of delegates shall be held at stated intervals and from time to time, as occasion may require, for the purpose of dealing with matters within the sphere of action of the League. Meetings of the body of delegates shall be held at the seat of the League, or at such other places as may be found convenient, and shall consist of representatives of the high contracting parties. Each of the high contracting parties shall have one vote, but may have not more than three representatives.

Article IV

The Council shall consist of representatives of the principal allied and associated powers, together with representatives of four other members of the League. These four members of the League shall be selected by the Assembly from time to time in its discretion. Until the appointment of the representatives of the four members of the League first selected by the Assembly, representatives of Belgium, Brazil, Spain and Greece shall be members of the Council.

With the approval of the majority of the Assembly, the Council may name additional members of the League, whose representatives shall always be members of the Council; the Council with like approval may increase the number of members of the League to be selected by the Assembly for representation on the Council.

The Council shall meet from time to time as occasion may require, and at least once a year, at the seat of the League, or at such other place as may be decided upon.

The Council may deal at its meetings with any matter within the sphere of action of the League or affecting the peace of the world.

Any member of the League not represented on the Council shall be invited to send a representative to sit as a member at any meeting of the Council during the consideration of matters specially affecting the interests of that member of the League.

At meetings of the Council, each member of the League represented on the Council shall have one vote, and may have not more than one representative.

Article V

Except where otherwise expressly provided in this covenant, or by the terms of the present treaty, decisions at any meeting of the Assembly or of the Council shall require the agreement of all the members of the League represented at the meeting.

All matters of procedure at meetings of the Assembly or the Council, including the appointment of committees to investigate particular

Article III

The Executive Council shall consist of representatives of the United States of America, the British Empire, France, Italy, and Japan, together with representatives of four other States, members of the League. The selection of these four States shall be made by the body of delegates on such principles and in such manner as they think fit. Pending the appointment of these representatives of the other States, representatives of—— shall be members of the Executive Council.

Meetings of the council shall be held from time to time as occasion may require, and at least once a year, at whatever place may be decided on, or, failing any such decision, at the seat of the League, and any matter within the sphere of action of the League or affecting the peace of the world may be dealt with at such meetings.

Invitations shall be sent to any power to attend a meeting of the council, at which matters directly affecting its interests are to be discussed, and no decision taken at any meeting will be binding on such a power unless so invited.

matters, shall be regulated by the Assembly or by the Council and may be decided by a majority of the members of the League represented at the meeting.

The first meeting of the Assembly and the first meeting of the Council shall be summoned by the President of the United States of America.

Article VI

The permanent Secretariat shall be established at the seat of the League. The Secretariat shall comprise a Secretary General and such secretaries and staff as may be required.

The first Secretary General shall be the person named in the annex; thereafter the Secretary General shall be appointed by the Council with the approval of the majority of the Assembly.

The secretaries and the staff of the Secretariat shall be appointed by the Secretary General with the approval of the Council.

The Secretary General shall act in that capacity at all meetings of the Assembly and of the Council.

The expenses of the Secretariat shall be borne by the members of the League in accordance with the apportionment of the expenses of the International Bureau of the Universal Postal Union.

Article VII

The seat of the League is established at Geneva.

The Council may at any time decide that the seat of the League shall be established elsewhere.

All positions under or in connection with the League, including the Secretariat, shall be open equally to men and women.

Representatives of the members of the League and officials of the League when engaged on the business of the League shall enjoy diplomatic privileges and immunities.

The buildings and other property occupied by the League or its officers or by representatives attending its meetings shall be inviolable.

Article V

The permanent secretariat of the League shall be established at———, which shall constitute the seat of the League. The secretariat shall comprise such secretaries and staff as may be required, under the general direction and control of a Secretary General of the League, who shall be chosen by the Executive Council. The secretariat shall be appointed by the Secretary General subject to confirmation by the Executive Council.

The Secretary General shall act in that capacity at all meetings of the body of delegates or of the Executive Council.

The expenses of the secretariat shall be borne by the States members of the League, in accordance with the apportionment of the expenses of the International Bureau of the Universal Postal Union.

Article VI

Representatives of the high contracting parties and officials of the League, when engaged in the business of the League, shall enjoy diplomatic privileges and immunities, and the buildings occupied by the League or its officials, or by representatives attending its meetings, shall enjoy the benefits of extra-territoriality.

Article VIII

The members of the League recognize that the maintenance of a peace requires the reduction of national armaments to the lowest point consistent with national safety and the enforcement by common action of international obligations.

The Council, taking account of the geographical situation and circumstances of each state, shall formulate plans for such reduction for the consideration and action of the several Governments.

Such plans shall be subject to reconsideration and revision at least every ten years.

After these plans shall have been adopted by the several Governments, the limits of armaments therein fixed shall not be exceeded without the concurrence of the Council.

The members of the League agree that the manufacture by private enterprise of munitions and implements of war is open to grave objections. The Council shall advise how the evil effects attendant upon such manufacture can be prevented, due regard being had to the necessities of those members of the League which are not able to manufacture the munitions and implements of war necessary for their safety.

The members of the League undertake to interchange full and frank information as to the scale of their armaments, their military, naval and air programs and the condition of such of their industries as are adaptable to warlike purposes.

Article IX

A permanent commission shall be constituted to advise the Council on the execution of the provisions of Articles I and VIII and on military, naval and air questions generally.

Article X

The members of the League undertake to respect and preserve as against external aggression the territorial integrity and existing political independence of all members of the League. In case of any such aggression or in case

Article VIII

The high contracting parties recognize the principle that the maintenance of peace will require the reduction of national armaments to the lowest point consistent with national safety, and the enforcement by common action of international obligations, having special regard to the geographical situation and circumstances of each State, and the Executive Council shall formulate plans for effecting such reduction. The Executive Council shall also determine for the consideration and action of the several Governments what military equipment and armament is fair and reasonable in proportion to the scale of forces laid down in the program of disarmament and these limits, when adopted, shall not be exceeded without the permission of the Executive Council.

The high contracting parties agree that the manufacture by private enterprise of munitions and implements of war lends itself to grave objections, and direct the Executive Council to advise how the evil effects attendant upon such manufacture can be prevented, due regard being had to the necessities of those countries which are not able to manufacture for themselves the munitions and implements of war necessary for their safety.

The high contracting parties undertake in no way to conceal from each other the condition of such of their industries as are capable of being adapted to warlike purposes or the scale of their armaments, and agree that there shall be full and frank interchange of information as to their military and naval programs.

Article IX

A permanent commission shall be constituted to advise the League on the execution of the provisions of Article VIII and on military and naval questions generally.

Article X

The high contracting parties shall undertake to respect and preserve as against external aggression the territorial integrity and existing political independence of all States members of the League. In case of any such aggression of any threat or danger of such aggression, the Council shall advise upon the means by which this obligation shall be fulfilled.

Article XI

Any war or threat of war, whether immediately affecting any of the members of the League or not, is hereby declared a matter of concern to the whole League, and the League shall take any action that may be deemed wise and effectual to safeguard the peace of nations. In case any such emergency should arise, the Secretary General shall, on the request of any member of the League, forthwith summon a meeting of the Council.

It is also declared to be the fundamental right of each member of the League to bring to the attention of the Assembly or of the Council any circumstance whatever affecting international relations which threatens to disturb either the peace or the good understanding between nations upon which peace depends.

Article XII

The members of the League agree that if there should arise between them any dispute likely to lead to a rupture, they will submit the matter either to arbitration or to inquiry by the Council, and they agree in no case to resort to war until three months after the award by the arbitrators or the report by the Council.

In any case under this article the award of the arbitrators shall be made within a reasonable time, and the report of the Council shall be made within six months after the submission of the dispute.

Article XIII

The members of the League agree that whenever any dispute shall arise between them which they recognize to be suitable for submission to arbitration and which cannot be satisfactorily settled by diplomacy, they will submit or in case of any threat or danger of such aggression the Executive Council shall advise upon the means by which the obligation shall be fulfilled.

Article XI

Any war or threat of war, whether immediately affecting any of the high contracting parties or not, is hereby declared a matter of concern to the League, and the high contracting parties reserve the right to take any action that may be deemed wise and effectual to safeguard the peace of nations.

It is hereby also declared and agreed to be the friendly right of each of the high contracting parties to draw the attention of the body of delegates or of the Executive Council to any circumstance affecting international intercourse which threatens to disturb international peace or the good understanding between nations upon which peace depends.

Article XII

The high contracting parties agree that should disputes arise between them which cannot be adjusted by the ordinary processes of diplomacy they will in no case resort to war without previously submitting the questions and matters involved either to arbitration or to inquiry by the Executive Council and until three months after the award by the arbitrators or a recommendation by the Executive Council, and that they will not even then resort to war as against a member of the League which complies with the award of the arbitrators or the recommendation of the Executive Council.

In any case under this article the award of the arbitrators shall be made within a reasonable time, and the recommendation of the Executive Council shall be made within six months after the submission of the dispute.

Article XIII

The high contracting parties agree that whenever any dispute or difficulty shall arise between them, which they recognize to be suitable for submission to arbitration and which cannot be satisfactorily settled by the whole subject matter to arbitration. Disputes as to the interpretation of a treaty, as to any question of international law, as to the existence of any fact which if established would constitute a breach of any international obligation, or as to the extent and nature of the reparation to be made for any such breach, are declared to be among those which are generally suitable for submission to arbitration. For the consideration of any such dispute the court of arbitration to which the case is referred shall be the court agreed on by the parties to the dispute or stipulated in any convention existing between them.

The members of the League agree that they will carry out in full good faith any award that may be rendered and that they will not resort to war against a member of the League which complies therewith. In the event of any failure to carry out such an award, the Council shall propose what steps should be taken to give effect thereto.

Article XIV

The Council shall formulate and submit to the members of the League for adoption plans for the establishment of a permanent Court of International Justice. The court shall be competent to hear and determine any dispute of an international character which the parties thereto submit to it. The court may also give an advisory opinion upon any dispute or question referred to it by the Council or by the Assembly.

Article XV

If there should arise between members of the League any dispute likely to lead to a rupture, which is not submitted to arbitration in accordance with Article XIII, the members of the League agree that they will submit the matter to the Council. Any party to the dispute may effect such submission by giving notice of the existence of the dispute to the Secretary General, who will make all necessary arrangements for a full investigation and consideration thereof. For this purpose the parties to the dispute will communicate to the Secretary General, as promptly as possible, statements of their case, all the relevant facts and papers; and the Council may forthwith direct the publication thereof.

The Council shall endeavor to effect a settlement of any dispute, and if diplomacy, they will submit the whole matter to arbitration. For this purpose the court of arbitration to which the case is referred shall be the court agreed on by the parties or stipulated in any convention existing between them. The high contracting parties agree that they will carry out in full good faith any award that may be rendered. In the event of any failure to carry out the award the Executive Council shall propose what steps can best be taken to give effect thereto.

Article XIV

The Executive Council shall formulate plans for the establishment of a permanent court of international justice, and this court shall, when established, be competent to hear and determine any matter which the parties recognize as suitable for submission to it for arbitration under the foregoing article.

Article XV

If there should arise between States, members of the League, any dispute likely to lead to a rupture, which is not submitted to arbitration as above, the high contracting parties agree that they will refer the matter to the Executive Council; either party to the dispute may give notice of the existence of the dispute to the Secretary General, who will make all necessary arrangements for a full investigation and consideration thereof. For this purpose the parties agree to communicate to the Secretary General, as promptly as possible, statements of their case, with all the relevant facts and papers, and the Executive Council may forthwith direct the publication thereof.

Where the efforts of the council lead to the settlement of the dispute, a such efforts are successful, a statement shall be made public giving such facts and explanations regarding the dispute and terms of settlement thereof as the Council may deem appropriate.

If the dispute is not thus settled, the Council either unanimously or by a majority vote shall make and publish a report containing a statement of the facts of the dispute and the recommendations which are deemed just and proper in regard thereto.

Any member of the League represented on the Council may make public a statement of the facts of the dispute and of its conclusions regarding the same.

If a report by the Council is unanimously agreed to by the members thereof, other than the representatives of one or more of the parties to the dispute, the members of the League agree that they will not go to war with any party to the dispute which complies with the recommendations of the report.

If the Council fails to reach a report which is unanimously agreed to by the members thereof, other than the representatives of one or more of the parties to the dispute, the members of the League reserve to themselves the right to take such action as they shall consider necessary for the maintenance of right and justice.

If the dispute between the parties is claimed by one of them, and is found by the Council, to arise out of a matter which by international law is solely within the domestic jurisdiction of that party, the Council shall so report, and shall make no recommendation as to its settlement.

The Council may in any case under this article refer the dispute to the Assembly. The dispute shall be so referred at the request of either party of the dispute, provided that such request be made within fourteen days after the submission of the dispute to the Council.

In any case referred to the Assembly all the provisions of this article and of Article XII relating to the action and powers of the Council shall apply to the action and powers of the Assembly, provided that a report made by the Assembly, if concurred in by the representatives of those members of the League represented on the Council and of a majority of the other members of the League, exclusive in each case of the representatives of the parties to the dispute, shall have the same force as a report by the Council, concurred in by all the members thereof other than the representatives of one or more of the parties to the dispute.

statement shall be published, indicating the nature of the dispute and the terms of settlement, together with such explanations as may be appropriate. If the dispute has not been settled, a report by the council shall be published, setting forth with all necessary facts and explanations the recommendation which the council think just and proper for the settlement of the dispute. If the report is unanimously agreed to by the members of the council, other than the parties to the dispute, the high contracting parties agree that they will not go to war with any party which complies with the recommendations, and that, if any party shall refuse so to comply, the council shall propose measures necessary to give effect to the recommendations. If no such unanimous report can be made it shall be the duty of the majority and the privilege of the minority to issue statements, indicating what they believe to be the facts, and containing the recommendations which they consider to be just and proper.

The Executive Council may in any case under this article refer the dispute to the body of delegates. The dispute shall be so referred at the request of either party to the dispute, provided that such request must be made within fourteen days after the submission of the dispute. In any case referred to the body of delegates, all the provisions of this article, and of Article XII, relating to the action and powers of the Executive Council, shall apply to the action and powers of the body of delegates.

Article XVI

Should any member of the League resort to war in disregard of its covenants under Article XII, XIII or XV, it shall *ipso facto* be deemed to have committed an act of war against all the other members of the League, which hereby undertake immediately to subject it to the severance of all trade or financial relations, the prohibition of all intercourse between their nationals and the nationals of the covenant-breaking State and the prevention of all financial, commercial, or personal intercourse between the nationals of the covenant-breaking State and the nationals of any other State, whether a member of the League or not.

It shall be the duty of the Council in such case to recommend to the several Governments concerned what effective military, naval or air force the members of the League shall severally contribute to the armaments of forces to be used to protect the covenants of the League.

The members of the League agree, further, that they will mutually support one another in the financial and economic measures which are taken under this article, in order to minimize the loss and inconvenience resulting from the above measures, and that they will mutually support one another in resisting any special measures aimed at one of their number by the covenant-breaking State, and that they will take the necessary steps to afford passage through their territory to the forces of any of the members of the League which are cooperating to protect the covenants of the League.

Any member of the League which has violated any covenant of the League may be declared to be no longer a member of the League by a vote of the Council concurred in by the representatives of all the other members of the League represented thereon.

Article XVII

In the event of a dispute between a member of the League and a State which is not a member of the League, or between States not members of the League, the State or States not members of the League shall be invited to accept the obligations of membership in the League for the purposes of such dispute, upon such conditions as the Council may deem just. If such invitation is accepted, the provisions of Articles XII to XVI inclusive shall

Article XVI

Should any of the high contracting parties break or disregard its covenants under Article XII it shall thereby *ipso facto* be deemed to have committed an act of war against all the other members of the League, which hereby undertakes immediately to subject it to the severance of all trade or financial relations, the prohibition of all intercourse between their nationals and the nationals of the covenant-breaking State and the prevention of all financial, commercial, or personal intercourse between the nationals of the covenant-breaking State and the nationals of any other State, whether a member of the League or not.

It shall be the duty of the Executive Council in such case to recommend what effective military or naval force the members of the League shall severally contribute to the armed forces to be used to protect the covenants of the League.

The high contracting parties agree, further, that they will mutually support one another in the financial and economic measures which may be taken under this article in order to minimize the loss and inconvenience resulting from the above measures, and that they will mutually support one another in resisting any special measures aimed at one of their number by the covenant-breaking State and that they will afford passage through their territory to the forces of any of the high contracting parties who are cooperating to protect the covenants of the League.

Article XVII

In the event of disputes between one State member of the League and another State which is not a member of the League, or between States not members of the League, the high contracting parties agree that the State or States, not members of the League, shall be invited to accept the obligations of membership in the League for the purposes of such dispute, upon such conditions as the Executive Council may deem just, and upon acceptance be applied with such modifications as may be deemed necessary by the Council.

Upon such invitation being given, the Council shall immediately institute an inquiry into the circumstances of the dispute and recommend such action as may seem best and most effectual in the circumstances.

If a State so invited shall refuse to accept the obligations of membership in the League for the purposes of such dispute, and shall resort to war against a member of the League, the provisions of Article XVI shall be applicable as against the State taking such action.

If both parties to the dispute, when so invited, refuse to accept the obligations of membership in the League for the purposes of such dispute, the Council may take such measures and make such recommendations as will prevent hostilities and will result in the settlement of the dispute.

Article XVIII

Every convention or international engagement entered into henceforward by any member of the League shall be forthwith registered with the Secretariat and shall as soon as possible be published by it. No such treaty or international engagement shall be binding until so registered.

Article XIX

The Assembly may from time to time advise the reconsideration by members of the League of treaties which have become inapplicable, and the consideration of international conditions whose continuance might endanger the peace of the world.

Article XX

The members of the League severally agree that this covenant is accepted as abrogating all obligations or understandings *inter se* which are of any such invitation, the above provisions shall be applied with such modifications as may be deemed necessary by the League.

Upon such invitation being given, the Executive Council shall immediately institute an inquiry into the circumstances and merits of the dispute and recommend such action as may seem best and most effectual in the circumstances.

In the event of a power so invited refusing to accept the obligations of membership in the League for the purposes of such dispute, and taking any action against a State member of the League, which in the case of a State member of the League would constitute a breach of Article XII, the provisions of Article XVI shall be applicable as against the State taking such action.

If both parties to the dispute, when so invited, refuse to accept the obligations of membership in the League for the purposes of such dispute, the Executive Council may take such action and make such recommendations as will prevent hostilities and will result in the settlement of the dispute.

Article XXIII

The high contracting parties agree that every treaty or international engagement entered into hereafter by any State member of the League shall be forthwith registered with the Secretary General and as soon as possible published by him, and that no such treaty or international engagement shall be binding until so registered.

Article XXIV

It shall be the right of the body of delegates from time to time to advise the reconsideration by States members of the League of treaties which have become inapplicable and of international conditions of which the continuance may endanger the peace of the world.

Article XXV

The high contracting parties severally agree that the present covenant is accepted as abrogating all obligations *inter se* which are inconsistent with inconsistent with the terms thereof, and solemnly undertake that they will not hereafter enter into any engagements inconsistent with the terms thereof.

In case members of the League shall, before becoming a member of the League, have undertaken any obligations inconsistent with the terms of this covenant, it shall be the duty of such member to take immediate steps to procure its release from such obligations.

Article XXI

Nothing in this covenant shall be deemed to affect the validity of international engagements such as treaties of arbitration or regional understandings like the Monroe Doctrine for securing the maintenance of peace.

Article XXII

To those colonies and territories which as a consequence of the late war have ceased to be under the sovereignty of the states which formerly governed them and which are inhabited by peoples not yet able to stand by themselves under the strenuous conditions of the modern world, there should be applied the principle that the well-being and development of such peoples form a sacred trust of civilization and that securities for the performance of this trust should be embodied in this covenant.

The best method of giving practicable effect to this principle is that the tutelage of such peoples should be intrusted to advanced nations who, by reasons of their resources, their experience or their geographical position, can best undertake this responsibility, and who are willing to accept it, and that this tutelage should be exercised by them as mandataries on behalf of the League.

The character of the mandate must differ according to the stage of the development of the people, the geographical situation of the territory, its economic condition and other similar circumstances.

Certain communities formerly belonging to the Turkish Empire have reached a stage of development where their existence as independent nations can be provisionally recognized, subject to the rendering of administrative advice and assistance by a mandatary until such time as they are able the terms thereof, and solemnly engage that they will not hereafter enter into any engagement inconsistent with the terms thereof. In case any of the powers signatory hereto or subsequently admitted to the League shall, before becoming a party to this covenant, have undertaken any obligations which are inconsistent with the terms of this covenant, it shall be the duty of such power to take immediate steps to procure its release from such obligations.

Article XIX

To those colonies and territories which, as a consequence of the late war, have ceased to be under the sovereignty of the States which formerly governed them and which are inhabited by peoples not yet able to stand by themselves under the strenuous conditions of the modern world, there should be applied the principle that the well-being and development of such peoples form a sacred trust of civilization and that securities for the performance of this trust should be embodied in the constitution of the League.

The best method of giving practical effect to this principle is that the tutelage of such peoples should be intrusted to advanced nations, who by reason of their resources, their experience, or their geographical position, can best undertake this responsibility, and that this tutelage should be exercised by them as mandatories on behalf of the League.

The character of the mandate must differ according to the stage of the development of the people, the geographical situation of the territory, its economic conditions and other similar circumstances.

Certain communities, formerly belonging to the Turkish Empire, have reached a stage of development where their existence as independent nations can be provisionally recognized, subject to the rendering of administrative advice and assistance by a mandatory power until such time as they to stand alone. The wishes of these communities must be a principal consideration in the selection of the mandatary.

Other peoples, especially those of Central Africa, are at such a stage that the mandatary must be responsible for the administration of the territory under conditions which will guarantee freedom of conscience and religion, subject only to the maintenance of public order and morals, the prohibition of abuses, such as the slave trade, the arms traffic and the liquor traffic and the prevention of the establishment of fortifications or military and naval bases and of military training of the natives for other than police purposes and the defense of territory, and will also secure equal opportunities for the trade and commerce of other members of the League.

There are territories, such as Southwest Africa and certain of the South Pacific Islands, which, owing to the sparseness of their population or their small size or their remoteness from the centers of civilization or their geographical contiguity to the territory of the mandatary and other circumstances, can be best administered under the laws of the mandatary as integral portions of its territory, subject to the safeguards above mentioned in the interests of the indigenous population. In every case of mandate, the mandatary shall render to the Council an annual report in reference to the territory committed to its charge.

The degree of authority, control or administration to be exercised by the mandatary shall, if not previously agreed upon by the members of the League, be explicitly defined in each case by the Council.

A permanent commission shall be constituted to receive and examine the annual reports of the mandataries and to advise the Council on all matters relating to the observance of the mandates.

Article XXIII

Subject to and in accordance with the provisions of international conventions existing or hereafter to be agreed upon, the members of the League (a) will endeavor to secure and maintain fair and humane conditions of labor for men, women and children both in their own countries and in all countries to which their commercial and industrial relations are able to stand alone. The wishes of these communities must be a principal consideration in the selection of the mandatory power.

Other peoples, especially those of Central Africa, are at such a stage that the mandatory must be responsible for the administration of the territory, subject to conditions which will guarantee freedom of conscience or religion, subject only to the maintenance of public order and morals, the prohibition of abuses such as the slave trade, the arms traffic, and the liquor traffic, and the prevention of the establishment of fortifications or military and naval bases and of military training of the natives for other than police purposes and the defense of territory, and will also secure equal opportunities for the trade and commerce of other members of the League.

There are territories, such as Southwest Africa and certain of the South Pacific Islands, which, owing to the sparseness of the population, or their small size, or their remoteness from the centers of civilization, or their geographical contiguity to the mandatory State and other circumstances, can be best administered under the laws of the mandatory State as integral portions thereof, subject to the safeguards above mentioned in the interests of the indigenous population.

In every case of mandate, the mandatory State shall render to the League an annual report in reference to the territory committed to its charge.

The degree of authority, control, or administration, to be exercised by the mandatory State, shall, if not previously agreed upon by the high contracting parties in each case, be explicitly defined by the Executive Council in a special act or charter.

The high contracting parties further agree to establish at the seat of the League a mandatory commission to receive and examine the annual reports of the mandatory powers, and to assist the League in insuring the observance of the terms of all mandates.

Article XX

The high contracting parties will endeavor to secure and maintain fair and humane conditions of labor for men, women, and children, both in their own countries and in all countries to which their commercial and industrial relations extend; and to that end agree to establish as part of the organization of the League a permanent bureau of labor.

extend, and for that purpose will establish and maintain the necessary international organizations; (b) undertake to secure just treatment of the native inhabitants of territories under their control; (c) will intrust the League with the general supervision over the execution of agreements with regard to the traffic in women and children, and the traffic in opium and other dangerous drugs; (d) will intrust the League with the general supervision of the trade in arms and ammunition with the countries in which the control of this traffic is necessary in the common interest; (e) will make provision to secure and maintain freedom of communication and of transit and equitable treatment for the commerce of all members of the League. In this connection the special necessities of the regions devastated during the war of 1914–1918 shall be in mind; (f) will endeavor to take steps in matters of international concern for the prevention and control of disease.

Article XXIV

There shall be placed under the direction of the League all international bureaus already established by general treaties if the parties to such treaties consent. All such international bureaus and all commissions for the regulation of matters of international interest hereafter constituted shall be placed under the direction of the League.

In all matters of international interest which are regulated by general conventions but which are not placed under the control of international bureaus or commissions, the Secretariat of the League shall, subject to the consent of the Council and if desired by the parties, collect and distribute all relevant information, and shall render any other assistance which may be necessary or desirable.

The Council may include as part of the expenses of the Secretariat the expenses of any bureau or commission which is placed under the direction of the League.

Article XXV

The members of the League agree to encourage and promote the establishment and cooperation of duly authorized voluntary national Red

Article XVIII

The high contracting parties agree that the League shall be intrusted with the general supervision of the trade in arms and ammunition with the countries in which the control of this traffic is necessary in the common interest.

Article XXI

The high contracting parties agree that provision shall be made through the instrumentality of the League to secure and maintain freedom of transit and equitable treatment for the commerce of all States members of the League, having in mind, among other things, special arrangements with regard to the necessities of the regions devastated during the war of 1914–1918.

Article XXII

The high contracting parties agree to place under the control of the League all international bureaus already established by general treaties, if the parties to such treaties consent. Furthermore, they agree that all such international bureaus to be constituted in future shall be placed under control of the League.

Cross organizations having as purposes improvement of health, the prevention of disease and the mitigation of suffering throughout the world.

Article XXVI

Amendments to this covenant will take effect when ratified by the members of the League whose representatives compose the Council and by a majority of the members of the League whose representatives compose the Assembly.

No such amendment shall bind any member of the League which signifies its dissent therefrom, but in that case it shall cease to be a member of the League.

Annex to the Covenant

One. Original members of the League of Nations.

Signatories of the Treaty of Peace.

United States of America, Belgium, Bolivia, Brazil, British Empire, Canada, Australia, South Africa, New Zealand, India, China, Cuba, Ecuador, France, Greece, Guatemala, Haiti, Hedjaz, Honduras, Italy, Japan, Liberia, Nicaragua, Panama, Peru, Poland, Portugal, Romania, Serbia, Siam, Czecho-Slovakia, Uruguay.

States invited to accede to the covenant.

Argentine Republic, Chile, Colombia, Denmark, Netherlands, Norway, Paraguay, Persia, Salvador, Spain, Sweden, Switzerland, Venezuela.

Two. First Secretary General of the League of Nations, The Honorable Sir James Eric Drummond, K.C.M.G., C.B.

Article XXVI

Amendments to this covenant will take effect when ratified by the States whose representatives compose the Executive Council and by three-fourths of the States whose representatives compose the body of delegates.

4

Plan for a League of Nations to Enforce Peace

Institutional advances in the progress of the world are rarely made abruptly. They are not like Minerva who sprang full armed from the brain of Jove. If they are to have the useful feature of permanence, they must be a growth so that the communities whose welfare they affect may come to regard them as natural, and so accept them. Our so-called Anglo-Saxon civil liberty, with its guaranties of the Magna Carta, the Petition of Right, the Bill of Rights, the Habeas Corpus Act and the Independence of the Judiciary, constituting the unwritten British Constitution, made our American people familiar with a body of moral restraints upon executive and legislative action to secure the liberty of the individual. The written limitations upon legislative action in colonial charters granted by the Crown and their enforcement by the Privy Council of England, probably suggested to the framers of our Federal Constitution that the principles of British Constitutional liberty be given written form and be committed to a supreme and independent Court to enforce them, as against the Executive and Congress, its coordinate branches in the Government. The step, epochal as it was, from judicially enforcing such limitations against a subordinate legislature under a written charter of its powers, to a judicial enforcement of the limitations imposed by the sovereign people on the legislature and executive that they, the people, had created in the same instrument, was not radical but seemed naturally to follow. The revolted colonies after the Revolution, though united by a common situation and a common cause in their struggle with Great Britain, and acting together through the Continental Congress in a loose and voluntary alliance, were sovereigns independent of one another. The Articles of Confederation which declared their union to be permanent were not agreed to and ratified in such a way as to be binding until some five years after the Declaration of Independence. Meantime, it had become increasingly evident that, strong as were their common interests, they had divergent ones, too, which might embarrass their kindly relations. The leagues of Greece had furnished an example of confederations of small states forced together by a common oppressor and foe, which had found it wise to settle their own differences by some kind of an arbitral tribunal. The office which the Privy Council and the Crown had performed in settling intercolonial controversies suggested an analogy less remote than those in Grecian history and prompted the adoption of a substitute. So there was inserted in the Articles of Confederation a provision for a "court to determine disputes and differences between two or more States of the Confederation concerning boundary jurisdiction or any other cause whatever." The complainant state was authorized to present a petition to Congress stating the matter in question, and praying for a hearing. Notice of this was to be given by order of Congress to the other state in the controversy and a day was assigned for the appearance of the two parties by their lawful agents who should agree upon judges to constitute a court for hearing the matter in question. If they could not agree, Congress was then to name three persons out of each of the thirteen states. From this list each party was required alternately to strike out one until the number was reduced to thirteen, and from these thirteen not less than seven or more than nine names, as Congress should direct, were in the presence of Congress to be drawn by lot, and the persons whose names were so drawn, or any five of them, constituted the court to hear and finally determine the controversy.

Proceedings were instituted under this provision before the Constitution by New Jersey against Vermont, by New York against Vermont, by Massachusetts against Vermont, by Pennsylvania against Virginia, by Pennsylvania against Connecticut, by New Jersey against Virginia, by Massachusetts against New York, and by South Carolina against Georgia. Only one of these cases came to hearing and decision by a court selected as provided. That was the case of Pennsylvania against Connecticut involving the governmental jurisdiction over the Valley of Wyoming and Luzerne County. The court met and held a session of forty-one days at Trenton, in New Jersey. Able counsel represented the parties, and the court made a unanimous decision in favor of Pennsylvania, without giving reasons. A compromise is suspected, because Connecticut promptly acquiesced and soon thereafter, with the approval of the Pennsylvania delegation, Congress passed an act accepting a cession by Connecticut of all the lands claimed by it west of the west line of Pennsylvania, except the Western Reserve, now in Ohio, which Connecticut was thus given ownership of, and which it sold and settled. A number of the other cases were compromised and, in some, no proceedings were taken after the initial ones.

In the Constitutional Convention the necessity for some tribunal to preserve peace and harmony between the states was fully conceded by all, but the form of the court was the subject of some discussion. One proposal was that the Senate should be a court to decide between the states all questions disturbing peace and harmony between the states while the Supreme Court was given only jurisdiction in controversies over boundaries. Ultimately, however, the judicial power of the United States exercised through the Supreme Court was extended to "controversies between States," without exception.

To those who do not closely look into this jurisdiction of the Supreme Court, it seems no different from that of the ordinary municipal court over controversies between individuals. The states are regarded merely as municipal or private corporations subject to suit process, trial and judgment to be rendered on principles of municipal law declared by statute of State Legislature or Congress, or established as the common law. It is assumed that the Constitution destroyed the independence and sovereignty of the states and made the arrangement a mere domestic affair. This is a misconception. The analogy between the function of the Supreme Court in hearing and deciding controversies between states and that of an international tribunal sitting to decide a cause between sovereign nations is very close. When the suit by one state against another presents a case that is controlled by provisions of the Federal Constitution, of course there is nothing international about it. But most controversies between states are not covered by the Federal Constitution. That instrument does not, for instance, fix the boundary line between two states. It does not fix the correlative rights of two states in the water of a non-navigable stream that flows from one of the states into another. It does not regulate the use which the state up stream may make of the water, either by diverting it for irrigation, or by using it as a carrier of noxious sewage. Nor has Congress any power under the Constitution to lay down principles by Federal Law to govern such cases. The legislature of neither state can pass laws to regulate the right of the other states. In other words, there is nothing but international law to govern. There is no domestic law to settle this class of cases any more than there would be if a similar controversy were to arise between Canada and the United States.

For many purposes the states are independent sovereigns and not under Federal control. They have lost the powers which the people in the Constitution gave to the Central Government; but in the field of powers left to them, each is supreme within its own limits, and by the exercise of that power may trespass on the exercise of similar power by its neighbor. How is such a conflict to be settled? It may be by diplomacy, i.e., by negotiation and compromise agreement; but this, under the Constitution, must be with the consent of Congress. It might be settled by war; but the Constitution forbids. And the state invaded by the forces of another state can appeal to the General Government to resist and suppress the invasion, no matter what the merits of the quarrel. In other words, one of the attributes of sovereignty and independence which the people in ordaining the Constitution took away from the states was the unlimited power to make agreements between each other as to their respective rights, and the other was that of making war on each other when other means of settlement failed.

What did the people through the Constitution substitute for these attributes of unrestricted diplomatic negotiation and compromise and the right to go to war over such interstate issues? The right of the complaining state to hale the offending state before the Supreme Court and have the issue decided by a binding judgment.

Now, can the complaining state bring every issue between it and another state before the Supreme Court? No. The only issues which the Court can hear and decide are questions which in their nature are capable of judicial solution. Mr. Justice Bradley first called such questions "justiciable"[1] and Chief Justice Fuller and Mr. Justice Brewer used the same term. There are issues between states of a character which would be likely to lead to high feeling and to war if they arose between independent sovereignties, and which the Supreme Court cannot decide because they are not capable of judicial solution. In such cases between states, of course there can be no war because the Federal Government would suppress it. Therefore, if an amicable understanding cannot be reached, the states are left with an unsettled dispute between them and no way of deciding it. They must put up with the existing state of things.

There have been several interesting cases before our Supreme Court illustrating the character of the jurisdiction I have been describing. Chicago built a sewage canal to drain her sewage with the aid of the waters of Lake Michigan into the Desplaines River, thence into the Illinois and thence into the Mississippi from which St. Louis and other Missouri towns derived their water supply. The State of Missouri brought suit in the Supreme Court of the United States to enjoin the State of Illinois and the Sanitary District of Chicago from continuing the flow, on the ground that the impurities added to the Mississippi water had greatly increased the typhoid fever in Missouri. It was held that this was a subject matter capable of judicial solution, that Missouri was the guardian of her people's welfare and had a right to bring such a suit and, if she made a clear case, to enjoin such use of the Mississippi and its tributaries.

Mr. Justice Shiras, in upholding the jurisdiction (*Missouri v. Illinois,* 180 U.S. 208, 241), spoke of the Court as follows:

> The cases cited show that such jurisdiction has been exercised in cases involving boundaries and jurisdiction over land and their inhabitants, and in cases directly affecting the property rights and interests of a state. But such cases manifestly do not cover the entire field in which such controversies may arise, and for which the Constitution has provided a remedy; and it would be objectionable, and indeed impossible, for the

court to anticipate by definition what controversies can and what cannot be brought within the original jurisdiction of this court.

An inspection of the bill discloses that the nature of the injury complained of is such that an adequate remedy can only be found in this court at the suit of the State of Missouri. It is true that no question of boundary is involved, nor of direct property rights belonging to the complainant state. But it must surely be conceded that, if the health and comfort of the inhabitants of a state are threatened, the state is the proper party to represent and defend them. If Missouri were an independent and sovereign state, all must admit that she could seek a remedy by negotiation, and, that failing, by force. Diplomatic powers and the right to make war having been surrendered to the general government, it was to be expected that upon the latter would be devolved the duty of providing a remedy and that remedy, we think is found in the constitutional provisions we are considering.

This hearing was on demurrer. When the case came before the Court again on the merits, Mr. Justice Holmes delivered the judgment of the Court and, while affirming the jurisdiction of the Court, points out the difficulties the Court has in exercising it and the care it must take in doing so. He said in the course of his opinion: "It may be imagined that a nuisance might be created by a state upon a navigable river like the Danube which would amount to a *casus belli* for a state lower down unless removed. If such a nuisance were created by a state upon the Mississippi, the controversy would be resolved by the more peaceful means of a suit in this court."

Speaking of this provision in the Constitution extending the judicial power to controversies between states, Mr. Justice Bradley in *Hans v. Louisiana* (134 U.S. 1–15) said:

> Some things, undoubtedly, were made justiciable which were not known as such at the common law; such, for example, as controversies between states as to boundary lines, and other question admitting of judicial solution. And yet the case of *Penn v. Lord Baltimore* (I Ves. Sen. 444), shows that some of these unusual subjects for litigation were not unknown to the courts even in colonial times; and several cases of the same general character arose under the Articles of Confederation, and were brought before the tribunal provided for that purpose in those articles (131 U.S. App. 1). The establishment of this new branch of jurisdiction seemed to be necessary from the extinguishment of diplomatic

relations between the states. Of other controversies between a state and another state, or its citizens, which, on the settled principles of public law, are not subjects of judicial cognizance, this court has often declined to take jurisdiction.

A very satisfactory discussion of the scope of the power of the Supreme Court to settle controversies between states is contained in Mr. Justice Brewer's opinion in the suit brought by Kansas against Colorado to restrain the latter from absorbing so much of the water of the Arkansas River flowing from Colorado into Kansas as to interfere seriously with the supply of water from the river for irrigation purposes in Kansas. He said (206 U.S. 95, 99):

> When the States of Kansas and Colorado were admitted into the Union they were admitted with the full powers of local sovereignty which belonged to other states, *Pollard v. Hagan,* supra; *Shively v. Bowlby,* supra; 190 U.S. 508, 519; and Colorado by its legislation has recognized the right of appropriating the flowing waters to the purposes of irrigation. Now the question arises between the states, one recognizing generally the common law rule of riparian rights and the other prescribing the doctrine of the public ownership of flowing water. Neither state can legislate for or impose its own policy upon the other. A stream flows through the two and a controversy is presented as to the flow of that stream. It does not follow, however, that because Congress cannot determine the rule which shall control between the two states or because neither state can enforce its own policy upon the other, that the controversy ceases to be one of a justiciable nature, or that there is no power which can take cognizance of the controversy and determine the relative rights of the two states. Indeed, the disagreement, coupled with its effect upon a stream passing through the two states, makes a matter for investigation and determination by this court. . . .
>
> As Congress cannot make compacts between the states, as it cannot, in respect to certain matters, by legislation compel their separate action, disputes between them must be settled either by force or else by appeal to tribunals empowered to determine the right and wrong thereof. Force under our system of Government is eliminated. The clear language of the Constitution vests in this court the power to settle those disputes. We have exercised that power in a variety of instances, determining in the several instances the justice of the dispute. Nor is our jurisdiction

ousted, even if, because Kansas and Colorado are states sovereign and independent in local matters, the relations between them depend in any respect upon principles of international law. International law is no alien in this tribunal.

One cardinal rule, underlying all the relations of the states to each other, is that of equality of right. Each state stands on the same level with all the rest. It can impose its own legislation on no one of the others, and is bound to yield its own views to none. Yet, whenever, as in the case of *Missouri v. Illinois,* 180 U.S. 208, the action of one state reaches through the agency of natural laws into the territory of another state, the question of the extent and the limitations of the rights of the two states becomes a matter of justiciable dispute between them, and this court is called upon to settle that dispute in such a way as will recognize the equal rights of both and at the same time establish justice between them. In other words, through these successive disputes and decisions this court is practically building up what may not improperly be called interstate common law.

Controversies between one state and another or its citizens which are not justiciable or capable of judicial solution find examples in the suits brought before the Supreme Court. One case of which the Supreme Court refused to take jurisdiction was *Wisconsin v. The Pelican Insurance Company* (1 U.S.), in which the State of Wisconsin sought to enforce against a Louisiana Insurance Company a judgment rendered in a Wisconsin court for penalties by a Wisconsin Statute upon Foreign Insurance Companies for failure to comply with statutory regulations of its business. It was held that neither under international comity nor law was one nation required to enforce extraterritorially the criminal law of another nation and therefore that the controversy presented was not one of which, as between the states of the Union, the Supreme Court could take cognizance. Again in *Louisiana v. Texas,* 176 U.S. 1, Louisiana sought to restrain the Governor of Texas from so enforcing a quarantine law as to injure the business of the people of Louisiana. The law itself on its face was a proper one for the protection of Texas. In dismissing the suit the Court said:

> But in order that a controversy between states, justiciable in this court, can be held to exist, something more must be put forward than that the citizens of one state are injured by the maladministration of the

laws of another. The states cannot make war, or enter into treaties, though they may, with the consent of Congress, make compacts and agreements. When there is no agreement, whose breach might create it, a controversy between states does not arise unless the action complained of is state action, and acts of state officers in abuse or excess of their powers cannot be laid hold of as in themselves committing one state to distinct collision with a sister state.

In our judgment this bill does not set up facts which show that the State of Texas has so authorized or confirmed the alleged action of her health officer as to make it her own, or from which it necessarily follows that the two states are in controversy within the meaning of the Constitution.

Controversies between independent nations suggest themselves which are not capable of judicial solution and yet are quite capable of leading to war.

Thus suppose C nation in the exercise of its conceded powers admits to its shores and indeed to its citizenship the citizens or subjects of A nation and excludes those of B nation from both. The discrimination is certainly within the international right of C nation, but it may lead to acrimony and war. This is not a justiciable question nor one that could be settled by a court.

The so-called General Arbitration Treaties negotiated by Secretary Knox with France and England used the word "justiciable" to describe the kind of questions which the parties bound themselves to submit to arbitration. They defined this to include all issues that could be decided on principles of law or equity. The issue whether a question arising was justiciable and arbitrable was to be left to the decision of a preliminary investigating commission. The term justiciable and indeed the whole scheme of these treaties were suggested by the provision for settling controversies between states in the Federal Constitution and the construction of it by the Supreme Court. The controversies between states, decision of which was not determined by rules furnished by the Constitution or by congressional regulation, were strictly analogous to questions arising between independent nations and were to be divided into justiciable and non-justiciable questions by the same line of distinction.

The treaties were not ratified but their approval by England and

France and by the Executive of this country constitute a valuable and suggestive precedent for the framing of the constitution and jurisdiction of an arbitral court to be one of the main features of a League of Peace between the great nations of the world.

Is it idle to treat such a league as possible? Well, let us take England and Canada. For a hundred years we have been at peace. For that period of time the frontier between us and Canada, four thousand miles long, has been entirely undefended by forts or navies. We have had issue after issue between the two peoples that, because of their nature, might have led to war. But we have settled them by negotiation or, when that has failed, by arbitration, until now it is not too much to say that the "habit" of arbitration between us is so fixed that a treaty to secure such a settlement in future issues would not make it more certain than it is. I concede that conditions have been favorable for the creating of such a customary practice. The two peoples have the same language and literature, the same law and civil liberty and the same origin and history. Each has had a wide domain, in the settlement and development of which their energies and ambitions have been absorbed. The jealousies and encroachments of neighbors in the thickly populated regions of Europe have not been present to stir up strife. And yet we ought not to minimize the beneficent significance of this century of peace by ignoring the fact that many of the issues which we have settled peaceably seemed at the time to be difficult of settlement and likely to lead to war. The Alabama Claims issue and the Oregon Boundary dispute were two of this kind.

It is interesting to note that we now have two permanent arbitral English-American Commissions settling questions. One of them is to determine the equitable rules to govern the use of waters on our national boundary, in which both nations and their citizens have an interest, and to apply them to causes arising. The analogy between the function which the Supreme Court performed in the Kansas and Colorado case in regard to the use of the Arkansas River and that of this Commission in respect to rivers traversing both countries and crossing the border is perfect. Having thus reached what is practically the institution of a League and Arbitral Court with England and Canada for the preservation of peace between us, may we not hope to enlarge its scope and membership and give its benefits to the world?

Will not the exhaustion in which all the belligerents, whether victors or vanquished, find themselves after this awful sacrifice of life and wealth make them wish to make the recurrence of such a war less probable? Will they not be in a mood to entertain any reasonable plan for the settlement of international disputes by peaceable means? Can we not devise such a plan? I think we can.

The Second Hague Conference has proposed a permanent court to settle questions of a legal nature arising between nations. But the signatories to the convention would, under such a plan, not be bound to submit such questions. Nor were the conferring nations able to agree on the constitution of the court. But the agreement on the recommendation for the establishment of such a court shows that the idea is within the bounds of the practical.

To constitute an effective League of Peace, we do not need all the nations. Such an agreement between eight or nine of the Great Powers of Europe, Asia and America would furnish a useful restraint upon possible wars. The successful establishment of a Peace League between the Great Powers would draw into it very quickly the less powerful nations.

What should be the fundamental plan of the League?[2] It seems to me that it ought to contain four provisions. First: It ought to provide for the formation of a court, which would be given jurisdiction by the consent of all the members of the League to consider and decide justiciable questions between them or any of them, which have not yielded to negotiation, according to the principles of international law and equity, and that the court should be vested with power, upon the application of any member of the League, to decide the issue as to whether the question arising is justiciable.

Second: A Commission of Conciliation for the consideration and recommendation of a solution of all non-justiciable questions that may arise between the members of the League should be created, and this Commission should have power to hear evidence, investigate the causes of difference, mediate between the parties and then make its recommendation for a settlement.

Third: Conferences should be held from time to time to agree upon principles of international law, not already established, as their necessity shall suggest themselves. When the conclusions of the Commission shall have been submitted to the various parties of the League for a reasonable period of time, say a year, without calling forth objection, it should be deemed that they acquiesce in the principles thus declared.

Fourth: The members of the League shall agree that if any member of the League shall bring war against any other member of the League, without first having submitted the question, if found justiciable, to the arbitral court provided in the fundamental compact, or without having submitted the question, if found non-justiciable, to the Commission of Conciliation for its examination, consideration and recommendation, then the remaining members of the League agree to join in the forcible defense of the member thus prematurely attacked.

First: The first feature involves the principles of the general arbitration treaties with England and France, to which England and France agreed, and which I submitted to the Senate, and which the Senate rejected or so mutilated as to destroy their vital principle. I think it is of the utmost importance that it should be embraced in any effective League of Peace. The successful operation of the Supreme Court as a tribunal between independent states in deciding justiciable questions not in the control of Congress, or under the legislative regulation of either state, furnishes a precedent and justification for this that I hope I have made clear. Moreover, the inveterate practice of arbitration, which has now grown to be an established custom for the disposition of controversial questions between Canada and the United States, is another confirmation of the practical character of such a court.

Second: We must recognize, however, that the questions within the jurisdiction of such a court would certainly not include all the questions which might lead to war, and that, therefore, we should provide some other instrumentality for helping the solution of those questions which are non-justiciable. This might well be a Commission of Conciliation, a commission to investigate the facts, to consider the arguments on both sides, to mediate between the parties, to see if some compromise cannot be effected, and finally to formulate and recommend a settlement. This may involve time; but the delay, instead of being an objection, is really one of the valuable incidents of the performance of such a function by a commission. We have an example of such a Commission of Conciliation in the controversy between the United States and Great Britain over the Seal Fisheries. The case on its merits as a judicial question was decided against the United

States; but the world importance of not destroying the Pribilof Seal Herd by pelagic sealing was recognized, and a compromise was formulated by the arbitral tribunal, which was ultimately embodied in a treaty between England, Russia, Japan and the United States. Similar recommendations were made by the court of arbitration which considered the issues arising between the United States and Great Britain in respect to the Newfoundland Fisheries.

Third: Periodical conferences should be held between the members of the League for the declaration of principles of international law. This is really a provision for something in the nature of legislative action by the nations concerned in respect to international law. The principles of international law are based upon custom between nations established by actual practice, by their recognition in treaties and by the consensus of great law writers. Undoubtedly the function of an arbitral court established as proposed in the first of the above suggestions would lead to a good deal of valuable judge-made international law. But that would not cover the whole field. Something in the nature of legislation on the subject would be a valuable supplement to existing international law. It would be one of the very admirable results of such a League of Peace, that the scope of international law could be enlarged in this way. Mr. Justice Holmes, in the case of *Missouri v. Illinois,* to which I have already referred, points out that the Supreme Court, in passing on questions between the states, and in laying down the principles of international law that ought to govern in controversies between them, should not and cannot make itself a legislature. But in a League of Peace, there is no limit to the power of international conferences of the members, except the limit of the wise and the practical.

Fourth: The fourth suggestion is one that brings in the idea of force. In the League proposed, all members are to agree that if any one member violates its obligation and begins war against any other member, without submitting its cause for war to the arbitral court, if it is a justiciable question, or to the Commission of Conciliation, if it is otherwise, all the members of the League will unite to defend the member attacked against a war waged in breach of plighted faith. It is to be observed that this does not involve members of the League in an obligation to enforce the judgment of the court or the recommendation of the Commission of Conciliation. It only furnishes the instrumentality of force to prevent attack without submission. It is believed that is more practical than to attempt to enforce judgment after the hearing. One reason is that the failure to submit to one of the two tribunals the threatening cause of war for the consideration of one or the other is a fact easily ascertained, and concerning which there can be no dispute, and it is a palpable violation of the obligation of the members. It is wiser not to attempt too much. The required submission and the delay incident thereto, will in most cases lead to acquiescence in the judgment of the court or in the recommendation of the Commission of Conciliation. The threat of force against plainly unjust war, for that is what is involved in the provision, will have a most salutary deterrent effect. I am aware that membership in this League would involve, on the part of the United States, an obligation to take part in European and Asiatic wars, it may be, and that in this respect it would be a departure from the traditional policy of the United States in avoiding entangling alliances with European or Asiatic countries. But I conceive that the interests of the United States, in view of its close business and social relations, with the other countries of the world, much closer now than ever before, would justify it, if such a League could be formed, in running the remote risk of such a war in order to make more probable the securing of the inestimable boon of peace to the world, an object of desire that now seems so far away.

Notes

Address before the World Court Congress, at Cleveland, Ohio, May 12, 1915.

1. A conventional French word. [Marburg]

2. This is the earliest public utterance of these four principles which correspond to the four articles of the program of the League to Enforce Peace as formally adopted at Phila., June 17, 1915. The principles were worked out at a series of meetings—the last of which, April 9, 1915, was attended by Mr. Taft—[and] were formulated by a small group on April 10th and immediately submitted to Mr. Taft who gave them the final form substantially embodied, later on, in the Phila. platform. [Marburg]

5

Proposals of the League to Enforce Peace

In calling this meeting my associates and I have not been unaware that we might be likened to the Tailors of Tooley Street who mistook themselves for the people of England. We wish, first, to say that we do not represent anybody but ourselves. We are not national legislators, nor do we control the foreign policy of this Government. But we are deeply interested in devising a plan for an international agreement by which, when the present war shall cease, a recurrence of such a war will be made less possible.

We are not here to suggest a means of bringing this war to an end; much as that is to be desired and much as we would be willing to do to secure peace, that is not within the project of the present meeting.

We hope and pray for peace, and our hope of its coming is sufficient to make us think that the present is a good time to discuss and formulate a series of proposals to which the assent of a number of the Great Powers could be secured. We think a League of Peace could be formed which would enable nations to avoid war by furnishing a practical means of settling international quarrels or suspending them until the blinding heat of passion had cooled.

When the world conference is held, our country will have its official representatives to speak for us. We, Tailors of Tooley Street, shall not be there; but, if in our postprandial leisure we shall have discussed and framed a practical plan for a League of Peace, our official representatives will be aided and may in their discretion accept it and present it to the Conference as their own.

There are Tooley Streets in every nation today and the minds of earnest men are being stirred with the same thought and the same purpose—we have heard from them through various channels. The denizens of those Tooley Streets will have their influence upon their respective official representatives. No man can measure the effect upon the peoples of the belligerent countries and upon the peoples of the neutral countries which the horrors and exhaustion of this unprecedented war are going to have. It is certain that they all will look with much more favorable eye to leagues for the preservation of peace than ever before. In no war, moreover, has the direct interest that neutrals have in preventing a war between neighbors been so clearly made known. This interest of neutrals has been so forced upon them that it would require only a slight development and growth in the law of international relations to develop that interest into a right to be consulted before such a war among neighbors can be begun. This step we hope to have taken by the formation of a Peace League of the Great Powers, whose primary and fundamental principle shall be that no war can take place between any two members of the League until they have resorted to the machinery that the League proposes to furnish to settle the controversy likely to lead to war.

If any member of the League refuses to use this machinery, and attacks another member in breach of his League obligation, all members of the League agree to defend the member attacked by force.

We do not think the ultimate resort to force can be safely omitted from an effective League of Peace. We sincerely hope that it may never become necessary, and that the deterrent effect of its inevitable use in case of a breach of the League obligation will help materially to give sanction to the laws of the League and to render a resort to force avoidable

We are not peace-at-any-price men, because we do not think we have reached the time when a plan based on the complete abolition of war is practicable. As long as nations partake of the frailties of men who compose them, war is a possibility and that possibility should not be ignored in any League of Peace that is to be useful. We do not think it necessary to call peace-at-any-price men cowards, or apply other epithets to them. We have known in history the most noble characters who adhered to such a view and yet the example of their physical and moral courage is a heritage of mankind. To those who differ with us in our view of the necessity for this feature of possible force in our plan, we say we respect your attitude. We admit your claim to sincere patriotism to be as just as ours. We do not ascribe your desire to avoid war to be a fear of death to yourselves or your sons; but rather to your sense of the horror, injustice and ineffectiveness of settling any international issue by such a brutal arbitrament. Nevertheless, we differ with you in judgment that, in the world of nations as they are, war can be completely avoided. We believe it is still necessary to use a threat of overwhelming force of a great League with a willingness to make the threat good in order to frighten nations into a use of rational and peaceful means to settle their issues with their associates of the League. Nor are we militarists or jingoes—we are trying to follow a middle and practical path.

Now what is the machinery, a resort to which we wish to force on an intending belligerent of the League? It consists of two tribunals, to one of which every issue must be submitted. Issues between nations are of two classes:

First: Issues that can be decided on principles of international law and equity, called justiciable.

Second: Issues that cannot be decided on such principles of law and equity, but which might be quite as irritating and provocative of war, called non-justiciable.

The questions of the Alaskan Boundary, of the Bering Sea Seal Fisheries, and of the Alabama Claims were justiciable issues that could be settled by a court, exactly as the Supreme Court would settle claims between States.

The questions whether the Japanese should be naturalized, whether all American citizens should be admitted to Russia as merchants without regard to religious faith, are capable of causing great irritation against the nation denying the privilege; and yet such nations, in the absence of a treaty on the subject, are completely within their international right and the real essence of the trouble cannot be aided by a resort to a court. The dispute is non-justiciable.

We propose that for justiciable questions we shall have an impartial court to which all questions arising between members of the League shall be submitted. If the court finds the question justiciable, it shall decide it. If it does not, it shall refer it to a Commission of Conciliation to investigate, confer, hear argument and recommend a compromise.

We do not propose, in our plan, to enforce compliance either with the Court's judgment or the Conciliation Commission's recommendation. We feel that we ought not to attempt too much. We believe that the forced submission, the truce taken to investigate and the judicial decision, or the conciliatory compromise recommended, will form a material inducement to peace. It will cool the heat of passion and will give the men of peace in each nation time to still the jingoes.

The League of Peace will furnish a great opportunity for more definite formulation of the principles of international law. The arbitral court will amplify it and enrich it in their application of its general principles to particular cases. They will create a body of judge-made laws of the highest value.

Then the existence of the League will lead to ever recurring congresses of the League, which, acting in a quasi-legislative capacity, may widen the scope of international law in a way that a court may not feel able or competent to do.

This is our plan. It is not complicated, at least in statement. In its practical application, difficulties now unforeseen may arise, but we believe it offers a working hypothesis upon which a successful arrangement can be made.

We are greeted first by the objection that no treaties can prevent war. We are not called upon to deny this in order to justify or vindicate our proposals as useful. We realize that nations are sometimes utterly immoral in breaking treaties and shamelessly bold in avowing their right to do so on the ground of necessity. But this is not always the case. We cannot give up treaties because sometimes they are broken any more than we can give up commercial contracts because men sometimes dishonor themselves by breaking them. We decline to assume that all nations are always dishonorable or that a solemn treaty obligation will not have some deterrent effect upon a nation which has plighted its faith, to prevent its breach. In every nation there are people who are in favor of peace and opposed to war, and when you furnish a treaty that binds the nation not to go to war, you strengthen the hands of the people in that nation that do not want to go to war and are in favor of preserving the honor of the nation. When we add to this the sanction of an agreement by a number of powerful nations to enforce the obligation of the recalcitrant and faithless member, we think we have a treaty that is much more than a "scrap of paper"—and we base our faith in this on a common sense view of human nature.

We have got to depart from the traditional policy of this country, I agree. But this war has borne in on us the fact that we are so near to all the nations of the world today that we are vitally interested in keeping war down as far as we can, and that we had better step forward and assume certain obligations in the interest of the world and in the interest of mankind, because there is a utilitarian reason for it—we are likely to be drawn in ourselves. Therefore we ought to depart from the policy of isolation that heretofore has served us so well, because we are a strong nation. We must bear our share of the responsibilities of the moment, and we must help along the world, and incidentally help along ourselves, for I believe, even if you view it from a selfish standpoint, in the long run it will be a better policy.

It is objected that we only propose to include the more powerful nations. We'll gladly include them all. But we don't propose to have the constitution of our court complicated by a demand for equal representation of the many smaller nations. We believe that when we have a League initiated by the larger powers, the smaller powers will be glad to come in and enjoy the protection that the League will afford against the unjust aggression of the strong against the weak.

Note

Address delivered at the Convention of the League to Enforce Peace which was held at Philadelphia, June 17, 1915.

6

Constitutionality of the Proposals

To me has been assigned the discussion of the constitutional objections to the proposals of the League to Enforce Peace. These objections, so far as I understand them, are directed against the first and third planks in our platform. The first plank reads as follows:

"First: All justiciable questions arising between the signatory powers, not settled by negotiation, shall, subject to the limitations of treaties, be submitted to a judicial tribunal for hearing and judgment, both upon the merits and upon any issues as to its jurisdiction of the question."

This looks to an organization of a permanent court by the signatories to the League. It contemplates the opportunity of any member of the League, having a cause of complaint against any other member of the League, to sue such member in this court and bring it into court by proper process. The complainant's pleading will, of course, state its cause of action. The defendant may wish to question the jurisdiction of the court on the ground, for instance, that the cause of action stated by the complainant does not involve a justiciable issue; that it can not be decided on principles of law or equity.

The court, upon this preliminary question, must decide upon its jurisdiction. If it finds the question not to be justiciable, it must dismiss the complaint; but it may properly refer its investigation to the Commission of Conciliation. If it finds that it is justiciable, it must require the defendant nation to answer.

What I have to discuss is whether the President and the Senate, constituting the treaty-making power for this Government, may consent, for and on behalf of the United States, to the settlement of any justiciable issue arising between the United States and any other member of the League by this permanent court; and whether it may leave to that court the power to decide whether the issue raised is a justiciable one. It was argued against a similar provision in the general arbitration treaties with England and France that such a stipulation constituted a delegation by the President and Senate of the authority reposed in them over the foreign relations of our Government and therefore that it was *ultravires*. Both upon reason and authority this objection is untenable. The United States is a nation, and, from a foreign standpoint, a sovereign nation, without limitation of its sovereignty. It may, therefore, through its treaty-making power, consent to any agreement with other powers relating to subject matter that is usually considered and made the subject of treaties. The well-known language of Mr. Justice Field, in the case of *Geofrey v. Riggs*, 133 U.S. 258, leaves no doubt upon this point. It is as follows:

> That the treaty power of the United States extends to all proper subjects of negotiations between our Government and the Governments of other nations, is clear. . . . The treaty power, as expressed in the Constitution, is in terms unlimited, except by those restraints which are found in that instrument against the action of the Government, or of its Departments, and those arising from the nature of the Government itself, and of that of the States. It would not be contended that it extends so far as to authorize what the Constitution forbids, or a change in the character of the Government, or in that of one of the States, or a cession of any portion of the territory of the latter without its consent. But with these exceptions, it is not perceived that there is any limit to the questions which can be adjusted touching any matter which is properly the subject of negotiation with a foreign country.

Issues that can be settled on principles of law and equity are proper subjects for decision by a judicial tribunal. Such issues have been settled by Boards of Arbitration, agreed to by independent sovereigns since there were governments. The first provision agreed to by the United States for an arbitration of this kind was in the Jay Treaty in 1794; and since that time there have been eighty-four international arbitrations to which an American nation was a party. In forty, or nearly one-half of these, the other party was an European Power, while the arbitrations between American nations were forty-four. To about two-thirds of all of these the United States was a party, the number of arbitrations between other American powers being fourteen. Of this number, there were ten that related to questions of boundary, which are, of course, questions capable of solution on principles of law and equity.

In such cases, it was never suggested that the Government was delegating any power at all to the tribunal. A submission to a judicial decision is not a delegation of power as to an agent. It is a submission of an issue to a judge. It is an error to call such a submission a delegation, or to determine its validity on principles of delegation of power as that is limited in constitutional law. In the discussion of the general arbitration treaties in the Senate, there was a suggestion that the agreement to submit to a court questions which had not yet arisen described only by definition and classification, with power in the court to take jurisdiction, was more of a delegation of power than the mere submission of an existing question to arbitrators. There is, however, not the slightest difference in principle between the two. If one is a delegation, the other is. If one is invalid, the other is; and if one is not invalid, the other is not.

Nor does the right to determine jurisdiction of the court involve in principle any more of a delegation than the mere voluntary submission of the issue to the court. It only somewhat enlarges the issues to be submitted. The question whether the court has jurisdiction of an issue is dependent on the question of law, involving the construction of the treaty, and such a subject matter is the commonest instance of the class of questions submitted to arbitration or a court. More than this, the Senate has consented from time to time to arbitrations on issues which may arise in the future and [are] defined by language of the treaty of submission.

The last notable instance, and the one which involved a really permanent court is the advice and consent by our Senate to the Hague International Prize Court Convention in which a permanent international prize court was established, and the United States bound itself to submit all questions, arising between it and foreign nations in respect to questions of prize in naval warfare, to this international prize court, and to abide the decision, even though that decision might involve, as it generally would, the reconsideration of an issue already decided by the Supreme Court of the United States. The treaty is not in force because England did not finally approve, but our Senate approved it. The International Prize Court must of necessity pass upon its own jurisdiction, and by agreement between the parties, its decision is to be accepted and to be carried out in good faith. The question as to whether commissioners of arbitration, under the Jay Treaty, had power to determine their own jurisdiction was brought by Rufus King, American Minister in London, to the attention of Lord Grenville who submitted the question to Lord Chancellor Loughborough. The Lord Chancellor resolved the difficulty by declaring:

"That the doubt respecting the authority of the Commissioners to settle their own jurisdiction was absurd; and that they must necessarily decide upon cases being within, or without, their competency."

A similar question was raised by the British Government in regard to the power of the Geneva Tribunal to deal with what were known as the "indirect claims," and her arbitrators decided that they did not have jurisdiction of the indirect claims, and this was acquiesced in by both Governments.

In correspondence with the Chilean Minister over an arbitration between this country and Chile, Mr. Olney, then Secretary of State, used this language:

But the question whether any particular claim is a proper one for the consideration and decision of an international commission is necessarily one which the commission itself must determine. The conventions under which such commissions are organized usually describe in general terms the class of cases of which the commission is to take jurisdiction, and whether any particular case presented to it comes within this class the commission must, of course, determine. The decisions of the late commission, both interlocutory and final, are binding upon both Governments, the latter absolutely so, the former unless reversed, after proper proceedings for a rehearing.

I come now to the other objection. The third plank of the platform is as follows:

"Third: The signatory powers shall jointly use forthwith both their economic and military forces against any one of their number that goes to war, or commits acts of hostility, against another of the signatories before any question arising shall be submitted as provided in the foregoing."

It is objected to this clause that it violates the Constitution in that the effect of such a treaty signed by the United States would take away from Congress the power, conferred upon it by section eight of article one, to declare war.

I had the pleasure and privilege of hearing Mr. Bryan advance this argument at the Lake Mohonk Conference. He said that we should need an amendment to the Constitution before we could agree to any such provision. He said that in order to carry out the provision we must have a joint council of the powers to determine when the time had arrived for military action and war, and that this would substitute the action of the council for the constitutional discretion of Congress.

I venture to think that this view is wholly without foundation. Although it is not necessary, I am willing to accept the assumption that some kind of a council would be appointed by the powers to make the announcements when the time had come for the use of economic and military forces against the recalcitrant member. Does that take away from Congress the power to declare war? It does not. If the war is a foreign war, it could not be begun under the Constitution until Congress had declared war. The President would not be authorized to direct the Army and the Navy to begin war until Congress had declared it.

What, then, would be the situation if the fact were announced upon which the obligation of the United States to make war arose under this treaty? It would be to make war by Constitutional means, that is, by preliminary declaration of Congress that war existed. Congress might decline to exercise that power and refuse to declare war. What would be the effect of that? It would merely be a breach of faith on the part of Congress, and so a breach of faith on the part of the United States and we would not go to war. The treaty-making power under the Constitution creates the obligation to declare war in certain contingencies. That obligation is to be discharged by Congress under its Constitutional power to declare war. If it fails to do so, and thus comply with the binding obligation created by the treaty-making power, then it merely breaks the contract of the Government. It is left to Congress to carry out that which we in a Constitutional way have agreed to do. Thus to impose in a Constitutional way by treaty an obligation on Congress is not to take away its power to discharge it or to refuse to discharge it.

In 1904 we entered into a treaty with the Republic of Panama, the first article of which is:

"The United States guarantees and will maintain the independence of the Republic of Panama."

What is the necessary effect of this guaranty? It necessarily means that if any nation attacks Panama and attempts to take territory from her or to subvert her Government, the United States is under treaty obligation to make war to defend Panama. Was it ever supposed that such an obligation took away from Congress the power to declare war? This treaty obligation makes it the duty of the Government to declare war under certain conditions that may arise, creates a contract obligation to the Republic of Panama that it shall do so, and this duty can only be discharged through the action of Congress in declaring war. Does that deprive Congress of its Constitutional power to declare war? It seems to me the question answers itself.

In our relations with Cuba we find in the present treaty:

Article I

"The Government of Cuba shall never enter into any treaty or other compact with any foreign power or powers which will impair or tend to impair the independence of Cuba, nor in any manner authorize or permit any foreign power or powers to obtain by colonization or for military or naval purposes or otherwise, lodgment in or control over any portion of said Island."

Article II

"The Government of Cuba consents that the United States may exercise the right to intervene for the preservation of Cuban independence, the maintenance of a government adequate for the protection of life, property and individual liberty, and for discharging the obligation with respect to Cuba imposed by the Treaty of Paris on the United States now to be assumed and undertaken by the Government of Cuba."

Article III

"To enable the United States to maintain the independence of Cuba, and to protect the people thereof, as well as for its own defense, the Government of Cuba will sell or lease to the United States, lands necessary for coaling or naval stations at certain specific points to be agreed upon with the President of the United States."

It is quite clear from these three articles that the Government of the United States binds itself to maintain the independence of Cuba and to exclude other governments from lodgment in the Island. If any Government attempts to filch territory from Cuba or to subvert the government, it becomes the duty of the United States to make war and defend against such invasion. Does this treaty obligation thus created take away from Congress the power to declare war? It only creates the obligation on the part of the United States to wage war, and in discharging this obligation Congress must act, or the Government must be recreant to its agreement.

Thus, by reason and precedent, it would appear clear that this third plank of the platform of the League is not in any way an attempt to take from Congress the power which it has to declare war under the Constitution. The suggestion that in order to carry out such an obligation on the part of the United States, it would be necessary to amend the Constitution, grows out of a confusion of ideas and a failure to analyze the differences between the creation of an obligation of the United States to do a thing and the due, orderly and Constitutional course to be taken by it in doing that which it has agreed to do.

Note

Address delivered at the First Annual Assemblage of the League to Enforce Peace, Washington, D.C., May 26, 1916.

7

A Constructive Plan for Human Betterment

What is International Law? It is the body of rules governing the conduct of the nations of the world toward one another, acquiesced in by all nations. It lacks scope and definiteness. It is found in writings of international jurists, in treaties, in the results of arbitration, and in the decisions of those municipal courts which apply international law, like the Supreme Court of the United States and courts that sit in prize cases to determine the rules of international law governing the capture of vessels in naval warfare. It is obvious that a Congress of the League with quasi-legislative powers could greatly add to the efficacy of international law by enlarging its application and codifying its rules. It would be greatly in the interest of the world and of world peace to give to such a code of rules the express sanction of the family of nations.

As to the submission of all questions at issue of a legal nature to a permanent international court, it is sufficient to point out that the proposal is practical and is justified by precedent. The Supreme Court of the United States, *exercising the jurisdiction conferred on it by the Constitution*, sits as a permanent international tribunal to decide issues between the States of the Union. The law governing the settlement of most of the controversies between the States cannot be determined by reference to the Constitution, to statutes of Congress, or to the legislation of the States. Should Congress in such cases attempt to enact laws they would be invalid. The only law which applies is that which applies between independent governments, to wit: International Law. Take the case of Kansas against Colorado, heard and decided by the Supreme Court. Kansas complained that Colorado was using more of the water of the Arkansas River which flowed through Colorado into Kansas than was equitable for purposes of irrigation. The case was heard by the Supreme Court and decided, not by a law of Congress, not by the law of Kansas, not by the law of Colorado, for the law of neither applied. It was decided by principles of International Law.

Many other instances of similar decisions by the Supreme Court could be cited. But it is said that such a precedent lacks force here because the States are restrained from going to war with each other by the power of the National Government. Admitting that this qualifies the precedent to some extent, we need go no further than Canada to find a complete analogy and a full precedent. There is now sitting to decide questions of boundary waters (exactly such questions as were considered in Kansas and Colorado) a permanent court, consisting of three Americans and three Canadians, to settle the principles of international law that apply to the use of rivers constituting a boundary between the two countries and of rivers crossing the boundary. The fact is, that we have gotten so into the habit of arbitration with Canada that no reasonable person expects that any issue arising between us and that country, after a hundred years of peace, will be settled other than by arbitration.

If this be the case between ourselves and Canada and England, why may it not be practical with every well-established and ordered government of the Great Powers? The Second Hague Conference, attended by all nations, recommended the establishment of a permanent International Court to decide questions of a legal nature arising between nations.

The second proposal of the League involves the submission to a Commission of Conciliation of all questions that cannot be settled in court on principles of law or equity. There are such questions which may lead to war, and frequently do, and there are no legal rules for decision. We have such questions giving rise to friction in our domestic life. If a lady who owns a lawn permits children of one neighbor to play upon that lawn and refuses the privilege to the children of another neighbor because she thinks the latter children are badly trained and will injure her lawn or her flowers, it requires no imagination to understand that there may arise a neighborhood issue that will lead to friction between the families. The issue is, however, a non-justiciable one. Courts cannot settle it, for the reason that the lady owning the lawn has the right to say who shall come on it and who shall be excluded from it. No justiciable issue can arise, unless one's imagination goes to the point of supposing that the husbands of the two differing ladies came together and clashed, and then the issue in court will not be as to the comparative training of the children of the families.

We have an analogous question in our foreign relations with reference to the admission of the Chinese and Japanese. We discriminate against them in our naturalization and immigration laws and extend the benefit of those laws only to whites and persons of African descent. This discrimination has caused much ill-feeling among the Japanese and Chinese. We are within our international right in excluding them; but it is easy to understand how resentment, because of such discrimination, might be fanned into a flame, if through lawless violence or unjust State legislation the Japanese should be mistreated within the United States.

We have had instances of the successful result of commissions of conciliation where the law could not cover the differences between the two nations. Such was the case of the Bering Sea controversy.[1] We sought to prevent the killing of female seals in the Bering Sea and asserted our territorial jurisdiction over that sea for this purpose. The question was submitted to international arbitrators and the decision was against us; but the arbitrators, in order to save to the world the only valuable and extensive herd of fur seals, recommended a compromise by treaty between the nations concerned, and accordingly treaties have been made between the United States, Great Britain, Russia and Japan which have restored the herd to its former size and value. So much, therefore, for the practical character of the first two proposals.

The third proposal is more novel than the others and gives to the whole plan a more constructive character. It looks to the use of economic means first, and military force if necessary, to enforce the obligation of every member of the League to submit any complaint it has to make against another member of the League, either to the permanent international court, or to the Commission of Conciliation, and to await final action by that tribunal before beginning hostilities. It will be observed that it is not the purpose of this program to use the economic boycott or the jointly acting armies of the League to enforce the judgment declared or the compromise recommended. These means are used only to prevent the beginning of war before there has been a complete submission, hearing of evidence, argument and decision or recommendation. We sincerely believe that in most cases, with such a delay and such a winnowing out of the issues and such an opportunity for the peoples of the different countries to understand the position of each other, war would generally not be resorted to. Our ambition is not to propose a plan, the perfect working out of which will absolutely prevent war; first, because we do not think such a plan would work; and second, because we are willing to concede that there may be governmental and international injustice which cannot be remedied except by force. If, therefore, after a full discussion and decision by impartial judges or a recommendation by earnest, sincere and equitable compromisers, a people still thinks that it must vindicate its rights by war, we do not attempt in this plan to prevent it by force.

Having thus explained what the plan is, let us consider the objections which have been made to it.

The first objection is that, in a dispute between two members of the League, it would be practically difficult to determine which one was the aggressor and which one, therefore, in fact, began actual hostilities. There may be some trouble in this, I can see; but what we are dealing with is a working hypothesis, a very general plan. The details are not worked out. One can suggest that an International Council engaged in an attempt to mediate the differences might easily determine for the League which nation was at fault in beginning hostilities. It would doubtless be necessary where some issues arise to require a maintenance of the *status quo* until the issues were submitted and decided in one tribunal or the other; but it does not seem to me that these suggested difficulties are insuperable or may not be completely met by a detailed procedure that, of course, must be fixed before the plan of the League shall become operative.

The second objection is to the use of the economic boycott and the army and the navy to enforce the obligations entered into by the members of the League. I respect the views of Pacifists and those who advocate the doctrine of non-resistance as the only Christian doctrine. Such is the view of that Society of Friends which, with a courage higher than that possessed by those who advocate forcible means, are willing to subject themselves to the injustice of the wicked in order to carry out their ideal of what Christian action should be. They have been so far in advance of the general opinions of the world in their history of three hundred years, and have lived to see so many of their doctrines recognized by the world as just, that I always differ from them with reluctance. Still, it seems to me that in the necessity of preserving our civilization and saving our country's freedom and individual liberty maintained now for one hundred and twenty-five years, we have no right to assume that we have passed beyond the period in history when nations are affected by the same frailties and the same temptations to cupidity, cruelty and injustice as men. In our domestic communities we need a police force to protect the innocent and the just against the criminal and the unjust, and to maintain the guaranty of life, liberty and property. The analogy between the domestic community and that of nations is sufficiently close to justify and require what is in fact an international police force. The attitude of those who oppose using force or a threat of force to compel nations to keep the peace is really like that of the modern school of theoretical anarchists, who maintain that if all restraint were removed and there were no government, and the children and youth, and men and women were trained to self-responsibility, every member of society would know what his or her duty was and would perform it. They assert that it is the existence of restraint that leads to the violation of right. I may be permitted to remark that with modern fads of education we have gone far in the direction of applying this principle of modern anarchy in the discipline and education of our children and youth, but I do not think the result can be said to justify the theory if we can judge from the strikes of school children or from the general lack of discipline and respect for authority that the rising generation manifests. The time has not come when we can afford to give up the threat of the police and the use of force to back up and sustain the obligation of moral duty.

The third objection is that it would be unconstitutional for the United States, through its treaty-making power, to enter into such a League. This objection is based on the fact that the Constitution vests in Congress the power to declare war. It is said that this League would transfer the power to declare war away from Congress to some foreign council, in which the United States would only have a representative. This objection grows out of a misconception of the effect of a treaty and a confusion of ideas. The United States makes its contract with other nations under the Constitution through the President and two-thirds of the Senate, who constitute the treaty-making power. The President and the Senate have a right to bind the United States to any contract with any other nation covering the subject matter within the normal field of treaties. For this purpose the President and the Senate are the United States. When the contract comes to be performed, the United States is to perform it through that department of the government which, by the Constitution, should perform it, should represent the government and should act for it. Thus, the treaty-making power may bind the United States to pay to another country under certain conditions a million dollars. When the conditions are fulfilled, then it becomes the duty of the United States to pay the million dollars. Under the Constitution, only Congress can appropriate the million dollars from the treasury. Therefore, it becomes the duty of Congress to make that appropriation. It may refuse to make the appropriation. If it does so, it dishonors the written obligation of the United States. It has the power either to perform the obligation or to refuse to perform it. That fact, however, does not make the action of the treaty power in binding the United States to pay the money unconstitutional. So the treaty-making power may bind the United States under certain conditions to make war. When the conditions arise requiring the making of war, then it becomes the duty of Congress honorably to perform the obligation of the United States. Congress may shirk this duty and exercise its power to refuse to declare war. It thus dishonors a binding obligation of the United States. But the obligation was entered into in the constitutional way and it is to be performed in the constitutional way.

It is said that to enter into such a compact would require us to maintain a standing army. I do not think this follows at all. If we become, as we should become, reasonably prepared to resist unjust military aggression, and have a navy sufficiently large, and coast defenses sufficiently well equipped to constitute a first line of defense, and an army which we could mobilize into half a million trained men within two months, we would have all the force needed to do our part of the police work in resisting the unlawful aggression of any one member of the League against another.

Fourth, it has been urged that for us to become a party to this League is to give up our Monroe Doctrine, under which we ought forcibly to resist any attempt on the part of European or Asiatic powers to subvert an independent government in the Western Hemisphere or to take from such a government any substantial part of its territory. It is a sufficient answer to this objection to say that a question under the Monroe Doctrine would come under that class of issues which must be submitted to a Council of Conciliation. Pending this, of course, the *status quo* must be maintained. An argument and recommendation of compromise would follow. If we did not agree to the compromise and proceeded forcibly to resist violation of the Doctrine, we should not be violating the terms of the League by hostilities thereafter. More than this, as Professor Wilson, of Harvard, the well-known authority upon international law, has pointed out, we are already under a written obligation to delay a year before beginning hostilities in respect to any question arising between us and most of the Great Powers, and this necessarily includes questions relating to a violation of the Monroe Doctrine. It is difficult to see, therefore, how the obligation of such a League as this would put us in any different position from that which we now occupy in regard to the Monroe Doctrine.

Finally, I come to the most formidable objection, which is that entering into such a League by the United States would be a departure from the policy that it has consistently pursued since the days of Washington, in accordance with the advice of his farewell address that we enter into no entangling alliances with European countries. Those of us who support the proposals of the League believe that were Washington living today he would not consider the League as an entangling alliance. He had in mind such a treaty as that the United States made with France, by which we were subjected to great embarrassment when France attempted to use our ports as bases of operation against England while we were at peace with England. He certainly did not have in mind a union of all the Great Powers to enforce peace; and while he did dwell, and properly dwelt, on the very great advantage that the United States had in her isolation from European disputes, it was an isolation which does not now exist. In his day we were only three and a half millions of people, with thirteen States strung along the

Atlantic seaboard. We were five times as far from Europe as we are now in speed of transportation, and many times as far in speed of communication. We are now one hundred millions of people between the two oceans and between the Canada line and the Gulf. We face the Pacific with California, Oregon and Washington, which alone makes us a Pacific power. We own Alaska, the northwestern corner of our continent, a dominion of immense extent with natural resources as yet hardly calculable and with a country capable of supporting a considerable population. This makes us a close neighbor of Russia across the Bering Straits; while ownership of islands in that sea brings us close to Japan. We own Hawaii, 2,000 miles out to sea from San Francisco, with 75,000 Japanese laborers constituting the largest element of its population. We own the Philippine Islands, 140,000 square miles, with eight millions of people, under the eaves of Asia. We are properly anxious to maintain an open door to China, and to share equally in the enormous trade which that country, with her 400 teeming millions, is bound to furnish when organized capital and her wonderful laboring populations shall be intelligently directed toward the development of her rich natural resources. Our discrimination against the Japanese and the Chinese presents a possible cause of friction, since the resentment that they feel may lead to untoward incidents. We own the Panama Canal in a country which was recently a part of a South American confederation. We have invested 400 millions in that great world enterprise to unite our Eastern and Western seaboards by cheap transportation, to increase the effectiveness of our navy and to make a path for the world's commerce between the two great oceans.

We own Puerto Rico, with a million people, and we owe to those people protection at home and abroad, as they owe allegiance to us.

We have guaranteed the integrity of Cuba, and have reserved the right to enter and maintain the guaranty of life, liberty and property and to repress insurrection in that island. Since originally turning over the island to its people we have had once to return there and restore peace and order. We have on our southern border the international nuisance of Mexico, and nobody can foresee the complications that will arise out of the anarchy there prevailing. We have the Monroe Doctrine still to maintain. Our relations to Europe have been shown to be very near by our experience in pursuing lawfully our natural rights in our trade upon the Atlantic Ocean with European countries. Both belligerents have violated our rights, and in the now nearly two years which have elapsed since the war began we have been close to war in the defense of those rights. Contrast our present world relations with those we had in Washington's time. It would seem clear that the conditions have so changed as to justify a seeming departure from advice directed to such a different state of things. One may reasonably question whether the United States, by uniting with the other great powers to prevent the recurrence of future world war, may not risk less in assuming the obligations of a member of the League than by refusing to become such a member in view of her world-wide interests. But even if the risk of war to the United States would be greater by entering the League than by staying out of it, does not the United States have a duty, as a member of the family of nations, to do its part and run its necessary risk to make less probable the coming of such another war and such another disaster to the human race?

We are the richest nation in the world, and in the sense of what we could do were we to make reasonable preparation we are the most powerful nation in the world. We have been showered with good fortune. Our people have enjoyed a happiness known to no other people. Does not this impose upon us a sacred duty to join the other nations of the world in a fraternal spirit and with a willingness to make sacrifices if we can promote the general welfare of men?

At the close of this war the governments and the people of the belligerent countries, under the enormous burdens and suffering from the great losses of the war, will be in a condition of mind to accept and promote such a plan for the enforcement of future peace. President Wilson, at the head of this administration and the initiator of our foreign policies under the Constitution, and Senator Lodge, the senior Republican member of the Committee on Foreign Relations, and therefore the leader of the opposition on such an issue, have both approved of the principles of the League to Enforce Peace. Sir Edward Grey and Lord Bryce have indicated their sympathy and support of the same principles, and we understand that M. Briand, of France, has similar views.

Notes

Address delivered before the National Educational Association, New York City, July 3, 1916.

1. In an address before the National Geographic Society in Washington, D.C., Jan. 17, 1919, Mr. Taft has the following to say in regard to this arbitration:

The United States, by a transfer from Russia, became the owner of the Pribiloff Islands, in the middle of the Bering Sea. Upon those islands was the breeding place of the largest herd of fur-bearing seals in the world. They were a valuable property and a considerable annual income was derived by the United States from the sale of the fur. Canadian schooners began what was called pelagic sealing. They shot the seals in the open Bering Sea. This indiscriminate hunting killed the females of the herd and was destroying it. Revenue cutters of the United States, by direction of the government, served such sealing vessels, brought them into a port of the United States, where were instituted proceedings to forfeit them. Great Britain objected on the ground that the United States had no legal jurisdiction. The case was submitted to an arbitration. The treaty contained a provision that the arbitrators, should they reach the conclusion that the United States had no legal right, might recommend a basis of compromise. The United States asserted its right, on the ground, first, that it had territorial jurisdiction over the open waters of the Bering Sea by transfer from Russia, which had asserted, maintained, and enjoyed such jurisdiction, and, second, that it owned the seals while in the sea in such a way that the Canadian schooners were despoiling its personal property. The court of arbitration held against the United States on both points, deciding that Russia never had any territorial jurisdiction over the open Bering Sea to transfer to the United States, and that when the seals left the islands and swam out into the open sea they were the property of no one and were subject to capture by any one. The judgment of the court, therefore, was against the United States and awarded damages. Pursuing, however, the recommendation of the treaty, the court made itself into a council of mediation. It said that while the killing of seals in the open sea was not a violation of the legal rights of the United States of which that country could legally complain, it was nevertheless a great injury to the common welfare of the world to destroy this greatest seal herd of the world, first, because the fur was valuable and useful for the garments of men and women, and, second, because the destruction of the herd would destroy valuable and useful industries in the preparation of the seal pelts for use. Therefore, they said it was good form and in the interest of the world that the four nations concerned should agree upon a compromise by which the United States might continue to maintain the herd and sell the seal pelts gathered on the islands and that pelagic sealing should be stopped, but that the United States, in consideration of the other three nations restricting their citizens from pelagic sealing, should divide with the other three nations some of the profits of the herd. Accordingly, Great Britain, Russia, Japan, and the United States made such a treaty, which is still in force and under which the herd has been restored to its former size and value. Here we have an example of a court passing on questions of legal right and deciding them against the United States. Then we have the court changing itself into a council of mediation and recommending a compromise, prompted by considerations of decency and good form and the public welfare of the world, which the nations appealed to have adopted and embodied in a treaty.

[Marburg]

8

The Purposes of the League

The purpose of the League to Enforce Peace is, after the present war, to organize the world politically so as to enable it to use its power to prevent the hotheadedness of any nation from lighting a fire of war which shall spread into another general conflagration. It proposes to effect this by securing membership in the League of all the great nations of the world. The minor stable nations will then certainly join because of the protection which the League would afford them against sudden attack by a great power. The League will then become a World League. If it does not, it will fail of its purpose. No member of the League is to begin war against any other member until after the question between them shall have been submitted to a Court, if the question is of a legal nature, or a Commission of Conciliation, if it can not be settled on principles of law. The members agree to await the judgment in the one case or the recommendation of a compromise in the other, before beginning hostilities. If any member violates this agreement and begins hostilities before the appointed time, the whole power of the League, by the joint use of the military and naval force of its members, is to be exerted to defend the nation prematurely attacked against the nation attacking it. The compulsion thus to be exercised is directed only to securing deliberation and delay sufficient to permit a hearing and judgment on questions of a legal nature, and a hearing and recommendation of compromise on other questions.

There would be practical difficulties in attempting to enforce judgments, difficulties which may some day be overcome but which the League has now no purpose to attempt to solve. It would be still more difficult to enforce compromises. The League contents itself, and believes that it will make a long step forward if it succeeds, in securing a world agreement by which hearings of the irritating issues may be had and a decision rendered before war is allowed to begin. It is confident that, in most cases, a war thus delayed for a full discussion of the issues and a fair decision will never come.

Mr. Roosevelt objects to the League with great emphasis. It would have added to the usefulness of his criticism if he had read carefully the proposals of the League. He assumes that the League proposes that the judgments and recommendations of compromise reached shall be enforced by the League. This is a fundamental error. We may therefore dismiss further consideration of Mr. Roosevelt's objections.

Senator Borah objects to the League because he says it will involve the United States in a surrender of the Monroe Doctrine and in momentous obligations which he does not think the people would be willing to assume. I quite agree that the League will involve momentous consequences, and I also quite agree that the people of the United States ought to understand exactly what those consequences are and the burdens that they would assume in entering such a League. It would be a great deal better not to enter such a League than to suffer the humiliation of having made an agreement and then repudiate it. There is no disposition on the part of those who are urging the adoption of the League to avoid a discussion of its necessary consequences. They, on the contrary, seek the fullest discussion because it would be idle for the treaty-making power to enter into a treaty of this kind until after Congress and all the people of the United States shall know and fully approve our participation in such a movement.

Senator Borah supposes three cases to show its dangers. In the first, Russia and Japan, being members of the League with all the other great nations of the World, have a controversy over a matter in Manchuria. Russia refuses submission to a Court or Commission, and begins hostilities against Japan. Under the League, England, France, Germany, Austria, Italy and the United States would unite forces with Japan to defeat Russia's attack. The United States would have to contribute men and vessels according to some equitable rule prescribed in the Treaty, proportioned to resources and geographical location. This is the extreme responsibility which the United States must face. This is the burden she might have. But it is improbable. With a knowledge of this union of tremendous forces against her, Russia would not be likely to violate her plighted faith. The moral effect of the power of the world would prevent her. Ought the United States not be willing to run the risk of being called upon to contribute her quota in such a remote contingency in order that the power of the world may become effective without actual use of force to stop war? Each instance of its successful exercise would strengthen its future moral influence.

The second case suggested by Senator Borah is this. Mexico transfers part of her territory to Japan, and Japan takes it. Thus the Monroe Doctrine is violated. The United States protests and Japan demands a submission under the League. The question is a political one; the Monroe Doctrine does not involve or rest on principles of international law. It would be submitted to the Commission of Conciliation which would, after needed time, recommend a compromise. The United States, if it did not subscribe to the compromise, might honorably refuse to accept it and begin hostilities against Japan. Under the thirty treaties initiated by Mr. Bryan, and consented to by the Senate, the United States could not even now begin such hostilities within a year. In what respect, therefore, is the United States at a disadvantage in the maintenance of the Monroe Doctrine?

The third case supposed by Senator Borah is that Argentine and a European government have a dispute and Argentine refuses to submit. If Argentine begins war against the European country, then the powers of the League must be used against her, and European forces jointly with our own will punish her for violating her plighted faith and treaty obligations. This is said to involve an abandonment of the Monroe Doctrine. Why? Mr. Seward in 1866, and Mr. Roosevelt in his administration, said most emphatically that the Doctrine can not be used to shelter South American countries against punishment by European countries for their shortcomings. The only limitation set by the Doctrine is that the punishment inflicted shall not involve subverting the independence of Argentine or appropriating and colonizing her territory. I submit, therefore, that the three cases suggested by Senator Borah do not present the difficulties he supposes.

The two questions for us are whether the League is practical and whether the United States ought to enter it. Of course it is only a general plan, and the details would have to be worked out in a world conference. That it is feasible, and that such details may be worked out, is indicated by the approval which the League has received from Germany, on the one hand, and from the Allies, on the other. There are of course very great difficulties in a practical union of the forces of the world to accomplish a definite single purpose, but they are not insuperable. The League is only applying to the international community the same principle that has been applied to the domestic community, that of using the force of all to suppress the lawless force of the few for the common good.

We are now entering upon a policy of preparation to defend ourselves against the unjust aggression of any nation. I believe this to be absolutely essential to our country's interest. The League has officially recognized that such preparation is necessary to its progress. When we have made this preparation and have the forces of our army and navy adequate to it, we shall be in a position to contribute our share to any force that we may be called upon to furnish in a joint exercise of power by the world to suppress war. President Wilson has said that in the next war there will be no neutrals. If the science of war advances in the next war as much as it has advanced in this over the last war, he is certainly right—there will be no room for neutrals. In this aspect, and from a selfish standpoint, therefore, our membership in the League in the future would prove to be safer for our interests than if we stayed out of it.

But is the selfish standpoint the only one from which we should view this question? We are potentially the strongest nation in the world. We have a vast population with high intelligence, solidarity and homogeneity. We have enormous resources and incomparable wealth. We are so situated that our position between the nations of Europe and between those of Asia is an impartial one and we could therefore exercise a just and commanding influence in a council of nations. We do not realize our power in this respect. Lord Grey says that we are necessary to the successful launching of such a League. We must lead it. Have we any right, therefore, to stay out of a world-arrangement calculated to make a world-war improbable, because we shall risk having to contribute our share to an international police force to suppress the disturbers of peace? Today war in any part of the world may rapidly manifest itself in another part, and the advantage of suppressing it or hedging it about so as to prevent its spread is inestimable.

Note

Address delivered at the dinner of the Chamber of Commerce of the Borough of Queens, New York City, Saturday evening, January 20, 1917.

9

Statement Made at Richmond, Virginia, March 21, 1917

[The following statement was made on the occasion of a mass meeting at Richmond, Virginia, Wednesday evening, March 21, 1917:]

The break with Germany and the imminence of war furnish the strongest arguments for the League to Enforce Peace.

Preparedness is one of the watchwords of the hour. The Executive Committee of the League to Enforce Peace has pronounced more than once in favor of national preparedness to meet all emergencies and pointed out the fact that the plan it puts forward makes preparedness a necessity.

The duty to support the President in his foreign policy is plain. The League has declared a thousand times that it is not a stop-the-war movement, and has pledged its support in the defense of civilization and the rights of our citizens.

The reason we have protested against Germany's ruthless submarine warfare and broken off relations with her is because her conduct is subversive of any peace that is worth having.

As we are forced into the war, our sole purpose must be to secure the right kind of a peace after the war, for ourselves and for the whole world—a permanent and righteous peace.

This fact is fundamental to the whole situation, and ought to be kept constantly before the minds of all our people. We are contending for a righteous and permanent peace and for nothing else whatsoever. Preparation for such a peace is the most important part of preparedness. The President has this strongly in mind. If, through the growth of hatred and the cry for vengeance, the world should lose sight of its real purpose and come to the end of the war not knowing what it most wants and needs, and so should fail to roll the burden of militarism off its shoulders and to establish lasting peace, it would be a tragedy in the history of the world.

The League to Enforce Peace presents the elements of a program that has been recognized as having in it the promise of a better future, a program that has the support in general terms not only of the President but of leading statesmen in all or nearly all of the leading nations. The latter have espoused it while their countries were at war and both they and the President are watching the growth and expression of public opinion in the United States as the deciding factor in the formation of a league.

During the present crisis and throughout the war which is at hand, the duty of the League to Enforce Peace is to stimulate military preparedness on the one hand, and on the other to spread its gospel of world organization for permanent peace after this conflict is over.

10

The Menace of a Premature Peace

We are engaged in the greatest war of history to secure permanent world peace. We are fighting for a definite purpose, and that is the defeat of German militarism. If the Prussian military caste retains its power to control the military and foreign policy of Germany after the war, peace will not be permanent, and war will begin again when the chauvinistic advisers of the Hohenzollern dynasty deem a conquest and victory possible.

Our Allies have made a stupendous effort and have strained their utmost capacity. Unready for the war, they have concentrated their energy in preparation. In this important respect they have defeated the plan of Germany "in shining armor" to crush her enemies in their unreadiness.

But the war has not been won. Peace now, even though it be made on the basis of the restoration of the *status quo,* "without indemnities and without annexations," would be a failure to achieve the great purpose for which the Allies have made heartrending sacrifice. Armaments would continue for the next war, and this war would have been fought in vain. The millions of lives lost and the hundreds of billions' worth of the product of men's labor would be wasted.

He who proposes peace now, therefore, either does not see the stake for which the Allies are fighting, or wishes the German military autocracy still to control the destinies of all of us as to peace or war. Those who favor permanent world peace must oppose with might and main the proposals for peace at this juncture in the war, whether made in socialistic councils, in pro-German conferences or by Pope Benedict. That the Pontiff of the greatest Christian Church should wish to bring to an end a war in which millions of its communion are on both sides is to be expected. That he should preserve a difficult neutrality is also natural. That his high purpose is to save the world from further suffering goes without saying. But the present is not the opportunity of an intervening peacemaker who must assume that compromise is possible.

The Allies are fighting for a principle the maintenance of which affects the future of civilization. If they do not achieve it they have sacrificed the flower of their youth and mortgaged their future for a century, and all for nothing. This is not a war in which the stake is territory or sphere of influence. The Allies cannot concede peace until they conquer it. When they do so, it will be permanent. Otherwise they fail.

There are wars like that between Japan and Russia, in which President Roosevelt properly and successfully intervened to bring about a peace that helped the parties to a settlement. The principle at stake and the power and territory were of such a character that a settlement might be made substantially permanent. But the present issue is like that in our Civil War, which was whether the Union was to be preserved and the cancer of slavery was to be cut out. Peace proposals to President Lincoln were quite as numerous as those of today, and were moved by quite as high motives. But there was no compromise possible. Either slavery and disunion lost or won. So today the great moral object of the war must be achieved or defeated.

An organization of citizens in the United States, known as the League to Enforce Peace, has been active for three years past in promoting its propaganda. There is a similar association in England. In that League are many persons who for years urged the settlement of all international controversies by arbitration or judicial decision. The vortex of death and destruction for the peoples of the world, which the breaking out of the war portended, roused these peace lovers and promoters to devise a plan for avoiding war after this should end. The English plan is more ambitious in providing that if the council of nations so decide they must enforce the judgment or settlement.

Whatever the detailed stipulations of such a league, its operation and success must depend on the obligations of the treaty stipulations. Unless their binding effect is recognized by the nations as a sacred principle, the stipulations of the league will be "writ in water." The revelations and disclosures of this war will satisfy the members of the league that as long as the present military caste controls the German military and foreign policy, the league is impracticable, and would not be worth the parchment on which its obligations would be recorded. Why have they reached this conclusion? Why, as citizens of the United States, and as citizens of the world anxious to promote peace, do they feel that any proposal of peace in the present situation would defeat permanent world peace and should be opposed by them with all the energy they can command? The answer to this question must be found in the causes of this war and the revelations it has made of Germany's purpose, stripped of confusing pretense and naked for the whole world to see.

Germany was long divided into little states, kingdoms, duchies, and other forms of one-man rule. She was the prey of political intrigue and manipulation of other powers. All her well-wishers hoped for and looked forward to her union. The Germans of yore had loved freedom. We Anglo-Saxons were Germans once and our representative system can be traced back to institutions found first in the forests of Germany. In the wars of the first Napoleon, Prussia, and other German states were subjected to a great humiliation. But the German youth rebelled, organized themselves into military reserves, and finally contributed much to the defeat of the man whose lust for universal power finds its counterpart in the aim of the Hohenzollerns of today. Later, the Holy Alliance, retaining the principle of the divine right of kings, and supporting it in all of Germany, left no opportunity for the free exercise of political power by these liberty-loving German youths. In 1848 democratic revolutions occurred throughout Germany and in Austria, but they were overcome. Many of the leaders came to the United States and with their followers became our best adopted citizens. When our Civil War came on, their hatred of slavery led them to volunteer for their adopted country, and every battlefield of the war was wet with German blood.

In Germany itself, however, the liberal element was not allowed to work out its hopes. It had looked to a united and liberal Germany with a government based on the representative system. It was not to be. Under the first William with his Prime Minister Bismarck, who came to power in 1862, a definite plan was adopted of perfecting the already well-disciplined Prussian army so that by "blood and iron" the unity of Germany should be achieved. The whole Prussian nation was made into an army, and it soon became a machine with a power of conquest equaled by no other. The cynical, unscrupulous, but effective, diplomacy of Bismarck first united Prussia with Austria to deprive Denmark of Schleswig-Holstein by force, then secured a quarrel with Austria over the spoils, and deprived her of all influence over the German states by humiliating defeat in the six weeks' war of 1866. After this war, several German states were annexed forcibly to Prussia and offensive and defensive alliances were made with others.

Then in 1870 the occasion was seized, when it was known that France was not prepared, to strike at her. France was beaten, and Alsace and Lorraine were taken from her. The German Empire was established with a Prussian King at its head. France was made to pay an indemnity of one billion dollars, with which the military machine of Germany was strengthened and improved. Then Germany settled down to a period of peace to digest the territory which by these three wars had been absorbed. Bismarck's purpose in maintaining the superiority of his army was to retain what had been taken by blood and iron, and at the same time by a period of prolonged peace to give to Germany a full opportunity for industrial development and the self-discipline necessary for the highest efficiency.

The marvelous work which the Germans have accomplished in their field of industrial activity is known to all. The prosperity which followed increased the population of Germany and crowded her borders. Bismarck was dismissed by the present Emperor, but his policy of maintaining the highest efficiency of the army was continued. And then, as the success of the German system in the material development of the Empire showed itself and became the admiration of the world, the destiny of Germany grew larger in the eyes of her Emperor and her people, and the blood and iron policy which had been directed first to the achievement of the unity of Germany and then to the defense of the German Empire in the enjoyment of what had been taken in previous wars, expanded into a dream of Germanizing the world. The German people were impregnated with this idea by every method of official instruction. A cult of philosophy to spread the propaganda developed itself in the universities and schools. The principle was that the state could do no wrong; that the state was an entity that must be sustained by force; that everything else must be sacrificed to its strength; that the only sin the state could commit was neglect and failure to maintain its power.

With that dogmatic logic which pleases the German mind, and to which it readily adapts itself, this proposition easily led to the further conclusion that there could be no international morality; that morality and its principles applied only to individuals, but that when the action of the state was involved, considerations of honor, of the preservation of obligations solemnly made, must yield if the interests of the state required. These were the principles taught by Treitschke in the University of Berlin and maintained by German economic philosophers and by the representative of the military regime in the person of Bernhardi.

Bismarck had been keen enough in his diplomacy to await the opportunity that events presented for seeming to be forced into a war which he had long planned. This was the case with Denmark. This was the case with Austria. This was the case with France. German diplomacy has lost nothing of this characteristic in the present war. Germany did not plan the killing of the Austrian Archduke and his consort; but the minute that that event presented the likelihood of war, Germany accepted it as the opportunity for her to strike down her neighbors, Russia and France, and to enlarge her power. She gladly gave her consent to the ultimatum of Austria to Servia that was sure to bring on war, and then posed as one driven into war by the mobilization of Russia.

She knew that Russia was utterly unprepared. She knew that France was unprepared. She knew that Great Britain was unprepared. She herself was ready to the last cannon and the last reservist. Therefore, when appealed to by Great Britain and by all the other Powers to intervene and prevent Austria from forcing a universal war, Germany declined to act. Not a telegram or communication between Germany and Austria has ever been given to the public to show the slightest effort to induce delay by

Austria. While Germany would pose as having acted only as Austria's ally and as unwilling to influence her against her interest and independent judgment, the verdict of history unquestionably will be that the war is due to Germany's failure to prevent it and to her desire to accept the opportunity of the assassination of the Austrian Archduke as a convenient time to begin a war she long intended. The revelation of their unpreparedness is sufficient to show that England, France and Russia did not conspire to bring on the war. On the other hand, before the war began Germany had constructed a complete system of strategic railways on her Belgian border, adapted not to commercial uses, but only to the quick invasion of Belgium.

Indeed, every fact as the war has developed forms one more circumstance in the irrefragable case against Germany as the Power responsible for this world-disaster. The preparation of fifty years, the false philosophy of her destiny and of the exaltation of force, had given her a yearning for conquest, for the expansion of her territory, the extension of her influence, and the Germanization of the world. She alone is responsible for the incalculable destruction of this war. She led on in the armament of the world that she might rule it. She promoted therefore the armament of other nations. Her system was followed, though not as effectively, by other countries in pure defense of their peace and safety.

And now her Emperor, her Prussian military caste, and her wonderful but blinded people, have the blood of the millions who have suffered in this world catastrophe on their heads. The German military doctrine, that when the interests of the state are concerned, the question is one of power and force, and not of honor or obligation or moral restraint, finds its most flagrant examples in Germany's conduct of this war.

Her breach of a solemn obligation entered into by her and all the powers of Europe, in respect to Belgium's neutrality, was its first exhibition. It was followed by the well-proven deliberate plan of atrocities against the men, women and children of a part of Belgium in order to terrorize the rest of the population into complete submission. It was shown in the prompt dropping of bombs on defenseless towns from Zeppelins and other aircraft; in the killing of non-combatant men, women and children by the naval bombardment of unfortified towns; in the use of liquid fire and poison gases in battle. All of these had been condemned as improper in declarations in the Hague treaties.

The Reptile Fund, which was used under Bismarck for the bribery of the press and for the maintenance of a spy system, has been enlarged and elaborated, so that German bribery has extended the world over, and the German espionage has exceeded anything known to history. The medieval use by the Hohenzollerns of dynastic kinship has paralyzed the action of the peoples of Greece and Russia. And now we know, by recent revelation, of the aid that Swedish diplomats are furnishing to Germany in her submarine warfare against neutral ships, and that it is made possible by the influence of the German consort of the Swedish King.

Intrigue, dishonor, cruelty, have characterized the entire military policy of Germany. The rules of international law have been cast to the winds. The murderous submarine has sunk without warning the non-combatant commercial vessels of the enemy and sent their officers, their crews and their passengers, men, women and children, to the bottom without warning. Not only has this policy been pursued against enemy commercial vessels, but also against neutral commercial vessels, and parts of the crew have been assembled on the submarines and then the submarine has been submerged and the victims left struggling in the ocean's waste to drown. We find a German diplomat telegraphing from a neutral port to the German headquarters advising that if the submarine be used against the vessels of that neutral Power it leave no trace of the attack. In other words, the murder of the crews must be complete, because "dead men tell no tales."

Having violated the neutrality of Belgium, having broken its sacred obligations to that country and her people, it is now enslaving them by taking them from Belgium and enforcing their labor in Germany. This is contrary to every rule of international law, and is in the teeth of the plainest principles of justice and honor. All these things are done for the state. It is not that the nature of the German people generally is cruel—that is not the case. But the minds of the German people have been poisoned with this false philosophy; and the ruling caste in Germany, in its desperate desire to win, has allowed no consideration of humanity or decency or honor to prevent its use of any means which in any way could by hook or crook accomplish a military purpose.

When the war began, Germany was able to convince her people and to convince many in the world that the issue in the war was not the exaltation of the military power of Germany and the expansion of her plan of destiny, but that it was a mere controversy between the Teuton and the Slav, and Germany asked with great plausibility, "Will you have the world controlled by the Slav or by the German?" Those who insisted that the issue was one of militarism against the peace of the world, of democracy against military autocracy, of freedom against military tyranny, were met with the argument: "Russia is an ally. She is a greater despotism and a greater military autocracy than Germany." As the war wore on, the real issue was cleared of this confusion. Russia became a democracy. The fight was between governments directed by their people on the one hand, and the military dynasties of Germany, Austria and Turkey, on the other.

President Wilson says the Allies are fighting to make the world safe for democracy. Some misconception has been created on this head. The Allies are not struggling to force a particular form of government on Germany. If the German people continue to prefer an Emperor it is not the purpose of the Allies to require them to have a republic. Their purpose is to end the military policy and foreign policy of Germany that looks to the maintenance of a military and naval machine, with its hair-trigger preparation for use against her neighbors. If this continues, it will entail on every democratic government the duty of maintaining a similar armament in self-defense, and, what is likely, the duty will be wholly or partly neglected. Thus the policy of Germany, with her purpose and destiny, will threaten every democracy. This is the condition which it is the determined purpose of the Allies, as interpreted by President Wilson, to change.

How is the change to be effected? By defeating Germany in this war. The German people have been very loyal to their Emperor, because his leadership accords with the false philosophy of the state and German destiny, with which they have been indoctrinated and poisoned. A defeat of the military machine, a defeat of the Frankenstein of the military dynasty to which they have been sacrificed, must open their eyes to the hideous futility of their political course. The German Government will then be changed, as its people will have it changed, to avoid a recurrence of such a tragedy as they have deliberately prepared for themselves.

Men who see clearly the kind of peace which we must have, in order to be a real and lasting peace, can have no sympathy therefore with a patched-up peace, one made at a council table, the result of diplomatic chaffering and bargaining. Men who look forward to a League of the

World to Enforce Peace in the future can have no patience with a compromise that leaves the promoting cause of the present awful war unaffected and unremoved. This war is now being fought by the Allies as a League to Enforce Peace. Unless they compel it by victory, they do not enforce it. They do not make the military autocracies of the world into nations fit for a World League, unless they convince them by a lesson of defeat.

When the war came on, there were a few in the United States who felt that the invasion of Belgium required a protest on the part of our government, and some indeed who felt that we should join in the war at once. But the great body of the American people, influenced by our traditional policy of avoiding European quarrels, stood by the Administration in desiring to maintain a strict neutrality. I think it is not unfair to say that a very large proportion of the intelligent and thinking people of the United States—and that means a great majority—sympathized with the Allies in the struggle which they were making. But many of German birth and descent, prompted by a pride in the notable advance in the world of German enterprise, German ingenuity, German discipline, German efficiency, and regarding the struggle as an issue between Teuton and Slav, extended their sympathy to their Fatherland.

As conscientiously as possible, the Administration and the country pursued the course laid down by international law as that which a neutral should take. International law is the rule of conduct of nations toward one another accepted and acquiesced in by all nations. It is not always as definite as one would like, and the acquiescence of all nations is not always as clearly established as it ought to be. But in the law of war as to capture at sea of commercial vessels, the principles have been established clearly by the decision of prize courts of all nations, English, American, Prussian and French. The right of non-combatants on commercial vessels, officers, crew and passengers, either enemy or neutral, to be secure from danger of life, has always been recognized and never contested. Nevertheless, by submarine attack on English and American merchant ships without warning, Germany sent to their death one hundred and fifty American men, women and children. We protested and Germany halted for a time. We thought that if we condoned the death of one hundred and fifty we might still maintain peace with that Power.

But it was not to be, and after more than a year Germany announced her purpose to resume this murderous and illegal course toward innocent Americans. Had we hesitated, we would have lost our independence as a people; we would have subscribed abjectly to the doctrine that might makes right. Germany left no door open to us as a self-respecting nation except that which led to war. She deliberately forced us into the ranks of her enemies, and she did it because she was obsessed with the belief that the submarine was the instrument of destruction by which she might win the war. She recked not that, as she used it, it was a weapon of murder. Making military efficiency her god, and exalting the appliances of science in the killing of men, she ignored all other consequences.

Germany's use of the submarine brought us into the war. But being in, we recognized as fully as any of our Allies do that its far greater issue is whether German militarism shall continue after this war to be a threat to the peace of the world, or whether we shall end that threat by this struggle in which we are to spend our life's blood. We must not therefore be turned from the stern necessity of winning this war.

When the war began and its horrible character was disclosed, there were many religious persons who found their faith in God shaken by the fact that millions of innocent persons could be headed into this vortex of blood and destruction without the saving intervention of their Creator. But the progress of the war has revealed much, and it has stimulated our just historic sense. It shows that the world had become, through the initiative of Germany and the following on of the other nations, afflicted with the cancer of militarism. God reveals the greatness of His power and His omnipotence not by fortuitous and sporadic intervention, but by the working out of His inexorable law. A cancer, if it is not to consume the body, must be cut out, and the cutting out necessarily involves suffering and pain. The sacrifices of lives and treasure are inevitable in the working out of the cure of the world malady. But we must win the war to vindicate this view.

We are now able to see the providential punishment and weakness that follows the violation of moral law. The crass materialism of the German philosophy that exalts force above morality, power above honor and decency, success above humanity, has blinded the German ruling caste to the strength of moral motives that control other peoples, and involved them in the fundamental mistakes that will cause their downfall. They assumed that England, burdened with Ireland, would violate her own obligation and abandon Belgium and would leave her ally France to be deprived of all her colonial possessions. They assumed that France was decadent, permeated with socialism, and unable to make a contest in her state of unpreparedness. They assumed that England's colonies, attached only by the lightest tie, and entirely independent, if they chose to be, would not sacrifice themselves to help the mother land in her struggle. How false the German conclusion as to England's national conscience and fighting power, as to France's supposed decadence and her actual patriotic fervor and strength, and as to the filial loyalty of England's daughters!

England and France since 1914 have been fighting the battle of the world and fighting for us of America. The war has drained their vitality, strained their credit, exhausted their man-power, subjected many of their non-combatants to suffering and destruction, and they have the war weariness which dulls the earlier eager enthusiasm for the principles at stake. Now, specious proposals for peace are likely to be most alluring to the faint-hearted, and most powerful in the hands of traitors.

The intervention of the United States, by her financial aid, has helped much; but her armies are needed and she, a republic unprepared, required time to prepare. The war is now to be determined by the active tenacity of purpose of the contestants. England showed that tenacity in the wars of Napoleon. Napoleon succumbed. General Grant, in his Memoirs, says that the battle is won not in the first day, but by the commander and the army which is ready, even after apparent defeat, to begin the next day. It is the side which has the nerve that will win. The intervention of the United States has strengthened that nerve in England, France and Italy. But delay and disappointment give full opportunity to the lethargic, the cowardly, the factious, to make the task of the patriot and the loyal men doubly heavy. This is the temper of the situation among our European Allies.

With us at home the great body of our people are loyal and strong for the war. Of course, it takes time to convince a people, however intelligent, when very prosperous and comfortable and not well advised as to the vital concern they have in the issue of a war across a wide ocean, thousands of miles away. But we have, for the first time in the history of our republic, begun a war right. We have begun with a conscription law which requires service from men of a certain age from every walk of life. It is democratic in principle, and yet it offers to the Government the means of selection so that those who shall be sent to the front may be best fitted to represent the nation there, and those best able to do the work in field and factory, essential to our winning at the front, may be retained. We have adopted a merit system of selecting from the intelligent and educated youth of the country the company officers. The machinery of the draft naturally creaked some because it had to be so hastily constructed, but on the whole it has worked well. Those who devised it and have carried it through are entitled to great credit.

The lessons of the war are being learned and applied in our war equipment and in neutralizing, by new construction, the submarine destruction of commercial transports. Adequate measures for the raising of the money needed to finance our Allies have been carried through Congress. Food conservation is provided for. But of course it took time for a hundred million of peace lovers and non-militarists to get ready, however apt, however patriotic, however determined.

"It is 'dogged' that does it." Reject all proposals of peace as ill advised or seditious, and then time will make for our certain victory.

While there has been pro-German sentiment in the United States, and while the paid emissaries of Germany have been busy trying to create as much opposition to the war as possible and have found a number of weak dupes and unintelligent persons, who don't understand the importance of the war, to aid them, our Allies should know that the whole body of the American people will earnestly support the President and Congress in carrying out the measures which have been adopted by the United States to win this war.

When the war is won, the United States will wish to be heard and will have a right to be heard as to the terms of peace. The United States will insist on a just peace, not one of material conquest. It is a moral victory the world should win. I think I do not mistake the current of public sentiment throughout our entire country in saying that our people will favor an international agreement by which the peace brought about through such blood and suffering and destruction and enormous sacrifice shall be preserved by the joint power of the world. Whether the terms of the League to Enforce

Peace, as they are, will be taken as a basis for agreement, or a modified form, something of the kind must be attempted.

Meantime, let us hope and pray that all the Allies will reject proposals for settlement and compromise of every nature; that they will adhere rigidly and religiously to the principle that, until a victorious result gives security that the world shall not again be drenched in blood through the insanely selfish policy of a military caste ruling a deluded people intoxicated with material success and power, there will be no peace.

Note

Address delivered at General Conference of Unitarian and other Christian Churches at Montreal, September 26, 1917.

11

World Peace Debate

A. Is the Platform of the League to Enforce Peace Feasible?

I

The platform is not a program to stop the present war. It looks to a treaty to be adopted at or after its close. Its purpose is to enforce deliberation, impartial investigation and judgment of a cause of international quarrel before hostilities. It does not seek to enforce the decision after it is rendered; but by making clear to the threatening nations and to the world what the real issue is, and what an impartial Tribunal thinks about it, the enforced procedure and the necessary delay will prevent most wars.

To make the platform work, the eight or nine great Powers should join the League. The weaker nations will then be glad to secure the benefit of its protection. Will the great belligerent Powers join? Lord Grey and Mr. Asquith of Great Britain, M. Briand of France, and Dr. Bethmann-Hollweg of Germany are representative of them. They have approved the principles of the League. Lord Grey says that the war should not end without it. President Wilson, Mr. Hughes and Mr. Lodge uphold it. These personal expressions do not bind the Nations; but they show that the general plan is feasible and supplies a want which the world feels.

The platform only lays down broad lines. Its machinery must be worked out in International Conference. Its feasibility is not successfully attacked by exceptional hypotheses under which it would fail of its purpose. The most practical plan of government may thus be shown to be futile. If the platform will work in most cases, the value of the result justifies its adoption.

Are the four planks considered in detail feasible?

1. A Court to administer international justice is not new. Our own Supreme Court is one. Questions arise between States not settled by the Federal Constitution or Federal statutes. In the Kansas-Colorado case, Congress had no power to control Colorado. International Law alone fixed the rights between the States; and the Supreme Court enforced these rights.

Our relations with Canada are such that we settle all questions by negotiation or arbitration. We have now two permanent Tribunals to decide controversies between us—one to adjudge questions of boundary waters like that between Kansas and Colorado, and the other to pass upon claims of the citizens of one country against the other. We have thus contracted the habit of arbitration; and, when negotiation fails, no one expects anything else. In our League, the quarrelling nations, moved by their obligation, sanctioned by the threat of compulsion by their associates, will contract the same habit.

2. There may be, however, political or other irritating and threatening issues between nations which cannot be settled on principles of law. They are to be submitted under the second plank for hearing and recommendation of compromise just as our Fur Seal Arbitration with England. . . .

3. The third or *"Force"* plank gives vitality to the platform. It appeals to practical men. It provides for economic pressure and a Police Force to hold off members of the League from war until the cooling and curative influence of the League's judicial procedure may have time to operate.

No matter how law-abiding a community, neither the statutes nor judgments of the Courts enforce themselves so as to dispense with police or sheriffs. The latter may be called on infrequently to suppress disorder or to remove obstruction to judicial decree. The fact that they are present, however, in the community, or in the Court, with the power to act and the intention to act when necessary, stays would-be disturbers or obstructors. Fear of police action is usually effective without actual use of force. "They also serve who only stand and wait."

4. No one will doubt the feasibility of the fourth plank. Successful Congresses for declaring the principles of International Law and enlarging their scope have been held before. Such was the Congress at Paris in 1856 in which privateering was abolished.

The agreement of all the powerful nations of the world to unite their armies and their navies to resist the premature hostilities of one or more nations against another must increase the binding effect of the obligation of the League members not to rush into sudden war. The fear of forcible restraint would thus, in most cases, render actual resort to it unnecessary.

The League is to be a world alliance. We have had precedents of successful alliances for the purpose of protecting the parties to them against outside attack. In various junctures in the past, these alliances have preserved peace. The fear of their united force has prevented others from attacking a single member.

Moreover, the binding effect of such alliances has shown itself. France, with no interest in Servia, and with the danger of being crushed by Germany, keeps the letter of her agreement with Russia. England, with no interest in Servia, maintains her obligation to Belgium; while Germany, without interest in Servia, upholds her word to Austria. Treaties may sometimes be broken; but as the best hope of securing international progress, we should not abandon them. The fear of another World War, which will lead the great Powers into our League, will also lead them to meet its obligation.

II

The League is not a defensive league against outside nations. It does not defend its members against non-members. Its purpose is to furnish a means of keeping peace among its own members only. It proposes to secure World Peace by attracting to its membership, first, all the Great Powers, and then the lesser Powers which will surely follow. The logic of circumstances must inevitably force the Great Powers engaged in this war to membership. In seeking permanent peace, whether they wish it or not, the League must be their common goal.

The Allies proclaim their purpose to be to secure a permanent basis for peace, safeguarded by practical guaranties, that is, of superior force. What is that but the League?

Germany's Chancellor avows her willingness to join a league to "suppress disturbers of peace." The League is only a wise preparation of the members, by organization of their united potential force, to frighten from its purpose a would-be disturber of the World's Peace, and thus probably make the use of actual force unnecessary.

Germany now proposes peace with suggestion of a limitation of armaments. In the Hague conferences, Germany declined to consider such a limitation. Such a suggestion by her now looks necessarily to a continuing "Bund" to exact the limitation. This is only a logical corollary to our proposals. Our League must deal with armaments and fix a minimum to secure effective joint action. Why not a maximum?

Again, whether Germany's present proposals are now to lead to peace or not, serious negotiations must sometime come; and then conditions will make for a League like ours. One of Germany's motives in offering peace is, of course, her desire to satisfy her own people that their Government is anxious to end their almost unbearable burdens. In Russia, the power of control is passing from the Bureaucracy to the Council and the Duma. When whole peoples constitute the armies and the makers of war supplies, as never before, and all of them are enduring the sweat and woe and blood, their will determines policies. Otherwise, dynasties fall. In all history, no time can find the contending peoples so anxious for guaranties of permanent peace as at the end of this war. Lord Grey's words, that the war cannot and should not end without such a League, will find an echo in all their hearts.

It is these circumstances that make the League feasible. Difficulties are suggested. They concern the detail of operation rather than the main principles. If the nations are determined to create such a League, as they will be, they can arrange the details.

Of course, a council or other joint body of representatives of the

League must act in case of strained relations between League members. It will naturally use diplomatic pressure to prevent a rupture. Such a body in negotiation with them will have excellent opportunity to learn which of the contestants intends a breach of its plighted faith. Upon the decision of such a council, all members of the League, in compliance with the third article, will withhold commerce or dealing with the recalcitrant. A boycott of this kind would be a powerful deterrent weapon and probably make resort to force unnecessary.

But it is said that force is not a feasible means of securing and maintaining peace. To say so is to ignore history and experience, domestic and international. Fear of forcible restraint and punishment is often an indispensable motive to strengthen moral impulse to obey the law and follow the right. That it may not be needed by some does not render it safe to dispense with it in the case of others. If we need restraint to keep men in paths of peace and law, why not nations? Nations are only men united in communities; and they have not the moral self-restraint of the average man. Force used for selfish, vicious or improper ends is, of course, to be deplored. But is there any method of defeating force used for such ends, except superior force threatened or applied for the common good? Has force, or fear of it, never done any good among the nations? What was it that kept Louis XIV's greedy hand out of the Spanish Netherlands but the fear of the league of England, Holland and Sweden? What was it that stopped Napoleon in his mad lust for universal domination but a league of all Europe, welded by England, against him? The fact that, after the Napoleonic wars, this league degenerated, as the Holy Alliance, into a selfish plot of an inner ring to promote the divine right of kings, does not detract from the useful purpose it originally served. What was it but force that cut out the cancer of slavery in our body politic? What was it but force that freed Cuba from oppression? Have men changed since these wars, that force or fear of force is not now needed at times to help a just cause to prevail?

Before the present war, the Triple Alliance on the one side and the Triple Entente on the other, divided Europe into two vast and powerful camps; and men spoke of their promoting peace on the theory that one sword would keep the other in its scabbard. These leagues did for a time prevent attack upon single members; but ultimately they failed. This war was precipitated because they were divided against each other; and there were other motives in their maintenance than a mere preservation of peace. Their failure offers no argument against the feasibility and success of our League. Its members could not organize separate leagues and be honest or consistent members of ours. The League's simple plan of unity of power, with but one purpose of forcibly maintaining World Peace by deliberation, hearing and decision before hostilities, distinguishes it in its aim and practical moderation from all others.

III

Mr. Bryan objects that if only a part of the nations entered the League, there would ensue a test of military strength between the League group of nations and other groups. This objection finds no warrant in our plan because the League deals not at all with non-members, but only with differences between League members. Of course, if but a part of the nations consented to join the League, the plan would not work. To be useful and accomplish its purpose, it must have world membership. In my last paper, I showed why it would have this, because the great Powers now in war, and then the lesser Powers, would and must seek such a League when peace comes.

Mr. Bryan objects that confidence in the armed support of the League would prompt a League member to acts rendering peaceful settlement impossible and precipitating war. This rests on the same misconception as to the League's attitude toward non-members. As between members, such motive would be slight. The Council of the League, in using diplomatic pressure to prevent a rupture between two members, would have full opportunity to know and report which was really forcing hostilities; and the League would act accordingly.

He also objects to a League with force in it because we have already made thirty-one treaties agreeing to investigation before war which contain no provision for force. An agreement for investigation and orderly procedure before war and a subsequent agreement providing a world police force to compel such procedure are not inconsistent.

Mr. Bryan asks what is meant by "economic pressure." I answer—a boycott of the unruly nation—an embargo threatened or imposed by all the members of the League on their trade with the recalcitrant member. Such an embargo must of necessity accompany war, because war means the cessation of commerce between the belligerent parties. The boycott or embargo may, however, precede war and prevent it. This is the part which it is intended to play in our plan.

Mr. Bryan's whole argument thus far against the League is an argument against the evils of war. But I submit this is not to the point if war persists. The use of force to suppress a small war, however undesirable, is better than a world war, and is justified in avoiding it. Mr. Bryan says, "Why not test the friendship plan among nations?" History has oftentimes tested it and found that it did not work. While peaceful means of avoiding war are becoming more successful than in the past, the present war has convinced the world that a plan for the peaceful settlement of international quarrels will be more certainly effective if the nations of the world unite in their own interest to compel the working of the plan. The present war has brought home to them their deep interest in stopping every war, however remote, in order to prevent the conflagration's spread.

Mr. Bryan says that force breeds violence and cites the useful change from the time when all men carried weapons to the time when they gave up the practice. The instance is not helpful to his argument. Men gave up weapons when they could rely on the police, exercising the force of the community, to protect them against violence. By analogy, if our plan becomes effective, it will offer a strong inducement to limit armaments—a proposal that Germany has already unofficially given out.

Would Mr. Bryan dispense with the police in city, state and nation? Does he think a state or national prohibition law would enforce itself without the arrest of offenders and their restraint and punishment? Will "the friendship plan," without any public force in the background, work well in any of our communities, however law-abiding? If not, why should it among the nations?

I agree that the analogy between the domestic police force and the union of the forces of the nations of the world is not complete because of the difficulty of effective international cooperation; but the essential principle which justifies and requires the use of force in each case is the same, to wit, that all the people have a right and duty to exert their united force to suppress violence between individuals disturbing the community, and that all nations have a right and duty to use their united forces to suppress a disturbance of international peace which may involve the whole world.

Mr. Bryan questions whether the President's words or those of Mr. Hughes, in respect to the League, are sufficiently specific to justify my use of them. They were used by the speakers with the League's proposals in mind, not only to approve them all, but especially the third or "Force" proposal, which is the one to which Mr. Bryan chiefly objects.

Of course, if the United States or any other nation is to join the League, its principles will be embodied in a treaty with all the necessary working details. This treaty should not be ratified unless it is approved, after full knowledge and consideration of the details, not only by the treaty-making agency of each power, but also by the great body of its people and its legislature or congress, upon whom must fall the serious burden of performance of the treaty obligations. This would be needed to give assurance that the League would really hold the nations when the strain comes.

B. Does the League Platform Offer the Most Practical Plan for Securing Permanent Peace?

IV

Is the platform of the League the most practical plan for securing permanent peace after the war?

Should the League attempt more than it does? Should it enforce the judgments of the Court and the recommendations for compromise by the Commission? The two must be distinguished. A judgment between nations, like a domestic judgment, might be enforced. But nations will reasonably object to final submission of vital interests to the discretion of arbitrators, however impartial, in recommending compromise of an issue not covered by principles of law. The Supreme Court of the United States renders and enforces judgments between the States on justiciable issues; but, although given broad authority to hear "controversies between States," it refuses to decide issues not involving the application of principles of law. They must be settled by agreement or go unsettled. A judgment binds the parties in honor to its terms. This helps to secure acquiescence. But a recommendation of compromise implies no such moral sanction.

The League has deemed it best not to attempt the enforcement of either judgments or compromises. It is wise for it not to try too much, lest being over ambitious, it fail.

There are said to be wrongs which only war can remedy. If so, our plan does not prevent such a remedy. It enforces investigation, discussion, deliberation and impartial decision before war is begun and avoids most wars. If a war between members of the League is inevitable and necessary, the delay secured will enable the remainder of the League to hedge it about so as not to permit its spread.

Is a plan *without force in it* more practical than that of the League? It is not practical at all because the present belligerent powers could not be induced to adopt it. They demand effective guaranties of future peace. They will not trust to the security of a League which depends for its maintenance of peace on the mere promises of its members to abide a judicial settlement. In their minds, nothing will be effective which will not unite the superior force of all for the common good to secure the world against the aggression of reckless and faithless disturbers of its peace. Without such a result, the war will, in their view, have been fought in vain.

The psychological effect of this war upon the world has not been to vindicate the purely non-resistant pacifists or to increase their number. It has been to increase "the militant pacifists," to use a paradox, who are now willing to consent to the use of force if it be directed to the maintenance of the just peace of the world.

Mr. Bryan objects to the obligation of every member of the League to be ready to do its share in creating the police force. What good could come from a police force if it had to be organized after the riot alarm was turned in? Each nation, therefore, must know what force it should furnish, and should in good faith keep in a state of reasonable preparation to respond to a call. The share of each member will have to be generally prescribed in the fundamental agreement of the League, and must vary in number and kind with the geographical location and resources of the member and other circumstances. A self-respecting nation, bound jointly with others to constitute an international police force, may agree without the least sacrifice of dignity, to keep ready a force to fulfill its obligation. It could well afford to do so, because the security afforded by the joint forces of the League will reduce the reasonable preparation needed for its own defence.

Mr. Bryan insists that our League with its obligation will increase armaments. On the contrary, it will reduce them and the taxes necessary to maintain them. Indeed the working out of our plan must inevitably furnish the strongest motive for an agreement to reduce and limit armaments, in accord with the intimation of Germany already referred to.

Mr. Bryan objects to the surrender by each member of its control over its own military and naval policy. If so, he objects to the reduction and limitation of maximum armaments supervised by the League,—a plan which I supposed had the approval of the most extreme pacifists. Every treaty between two nations which accomplishes any good involves a surrender on the part of each of some right which it is willing to limit to accomplish a greater benefit.

The fear, expressed by Mr. Bryan and others that such a league would degenerate into a trap for the peaceful nations, causing them to serve the purpose of designing and ambitious warlike members, has little to justify it. The unity, strength and permanence of the League must depend on its justice and fairness. The perversion of its high purpose, shown in the action of any group attempting its control, must inevitably and promptly lead to its dissolution.

A league for judicial settlement of international disputes without force would prove a step forward; but it would be far short of our League in efficacy and scope. It would cover only questions of legal nature. Many issues likely to provoke war would not come within its scope. The element of force in our League gives it an advantage not measured solely by the sanction it adds to its obligations. It will give to every member of the League a sense of responsibility for the peace of the world. It will create a union of interest among the members, wholly absent in a league for judicial settlement in which a refusal to submit to the court concerns only the refusing member and its opponent and involves the other members of the league in no responsibility. Our League, through the active and stimulated concern of every member in the continuing friendship of all, would bring the nations much nearer to "the Parliament of Man and the Federation of the World."

V

Mr. Bryan suggests a League of Nations of which the members agree to delay war for a year of investigation and report by a permanent tribunal.

This is on the basis of the stipulations of treaties negotiated by him as Secretary of State with thirty-one separate nations. Our League's proposals recognize the value of delay and investigation in avoiding hotheaded resort to war. But Mr. Bryan's plan did not include a judgment by a Court or a recommendation of compromise by a Commission. Thus he has advanced some, but little. He suggests that an arbitral judgment or recommendation after investigation and hearing is less likely to secure a peaceful adjustment than a mere investigation and report without conclusion and decision. This is not sound. The decision of an impartial tribunal must always be of some moral weight in securing from the disputing parties peaceful acquiescence in a settlement. He says that investigators will appeal to the reason and sense of justice of the parties, while arbitrators, in dealing with parties bound to abide their decision, are not so likely to do so. On the contrary, the most searching and just criticism of international arbitrations is that their judgments are compromises, intended to appeal to the acquiescence of the parties, rather than straight decisions on principles of law.

Mr. Bryan urges that a treaty obligation of two nations to maintain a period of delay and investigation before hostilities, is inconsistent with a compact of all other nations forcibly to require the two nations to keep their engagement. Why should this make the delay and investigation less likely than when dependent on the naked promises of the two nations in the heat of quarrel? How is the insistence of all other nations upon the delay likely to create war between the quarrelling nations? Mr. Bryan says "the League to Enforce Peace violates the spirit of our treaty plan; it would send forth a dove of peace, to be sure, but its dove would carry a sword instead of an olive branch." With deference, this is mere rhetoric. It is not dealing with facts as they are, or with human nature as it is. If it be a logical argument, then the presence of a policeman in a community to arrest law breakers and of a court to punish them violates the spirit of the law which all are under a moral obligation to obey. Mr. Bryan says that when two neighbors fall out they call in their friends and allow time for investigation and friendly advice, each party reserving the right of independent action after the conference, and that the prospect of settlement is much lessened if the conference is opened with a display of weapons. This is not the usual way of settling such disputes, but assume that it is. Would Mr. Bryan contend that the prospect of a settlement would be improved if the disputants knew that, in their failure to agree, there were no law and no courts and no police to enforce their mutual rights and duties? In our League to Enforce Peace, there is no display of weapons by one party to the controversy against the other. The element of world force in the third article is no more obtrusive and no more provocative of temper or heat than the machinery of justice in the domestic environment of the two supposed neighbors.

There is no proof of the feasibility of Mr. Bryan's World League in his thirty-one treaties between other nations and the United States. Many, but not all, nations were willing to sign such treaties because they were revocable within a short period, and because they were made with the United States which is notoriously unprepared for war. They would, doubtless, decline to make such an agreement with their immediate and powerful neighbors; and no such treaties have been made between other important nations. Mr. Bryan says that all nations would enter such a League if they would enter ours. On the contrary, the sanction of the world's united command in securing performance of the promises under our League will induce nations to yield their power to strike at once for their rights in the confidence that any opponent, however tricky or faithless, will not be permitted to take advantage of their concession. What the belligerent nations, in ending this war, are yearning for is a guaranty of peace, not only in the promise of each nation but in the assurance of the sanction of a superior force of all for the common good to compel observance of its promise. Mr. Bryan's proposal in this aspect would seem to them a rope of sand; and they would have none of it as a practical object in ending the war.

Mr. Bryan thinks that the present war demonstrates the fallacy of what he calls "peace by terrorism." What the present war really demonstrates is the truth of the conclusion of Immanuel Kant, the great philosopher, that universal peace cannot be expected until the world is *politically organized,* that is, until the nations of the world use the prestige and force of all for the common good to suppress disturbers of peace. The League to Enforce Peace, if it becomes an accomplished fact, will be a step in *this world political organization.*

Mr. Bryan's League would be nothing but a series of treaties between "couples" of nations. If two nations fell out, the nations of the world other than the disputants, would have no active function except to watch the two quarrelling nations keep or break their promises to wait a year. There would be no *"political organization"* of the world to preserve and secure peace. Our League makes every member active and selfishly interested in maintaining peace to escape the burden of acting as policeman. Thus we have the "team work" of the world.

VI

Mr. Bryan proposes four plans which he thinks more practical than that of our League. The first one I have already considered.

The second is a World Court, in which all nations are to be represented, to consider and decide justiciable issues, and to investigate and make findings on non-justiciable issues, the judgment or finding to be enforceable only by the parties. This is similar to the first two proposals of our League, with the force article left out. There is no sanction, beyond its agreement, that any nation will delay hostilities until hearing and judgment. It does not differ from Mr. Bryan's first proposal except that his tribunal gives a decision here; and, in his first, it did not. This is an improvement; but, with that exception, it is open to the same objections. It lacks the essential quality of world organization and pressure for peace. It is a mere combination of separate treaties of arbitration between every two nations. This suggestion of force adds nothing. The optional use of force by one party to an arbitration to compel performance by the other of an award would be implied. Mr. Bryan says, "If the nations agreed to such a plan, the chances against war would be a hundred to one, if not a thousand to one." Mr. Bryan's "if" is a formidable obstacle. The view of both the Allies and the Central Powers, shown in the peace correspondence, is clear. They both demand sanctions of force. Germany will enter a league to suppress disturbers of peace. The Allies declare in favor of "international agreements implying the sanctions necessary to insure their execution and thus prevent an apparent security from only facilitating new aggressions." Lloyd George, in his Guildhall speech on January 11th, said: "The peace and security for peace will be that the nations will band themselves together to punish the first peace breaker who comes out. As to the armies of Europe, every weapon will be a sword of justice in the Government of men; every army will be a constabulary of peace." . . .

Mr. Bryan's third plan is that all the nations shall agree to a referendum before declaring war. Mr. Bryan can hardly think that the Great Powers, Russia, Germany, France, England, Austria, Japan and Italy, or any of them, whose consent is necessary to form as effective league, would agree not to begin a war until the question should be left to a vote of their respective electorates and an affirmative vote given. If not, his proposal is not feasible. Suppose the electorate of one country decides for war and that of the other does not. Shall another vote be taken? In which country? Or shall it be in both? The difficulty in answering these questions shows how chimerical the proposal is, and how ill adapted to the settlement of a pressing international issue between two governments. The Federal Constitution gives to Congress the power to declare war. Without amendment, Mr. Bryan's proposal could not be seriously entertained. Such an amendment is not likely before this war ends.

As a fourth plan, Mr. Bryan suggests a reduction of armaments. We all strongly favor this. But Mr. Bryan offers no plan for securing and maintaining the reduction. Until all strongly-armed nations reduce their armaments, every wise nation will insist on providing and maintaining an armament enabling it to make effective defense against the possible unlawful aggression of any other armed nation. A general reduction of armaments is entirely impractical under a league unless the league offers to each country a security of peace equivalent to the armament it abandons. I have already pointed out that Germany has expressed a willingness to consent to a limitation of armament. The Allies, in their answer to President Wilson, have intimated that agreements as to armament should be one of the sanctions of a secure peace. How is the reduction to be continuously maintained unless by the united and enforceable command of all the members of the League? An agreed reduction of armament is a corollary to our League's proposals, because a world compact embodying them will furnish the security to each nation it requires, and justify a lessening of its self-protection. But Mr. Bryan suggests no such security.

Mr. Bryan, irrelevantly, as it seems to me, charges that all army and navy officers, including our own, "make it their business to imperil peace." This is prompted by their insistence on due preparedness. Applied to our officers, it is a grave injustice to a fine body of men, fully imbued with the true American spirit of subordination of the military to the civil. If war were to come, our sudden sense of dependence on their tried skill, courage and high patriotism would cause us deep humiliation for such words, uttered merely because they had warned their countrymen truly.

The practical advantage of the League is in its organizing the political, economic and military forces of the world to command resort to impartial tribunals for the decision and settlement of all irritating questions between nations before they begin war. The educational effect of this practice will accustom them to such a mode of settlement.

They will acquire the habit of arbitration as Canada and the United States have done. The sanction of world force, though present, will thus become less compulsive upon the nations; and they will, as a matter of due course, as a habit and by preference, seek only a peaceful form.

C. Should the United States Become a Member of the League to Enforce Peace?

VII

The war in Europe will have weakened all nations engaged in it by the loss of the flower of their youth and by the destruction of industries and homes in the thousands of miles in its train, the cost of the rehabilitation of which can hardly be measured. The belligerents will stagger under a stupendous debt and interest charge. The primacy of the United States among the nations of the world will thus become clearer than it ever was; and this, taken with its real neutrality, must give it a great influence in a council of nations which can and ought to be exerted for the world's benefit. Its advocacy of such a League will strongly make for its acceptance by the other Great Powers, but only on condition that it becomes a member and bears its share of the risk and receives its share of the benefit of membership.

Our wealth in the last three years has been added to by billions in the profits that have been reaped from the sale of war material and war equipment to the nations of Europe and thus from the blood and the suffering of the people of these stricken countries. We had the right to take advantage of the situation for which we were not responsible; but the fact should make us sensitive to our duty when occasion and opportunity arise for us to help our brethren of Europe to avoid a recurrence of such woe. We have been blessed beyond any other nation. Our good fortune seems to have no limit. We shall not be worthy of it unless we recognize our responsibility and run our share of risk in securing the world from a return of the scourge visiting it now. Of course, the first duty of a nation is to its own people and to itself; and it should not, out of a mere ideal of self-sacrifice, endanger the integrity of its government or its civilization. But it has a duty as a member of the family of nations; and that duty is commensurate with its power for good to the world.

Moreover the risk which the United States would run in joining such a League should not be exaggerated. If the United States makes adequate preparation, as it intends to do, to defend itself against the unlawful aggression of any nation, the army and navy which it has projected will furnish ample constabulary force to fill any quota which may be allotted to it in the formation of the world police to suppress the beginnings of war in violation of the regulations of the League.

In the preliminary conference as to the proposals of the League, one member present put this question to another: Would you be willing that your boy, the apple of your eye and the pride of your heart, should lay down his life in a struggle over a question between Servia and Austria in which America has no concern? The answer was: "If the suppression of that struggle by the police force of the world would prevent a spread of the local fire into a general world conflagration, my boy's life could not be sacrificed in a higher cause." It is the duty of the United States, in its own interest and in the interest of mankind, to lead the nations into a League to Enforce Peace.

VIII

Washington's advice has no application to the League. The alliances which he condemned were like that with France during the Revolution because of which we were called on twenty years later to serve the selfish motive of our ally. Jefferson advocated a permanent alliance with Great Britain to maintain the Monroe Doctrine. Our League is a league of all nations to support the selfish purposes of none. It has only one object: to prevent unnecessary wars. . . .

The Monroe Doctrine rests ultimately on force. The traditions of ninety-three years strengthen it; but the Zimmermann note advises us that they may not be sufficient. Indeed our interests the world over require us to protect and maintain them. Our enormous trade with all the countries of Europe makes it most difficult, in a European war, to preserve our rights and interests as neutrals, and is most likely to involve us in the war. We are now on the brink of hostilities with Germany. Why, then, should Washington's advice be controlling, advice given us in a day of small things, based on an isolation and a remoteness from the rest of the world which has ceased? Our coming war with Germany demonstrates, from the selfish point of view alone, the wisdom of our joining in a world movement to prevent the recurrence of another European war, even though it imposes on us the burden of contributing our quota to an international police force.

But Mr. Bryan says that in joining the League we would abandon the Monroe Doctrine. The Monroe Doctrine, shortly described, is our national policy of preventing, by protest and by force if necessary, any non-American Power from subverting any independent American government and from colonizing, by such means or by purchase, American territory under a government of its own. Our reason for maintaining the Doctrine is that we think such a course by a non-American Power would endanger our interests. The Doctrine does not rest on International Law. Should a question arise as to its enforcement between us and a non-American Power, therefore, it would be non-justiciable and must go to the Commission under the second article for a recommendation of compromise in which we would not be bound in honor to acquiesce. We would then have the same opportunity to maintain the Doctrine by force as if there were no league. Under the thirty-one treaties of Mr. Bryan, we would now have to abide a year of investigation before using force. The disadvantage to us, if any, of delay, therefore, will certainly be no greater under the terms of the League.

Instead of hampering our maintenance of the Doctrine, the League would help us in any case where its violation might be attempted, for by the terms of the League, the non-American Power must submit its cause for hearing to one of the Tribunals of the League before hostilities; and, if it failed to do so, we could summon the international police force to drive it off American shores.

But it is said that, if we mix in European politics to the extent required by this League, we cannot exclude European Powers from taking part in those of this hemisphere. There is nothing in the League requiring us or authorizing us to participate in the internal politics of any European country or to do other than to use our good offices to prevent a war between any two of such countries. We are to furnish our quota to suppress a premature war between them. They are to exercise the same functions in this hemisphere. In what respect does that violate the Monroe Doctrine? The League does not enable us nor authorize us to acquire and colonize territory in Europe by purchase or conquest any more than it authorizes a European nation to do so on this side; and that is all the Monroe Doctrine forbids.

Mr. Bryan suggests that we should not join a World League because our citizens of foreign nativity would divide in their sympathies as between European nations. If our foreign policies, needed for our protection and for that of the world, are to be abandoned because of race prejudice in a comparatively small group of our foreign-born citizens, we have failed in our experiment of naturalization. I cannot acquiesce in such a view. This would indeed be a humiliating surrender to the so-called "hyphen."

IX

Mr. Bryan's eighth article commends the attitude of the President in his message read to the United States Senate on January 22nd. I have altogether misinterpreted the notes of the President to the belligerent powers, his speech at the dinner of the League to Enforce Peace in May 1916, as well as the message of January 22nd last, if he has not, in all of these, intended to approve the general principles of our League. His reference to "the major force of the world" was certainly an approval of the political organization of the world to the extent of creating an international police force to secure compliance with a peaceable procedure for the settlement of international questions likely otherwise to lead to war. Mr. Bryan's citation of the President as authority does not sustain his contention. . . .

The question who shall command the joint military force in a campaign is not material, provided it be understood in advance, as it must be, what the purpose of the campaign is. The United States has had no difficulty in the past in acting with other nations to carry out a common purpose of a military character, as the taking of Pekin by the Allied force during the Boxer trouble proves. Nations have acted together often in history; and the question who shall have the military command or how the joint armies should be directed is a practical military question to be agreed upon by the joint powers in war council. The purpose of League campaigns would be settled by the terms of the League before the mobilization begins. It would be to restrain the warlike activities of a nation unlawfully breaking a peace to which it is pledged. To characterize this as placing the destiny of the toiling millions of the United States in the hands of aliens for their selfish purposes is to reveal a complete misunderstanding of the normal operation of the League. The United States retains complete control of its forces and can withdraw them whenever the lawful and commendable purpose of preserving the peace of the world shall cease to be the object of the military campaign. . . .

Those who are promoting the League are not committed to any particular means by which the necessary military preparation shall be secured. Personally, I favor universal compulsory military training, for a year, of our youth between the ages of nineteen and twenty-four as the most effective and most democratic plan that can be adopted. It will fall equally upon the rich and poor. It will give a year of valuable disciplinary education to our youth who need it much. It will furnish a citizenship from which we can summon a trained army to defend our country. I repeat, however, this is not a part of the League plan.

The war with Germany which we now face, after every effort to escape it and when our national conscience is wholly void of offence toward her, is a sufficient answer to Mr. Bryan's view that love is all that is needed to make effective a world league to insure peace. If this war teaches us anything, it is that our civilization has not advanced beyond the time when the major force of the world is sometimes needed for defense against selfish greed and ambition on the part of nations. If we fail to prepare ourselves to defend our rights against lawless aggression by ruthless military and naval power, we are blind to the simplest lessons of current history. If we can avail ourselves of the same preparation to do our part in defending the peace of the world, should we not seize the opportunity?

X

We have now reached the end of the discussion. This tenth article offers an opportunity for a summary of the positions taken in the previous papers. The program of the League looks to a treaty binding all nations to adopt, in the settlement of controversies likely to lead to war between them, a peaceable procedure for the hearing and decision of issues capable of being settled on principles of law and of issues that may not be so settled. It does not attempt to enforce the decisions. The aim of the League is, by elucidation of the facts and arguments on both sides of the issue and by a decision of it by an impartial tribunal, to practice nations in the art of settling irritating questions by judicial investigation and conclusion. The example of our relations with Canada and the constant use of arbitration to settle our difficulties—which has become a habit—offer a precedent from which we believe that, when such a procedure is enforced, it will train all nations to adopt it rather than to resort to war. . . . The force of the world is to be used to compel nations to adopt this procedure before resorting to hostilities. . . . A pacifist who will admit a policeman to be a proper official in the community yields the whole case against the creation of an international police force in our League.

Mr. Bryan attempts to meet this argument by saying that the analogy is misleading and uses these words:

> The nations cannot, in fairness, be likened to criminals, although we often describe their public acts as criminal, especially in time of war. The criminal is one who intentionally violates a law duly enacted by those having authority to make laws. He disregards an obligation confessedly binding upon him; and the policeman, acting for the outraged community, arrests the guilty party and brings him before the bar of justice. There is no international law-making power; and, if such a law-making power existed, there are certain questions upon which it would not assume to act—certain questions upon which each nation, whether large or small, is conceded the right to decide for itself without regard to the views or interests of other nations. Our arbitration treaties, the most advanced in the world, contain exceptions, questions of honor, questions of independence, vital interests and the interests of third parties. These questions are not to be submitted to arbitration; and yet these are the very questions out of which wars grow.

Of all men in the world, Mr. Bryan, by reason of his general views, is the one least entitled to put forth these reasons in order to escape the analogy of state police. No one has spoken more eloquently against war as a crime than Mr. Bryan. No one has upheld more fully international law as a binding force upon the nations. International law is the law of nations agreed to between the nations and deriving its sanction from their general acquiescence. A nation which violates international law is a criminal before the bar. The exceptions from our existing treaties of arbitration of questions of vital interest and national honor, to which Mr. Bryan refers, were exceptions which were not recognized in the unratified general arbitration treaties made with France and Great Britain which Mr. Bryan approved and to which he gave effective support. More than that, the Senate itself did not seek, in its proposed amendments, to except questions of honor and vital interest from arbitration. Mr. Bryan's distinction is a forced one and has no foundation, certainly as applied to the plan of the League to Enforce Peace. The treaty forming the League is an agreement by all nations to comply with its stipulations and not only to comply with its stipulations, but, in case of non-compliance by any member, to contribute their quotas to an international police to restrain and punish that member for non-compliance. In other words, it furnishes an international constitution. It creates an international law and denounces as a crime violation of the legal obligations into which the nations voluntarily enter. The very object of the League is to organize the world politically; and that means to enact law and to provide for its enforcement. I submit that the analogy of the state police is not only a fair one but a clinching and convincing one in showing the fundamental fallacy and error of those who have the international pacifist views of Mr. Bryan and still are in favor of a state and city police.

That the League is practical may be inferred from the approval which its general principles have received from the leading statesmen of the Great Powers in answer to direct questions upon the subject, and also in official expression in the correspondence between President Wilson and the belligerent Powers engaged in the present war. It is practical because there is precedent for every detail in the League, and because it embodies the elemental principle of government as it should be in city, state, and nation and in the world: to wit, the organization of the force of all to suppress lawless force of the few. The lines upon which the League has been framed are very general; the plan is only a working hypothesis. That it may be changed in international conference in detail goes without saying. But that it furnishes a broad and correct foundation for the political organization of the world, as Kant foresaw it, I submit, is clear.

The United States should enter the League; first, because of all nations in the world, it wishes to avoid war and to make it as remote as possible; second, because its interests have now become so world-wide and it has become so close a neighbor of all the Great Powers of Europe and of Asia that a general war must involve the United States. It is therefore of the highest importance to the United States, viewed from the standpoint of self-interest, to secure the joint effort of the world to prevent such a war or to confine it to a local struggle. The present difficulty with Germany is a most striking demonstration of the danger in which the United States will be involved in every general war in the future, struggle as it may to escape being drawn in. . . .

Nor does the League involve the delegation to an international council, in which the United States has but one vote, of the power to hurry this country into war. The President and the Senate sign the treaty of the League and bind the United States to its obligations. Congress is the authority which will decide whether the fact exists, calling for action by the United States, and then will take such action as the obligation requires. Should the purpose of the International Police under the League be perverted to anything other than enforcing the peaceable procedure in the settlement of international controversies, Congress will have full power to withdraw the United States forces and decline further to take part in the proceedings. . . .

With the blessings which God has showered on this country, it should not hesitate to help the world and the family of nations to protect itself against the recurrence of such an awful disaster and retrograde movement in Christian civilization as the present war.

XI

Since this discussion began, and indeed since the tenth paper was written, the plot of the world drama now being enacted has developed with startling rapidity. Even as we have been arguing, a World League to Enforce Peace has been formed; and the United States has taken its proper place therein. The absolutism of Russia has toppled over in the twinkling of an eye; and the Russian people have taken charge. Germany, in a ruthless disregard of the rights of American citizens, has forced the United States, as a self-respecting nation, to take up the sword against her. The United States is thus driven into an alliance with the Entente Allies. The democracies of Russia, Italy, France, England and the United States are now engaged in a death struggle with the dynasties of the Hohenzollerns and the Hapsburgs to end the only substantial military absolutism remaining in the world. Military dynasties are a threat against the peace of the world. With their lust for power and the selfish considerations that affect their policies, their respect for the solemn obligations of a treaty are much less than that of democracies. Democracies are not perfect in their sense of justice, in the certainty of peaceful policies, nor in their exact observance of treaty obligations; but they are a vast improvement in these respects over an autocracy dependent on military force.

The Prussian autocracy of Germany is the great international criminal. It has sacrificed honor; it has murdered men and women and has, in numberless ways, violated with ruthless cruelty the principles of international law to accomplish its dynastic purposes. It has dragged its allies with it, and made them *participes criminis.* The League of the United States and the Entente Allies, and the Central and South American countries that may join us, is an organization of world power to visit destruction on the dynasties whose continued existence constitutes an obstruction to Law and Peace. We are properly separating the Hohenzollerns and the Hapsburgs, from the great German people and the great people of the Dual Monarchy. If we succeed, as we must, the war, dreadful as it has been in the losses and suffering it has entailed, painful and destructive as it is likely to be, will be worth all it cost. It will make the future of the world depend upon the rule of the peoples of the world, will exalt the reign of international justice, and will organize the joint forces of the world to maintain it. With the German and the Austrian and Hungarian peoples on the one hand, and the American, English, French, Italian and Russian peoples on the other, in an international conference, none will hesitate to enter a League to Enforce Peace. The popular character of all the governments, in and of itself, will render war between them less probable, will give greater sanction to their promises, and will make more practical and less burdensome a League having for its purpose compulsory procedure for the settlement of irritating international disputes.

"Whom the gods wish to destroy they first make mad." The people of the United States, immersed in business, lethargic with prosperity, naturally averse to war and its new horrors as shown in the present struggle, have been loath to take up the sword. They have made every honorable effort to keep out of the vortex. But Germany, in her mad desperation and with a lack of foresight that has characterized all her diplomatic politics, has forced an unwilling people to join the league of her opponents. The triumph of Democracy in Russia and the entry of the United States into the war make clear to the world and to history that this is a war for the benefit of mankind.

The rulers of Germany have undervalued the power of the United States. They have made military efficiency their national god. A country which has, up to this time, ignored military science, and failed to maintain a trained army, arouses in them contempt. In their mad rage at England and in their desire to starve her people, they have stupidly aroused against themselves the only dangerous antagonist remaining. When money and food and supplies are more clearly the determining factor in the war than ever before, they deliberately make an enemy of the country which has greater capacity to furnish them than all other countries combined. The military unpreparedness of the United States blinds them to the enormous advantage which her accession to the ranks of their opponents gives in the test of endurance which must decide the struggle. Within a month after her declaration of war, the United States will place at the disposal of her allies the enormous sum of three billions of dollars to replenish their depleted treasuries and to strengthen the effectiveness of their serried hosts. Her resources in the production of food and war supplies are being promptly organized so that the energies of this country will be directed to feeding the peoples of her allies and supporting and maintaining the equipment of their armies. The skill and courage of her navy, with the ingenuity of her inventors, will be directed to the suppression of the sole hope of the Prussian military hierarchy, their cruel, lawless and murderous submarine.

The broad conception of the world-cause for which the United States is fighting will send the blood tingling through her giant limbs and awaken in her that moral strength which the Hohenzollern in his plan to conquer the world has consistently ignored.

The struggle may be a long one. We do not aid our cause by underestimating the power of our enemy or the perfection attained by her in the organization and use of physical and material resources, and of a people educated and moulded to the needs of a military autocracy. We hope the contest may end in a year. It may last double that or longer; but however long it lasts, the end is not in doubt. We were slow in getting in. We will never quit until our high purpose is attained; and the cause of Democracy is triumphant. We should not rely on the pleasing hope that our losses will chiefly be in money. We should organize our efforts and make our plans with the stern thought that many of our best lives and the flower of our youth will figure largely in the cost of our victory; but the greatness of our cause should reconcile us to every sacrifice. When we, by our intervention, shall have contributed largely to the victory, when our real enemies shall have disappeared in the deposition of the Hohenzollerns and the Hapsburgs, the influence for good that we, without motive of aggrandizement, without hope or wish to increase our territory or power, can wield in the councils of the world will be commanding and will make for a just peace and a world league to maintain it.

"God works in mysterious ways his wonders to perform." It would seem that there was now being disclosed the providential plan for securing the future peace of the world. Everything that has happened is forcing on the adoption of a League to Enforce Peace. Events are shaping themselves so that when the Congress of Nations meets, after the end shall have come, the League will be as natural a result as peace itself. How futile in the face of the facts of today seem the arguments that we must preserve our isolation and avoid entangling alliances! How inapplicable Washington's words, wise when uttered, become to the needs and policy of the present! The League to Enforce Peace is formed; and we have joined it. On its success and permanence depends the future peace of the sons of men.

Note

Written debate between Mr. Taft and Mr. Bryan during the first four months of 1917. *World Peace* (New York: George H. Doran Company, 1917).

12

Victory with Power

No one in the wildest flight of his imagination now can think of unde-
feated Germany yielding either proper indemnity to Belgium or justice to
Alsace-Lorraine, each of which Great Britain and the United States have
made a *sine qua non*. Nor will the unconquered German ruling class consent to lift the German paw and remove its crushing weight from prostrate
Russia or give over to decent rule the blood-stained Christian provinces of
Turkey. If the wrongs of Belgium and Alsace-Lorraine, and of Russians,
Italians, Poles, Armenians, Serbians and other Slav peoples are not righted,
the sacrifices of the war will have been for naught. We must, therefore,
conquer the Germans if a just and lasting peace is to be secured. Therefore,
the slogan of the Allies, and the cry of this country must be "Victory with
Power."

Our Society was organized to make this war an instrument for the
promotion of peace. It holds that the horrors of the war and the awful
misery it involves must make the nations bind themselves to a common
obligation for the future to suppress war. We call for a primitive political
organization of the world, affording judicial and mediating agencies and

an international police to stamp out the beginnings of every riot of world violence. A member of the family of nations which looks upon war as a normal means of acquiring power and a justifiable condition of growth destroys hope for the future. Such member must be whipped into a different view and into conformity with the public opinion of the world. Nothing but force can cure the brutality and ruthlessness of force. In such a case the maxim *Similia similibus curantur* has full application. The peaceful countries of the world are obliged to assume the habits and the panoply of war. When they, in spite of their lack of preparation, in spite of their peace-loving instincts, shall strike down in battle a people that makes war its god, the cure of that people will be complete, the scales will fall from their eyes, and with a clear vision they will see that he whom they have ignorantly worshipped is the devil and not God. Until so cured, the Central Powers can never be amenable and law-abiding members of a peaceful world community.

Note

Extracts from an address before League to Enforce Peace Convention, Philadelphia, May 1918.

13

Our Purpose

We are in the war first of all to make the world safer and a better place to live in. We are fighting to bring about a lasting peace. There was a time when many cherished the hope that such a peace could be established by the moral force of public opinion. Now we know that peace has a more terrible price, and we are ready to pay the price.

We have had nothing to do with the politics of Europe; but this war is not a matter of European politics. It is world politics; and we announced ourselves as citizens of the world when we declared war against Germany. World politics, after all, are only fundamental questions of right and wrong. We are for the right against the wrong.

We are fighting to make it impossible for military autocracy ever again to endanger the peace of the world. Republics make mistakes, but this war has proved that they are slow to fight.

One thing this war will accomplish: when it is over we shall hear no more talk about the advantages of national isolation. In taking our place among the nations we have come with an international policy already prepared and we have made it clear to the world that the success of this policy is our main purpose. We are fighting, as our President has put it, "To make the world safe for democracy."

We have not tried to set a price upon our participation in the war. We have made no bargain. Europe knows our purpose. When the war is over we expect to cast our vote at the peace council for what the President called "such cooperation of force among the great nations as may be necessary to maintain peace and freedom throughout the world."

The war has demonstrated the weakness of international law unsupported by force. Such support can be furnished by a system of international police.

I do not pretend to know just what our views will be when the war is over. Nobody realized where the Spanish war would carry us. We went into it in Cuba and came out in the Philippines. But this is how the thing looks now. The policy and the purpose I have explained are so broad and their application so universal that it is difficult to see how any event can change them.

In principle this policy and purpose have been endorsed by many of the leading European statesmen who may sit at the peace council beside the delegates from this side of the Atlantic. In his speech before the United States Senate, M. Viviani, the former premier of France and head of the French mission, said: "Together we will carry on that struggle; and when by force we have at last imposed military victory, our labors will not be concluded. Our task will be—I quote the noble words of President Wilson—to organize the society of nations. . . . We will shatter the ponderous sword of militarism; we will establish guarantees of peace; and then we can disappear from the world's stage, since we shall leave at the cost of our common immolation the noblest heritage future generations can possess."

And Russia has joined the consensus of the enlightened nations with this declaration by Prof. Milyukoff, first Foreign Minister of the young Republic: "The definition by President Wilson of the purposes of the war corresponds entirely with the declarations of the statesmen of the allied powers: M. Briand, Mr. Asquith and Viscount Grey all expressed themselves continually on the necessity of seeking to prevent conflicts of armed forces by providing peaceful methods of solution for international disputes and creating a new organization of nations based upon order and justice in international life. The democracy of free Russia is able to associate itself completely with these declarations."

Our allies have accepted the definition of the high purpose of the war as it came to them from this side of the Atlantic. Now let us show them that we can wage war as well as analyze and define it.

Note

Newspaper article, June 30, 1918.

14

Self Determination

The task of the League of Nations called to decide the terms of peace will be as huge as that of the war which the peace will end. The issues as to Alsace-Lorraine, the Trentino and Trieste will be simple as compared with the Czecho-Slovak and Jugo-Slav questions. The restrictions of the Turkish domain, the protection and freedom of Armenia, the Balkan boundaries and the government of Albania will try the ingenuity of statesmen in working out a just result. Above all in difficulty will be the settlement of the questions as to Russia. Shall it be a confederation of States like ours, or shall they be independent? Who shall determine this?

"Let the people themselves decide," it is said. Every one agrees that this general rule should prevail in post-war arrangements. But how large or how small shall the unit of a people for such decision be? Shall units be racial or geographical? Suppose a people as small in number as the Belfast Orangemen compared with the whole population of Ireland insists on a separate government, though geography, trade conditions and every consideration but religious difference and tradition require that the whole island be under one Government?

It becomes apparent at once that the general principle of popular rule is not a panacea and that many issues will have to be settled by the Congress of Nations, according to expedient and practical justice, over the objection of some part of the people affected. The result will illustrate the inherent error in the frequent assumption that a Government by the people is a Government in which that which is done is the will of each one. A practical Government by the people is a Government by a majority of the voters. The rest of the people must yield their will to the will of this majority. However, in the purest democracy, the voters are not a half of the population, and the prevailing majority is usually not more than 20 percent of all. The guide of the popular will is still less helpful when the issue is the fixing of the proper self-governing unit. In the intoxicating fumes of a new freedom, municipal Councils in Russia declared themselves independent governments. Should Lithuania, Estonia, the Ukraine and Great Russia be separate entities? This cannot be certainly and properly determined by a plebiscite of the population of the particular district, if its relation to the neighboring communities or to Russia as a whole make it best for all concerned that they be united. More than this, an ignorant people without the slightest experience in the restraints necessary in successful self-government and subject to the wildest imaginings under the insidious demagoguery of venal leaders may well not know what is best for them.

Thus, flowing phrases as to liberty and the rule of the people do not offer a complete solution for all the problems which the world's peacemakers will face. Still, if we can make the adjustment to depend on just provision for the welfare of the peoples affected instead of on the greed of the parties, we shall secure an enormous advance over past international settlements.

Note

Philadelphia Public Ledger, October 3, 1918.

15

Peril in Hun Peace Offer

The European situation is working out exactly as one might have antici-
pated. Indeed, when we read the resolutions of the League to Enforce
Peace, adopted in the convention which the League held in this city in
May, their language is like a prophecy. The league in its platform said:—

> Apprehensive of the lure of an inconclusive peace, which would en-
> able the present masters of Germany to continue their dominion of
> Central Europe and sooner or later again to menace the peace and free-
> dom of the world, the league feels that our people should be forewarned
> in case Germany should propose to make peace on terms that might
> well deceive the unsuspecting. Suppose she should offer to retire from
> Belgium and France; to cede the Trentino to Italy; even to relinquish all
> claims to her captured colonies and to promise some kind of autonomy
> to the various races of Central and Eastern Europe. Such an offer would
> be highly seductive, and if we are not prepared to understand what it
> means might well beguile the Allies into a peace which would be incon-
> clusive, because unless the principle of militarism is destroyed the prom-
> ise would be kept no better than those broken in the past. Autonomy of

the other races would mean their organization for the strengthening of Germany until she had control of the resources of 200,000,000 for her next war. . . . Such a settlement would be a mere truce pending a strife more fierce hereafter. So long as predatory militarism is not wholly destroyed no lasting peace can be made.

Germany now proposes an armistice in order to enable the representatives of the Central Powers and the Allies to negotiate a peace on the general basis of peace indicated by President Wilson in his address to Congress on January 8, 1918. This does not really commit Germany to anything except that she is willing to talk about the subject matter covered in the fourteen points by President Wilson in that address. It involves an interminable discussion of what his fourteen points mean and include. That address was made nearly nine months ago. It was made before the Czecho-Slovak and Jugoslav movements had crystalized into a demand for independent governments. The President in his reference to a settlement of an Austrian peace asked for "the freest opportunity for autonomous development." Austria evidently looks to a confederation under the dual monarchy. We have now gone further as to the Czecho-Slavs and recognized their independence. The message of January 8 was made before the full revelations as to Germany's policies in respect to Russian and the Baltic provinces, which reek with bad faith, cruelty and a murderous plotting with the insane Bolsheviki against the decent people of Russia.

The President's fourteen points are stated in general words, the only ones which he could use at such a time. They are not stated in the specific terms upon which a treaty of peace could be formulated or upon which any offer of the Germans could be accepted. The Germans do not agree to submit to the terms stated by the President, general as they are. All they agree to is to negotiate after an armistice, a treaty "on the basis" of the President's address. Nothing could be more unsatisfactory and uncertain.

The attitude of the German Kaiser is important only as it shows the iron ring closing about him. He sees the handwriting on the wall, and he struggles in a peace offensive for a halt which shall enable him to rehabilitate his forces. Then, if he does not secure peace, with the Hohenzollern dynasty still in the saddle, he can resist with a rested army to the last. He sets his snare in the sight of the bird. His offer should be rejected with the same curt rejoinder as that which met the Austrian approach. We, of course, should not deceive ourselves. A prompt and decided refusal on our part to accept this offer of the Kaiser will be used by him to arouse his people to further resistance. This is the great alternative object which he has in mind. He will say that this refusal indicates that the Allies seek to annihilate the German people. He hopes that this will stiffen all his subjects to further effort. In his dire extremity he has called on the most peaceful and the most liberal of the prominent political personages in his empire.

But this personage is a cousin of the Emperor, is a Hohenzollern and would, of course, maintain the dynasty. His speech reads well, but we who have at hand the damning evidence of the militaristic treachery and the wicked ambition of the Kaiser and his crew know that the Prince is but a pawn advanced now for the single purpose of securing a negotiated peace. The Prince will not sit at the council table to carry out his own ideas. Surrounding him and at his back will be the Kaiser, Hindenburg, Ludendorff and the Crown Prince, the leaders of Junkerdom, ready to refuse any terms in the treaty which will hamstring the dynasty or prevent the possibility of the resurrection of the German army and a future renewal of the Potsdam conspiracy.

We should read the spirit of the Kaiser's offer in the light of burning Douai and the cruel looting and devastation of Belgium and Northern France. He says he will consent only to "an honorable peace." What does that mean? It means a settlement which assures for the German High Command and the Kaiser the position of honorable and trustworthy foes. This, in view of their conduct, is impossible if we are to achieve what this war is fought for. The Kaiser's offer should be sternly rejected and he and Austria should be advised that in the present situation we can have no armistice and no negotiation except upon the same terms as those which were meted out to Bulgaria. Any other result will be a profound disappointment to the American people and our allies.

Note

Philadelphia Public Ledger, October 8, 1918.

16

The Obligations of Victory

The international compact which is to follow this war is to be more ambitious than any ever made before. The world is larger, the nations are more numerous, the field of war has been greater, and the political changes are to be far more extensive than the world has ever known.

The only peace comparable with this is that which was made after Napoleon's fall by the monarchs who constituted the Holy Alliance. That was a League of Nations, with a high sounding declaration of disinterestedness and love of peace. It was a failure because the real purposes which governed its formation and life were wrong and unstable. It rested on the divine right of kings, and its objects were to recognize dynastic claims and to establish and maintain them. It took into consideration neither the interest nor the will of the peoples under the governments which it was setting up and proposed to maintain. After a few years it became a by-word of reproach.

The difference between the Holy Alliance and the League of Nations we now propose is in the purpose and principle of its formation. Our League looks to a union of the democratic nations of the world, to the will of the peoples, expressed through their governments, as its basis and sanction. It looks to the establishment of new governments by popular choice and control. It is to be founded on justice, impartially administered, and not on the interests of kings or emperors or dynasties. It is to rise as a structure built upon the ashes of militarism, and it is to rest on the pillars of justice and equality and the welfare of peoples.

I have referred to the Holy Alliance not only to answer an argument, but also as a precedent to prove that a treaty of peace rearranging the map of Europe cannot be made without a League of Nations. Think of what this present peace has to compass. We can realize it by considering the points of President Wilson's message of January 8th, outlining the terms of the future peace.

In the first place, we are to have disposition of the German colonies in accord with the interests of the people who live in them. Germany has made such cruel despotisms of her colonies that it is quite likely the Allies will insist that they shall be put under some other power more to be trusted in securing the welfare of backward peoples. Thus we are to set up a new government in East and West Africa, in Australasia, in China, and in some of the islands of the Pacific. Then we are to deal with Russia. If we separate from her the Ukraine, and the Baltic Provinces and Finland, there are three or four new nations to establish. Great Russia is now under the domination of bloody anarchists, and we must free her and give to her good people the opportunity to organize and establish a free and useful government. This is a problem of the utmost complexity. In Austria we are to create a nation of the Czecho-Slavs, embracing Bohemia, Moravia and Slovakia. We are to cut this nation out of the Dual Empire, and take it from Austria and from Hungary. We are to do the same thing with the Jugo-Slavs on the south of Austria and Hungary and establish new boundaries there. We are to settle the boundaries of the Balkans. We are likely to give to Rumania the Rumanians of Hungary and of Bessarabia. We are to establish a new state of Poland out of Russian, Austrian and German Poland, and we are to give this state access to the sea. The fixing of these boundaries and the determination of the method of reaching the sea present issues of the utmost delicacy and difficulty. We are to determine the status of Constantinople and the small tract now known as Turkey in Europe. We are to fix the limits of Turkey in Asia, to set up a new government in Palestine, to recognize a new government of Arabia, to father, it may be, the creation of a new state in the Caucasus and to establish the freedom of Armenia.

The mere recital of them is most convincing of the intricacy of these problems. The Congress of Nations will probably find it impossible definitely to settle them all. It will have to create Commissions, with judicial and conciliatory powers, able to devote time enough to make proper investigation and thus to reach just, defensible and practical conclusions. When the boundaries are all fixed, when the innumerable rights growing out of access to the Baltic, access to the Danube, access to the Black Sea and access to the Aegean, together with rights of way across neighboring states for freedom of trade, are defined, with as much clarity as possible, there still will arise, in the practical operation of the treaty, a multitude of irritating questions of interpretation. In fixing boundaries on distinctions of race and language, the Congress will encounter the obstruction of racial prejudice and blindness to reasonable conclusions. Lines of race and of language are not always so clearly drawn that convenient and compact states may be established within them. To attempt in a great world-agreement to settle the boundaries and mutual rights of so many new nations, without providing a tribunal whose decisions are to control and are to be enforced by the major force of the world, will be to make a treaty that will become a laughing stock.

We know that we have got to rearrange the map of Europe, and, in so far as it is practicable in that arrangement, to follow popular choice of the peoples to be governed. But such a flowing phrase will not settle the difficulty. It is merely a general principle that in its actual application often does not offer a completely satisfactory solution; and after the Congress shall have made the decisions, sore places will be left, local enmities will arise, and if that permanent peace which is to justify the war is to be attained, the world compact must itself contain the machinery for settlement of such inevitable disputes. In other words, we do not have to argue in favor of a League to Enforce Peace—the nations which enter this Congress cannot do otherwise than establish it. It faces them as the only possible way to achieve their object.

Germany and Austria and Bulgaria and Turkey are to indemnify the countries which they have outraged and devastated. Commissions must be created, judicial in their nature, to pass upon what the amount of the indemnity shall be, and then an international force must exist to levy execution if necessary for the judgment upon the countries whose criminal torts are to be indemnified. We must, therefore, not only have, as a result of the Congress, the machinery of justice and conciliation, but we must retain a combined military force of the Allies and victors to see to it that these just judgments are carried out. Moreover, the Congress cannot meet without enlarging the scope of international law and making more definite its provisions. The very functions which the Congress is to exercise in fixing the terms of peace will necessitate a statement of the principles upon which it has been guided. That will lead to a broadening of the scope of existing principles of international law and a greater variety in their applications. Therefore, whether those who are in the Congress wish it or not, they cannot solve the problems which are set before them without adopting the principles of our League to Enforce Peace as embodied in the four planks of our original platform—Court, Commission of Conciliation, enforcement of submission and a Legislative International Congress to make International Law. They will have to create such machinery for the administration and enforcement of the treaty as to the Central Powers, the new nations created and Russia. Having gone so far as they must, can they fail to extend their work only a little to include the settlement of all future differences between all the nations that are parties to the League? A League for such future purposes will be no more difficult to make and maintain than the temporary League into which they are driven by the necessities of the situation.

Now I want to take up some of the arguments made against the League. In the first place, a good many have created a straw League which they have knocked down without difficulty. They have attributed to us the views and principles held by extremists who perhaps support our League, but whose extreme views we do not and need not adopt. Thus it is said that we favor internationalism, that we are opposed to nationalism, that we wish to dilute the patriotic spirit into a vague universal brotherhood. That there are socialists and others who entertain this view, and who perhaps support the League to Enforce Peace, may be true; but the assumption that such views are necessary to a consistent support of the League is entirely without warrant. I believe in nationalism and patriotism, as distinguished from universal brotherhood as firmly as any one can. I believe that the national spirit and the patriotic love of country are as essential in the progress of the world as the family and the love of family are essential in domestic communities. But as the family and the love of family are not inconsistent with the love of country, but only strengthen it, so a proper, pure and patriotic nationalism stimulates a sense of international justice and does not detract in any way from the spirit of universal brotherhood.

Again, it is said that in the League we injure nationalism by abridging the sovereignty of our country in that we are to yield to an international council and an international tribunal, in which we have only one representative, the decisions of questions of justice and of national policy.[1] Sovereignty is a matter of definition. The League does not contemplate the slightest interference with the internal government of any country. The League does not propose to interfere, except where the claims of right of one country clash with the claims of right of another. To submit such claims of right to an impartial tribunal no more interferes with the sovereignty of a nation than the submission of an individual to a hearing and decree of court interferes with his liberty. The League is merely introducing, into the world's sphere, liberty of action regulated by law instead of license uncontrolled except by the greed and passion of the individual nation.

It is said that we are giving up our right to make war or to withhold from making it. We cannot take away from our Congress the right to declare war, and no one would wish to do so. But that is no reason why we should not enter into an agreement to defend the impartial judgments of the League and to repress palpable violations of its covenants by those who have entered it. The question must always be for the decision of Congress whether our obligations under the League require us in honor to make war. We have guaranteed the integrity of Cuba, we have guaranteed the integrity of Panama. Does that deprive us of sovereignty? Yet we are under an obligation to make war if another country attacks them.

The fourth of the President's fourteen points contains the provision that adequate guaranties must be given and taken that national armaments will be reduced to the lowest point consistent with domestic safety. That cannot be done immediately. It represents an aim and an aspiration. We are the victors in this war which grew out of the extensive armament and military power of Germany. It will be a legitimate condition of peace exacted by the victors that Germany shall substantially disarm and leave the Allied Powers in a position with armament sufficient to keep Germany within law and right. How far disarmament can be carried must be determined by experience. Disarmament will be accomplished effectively in great measure by the economic pressure that will be felt intensely by all nations after this war, by such mutual covenants and general supervision of an international council as experience may dictate, and ultimately by a sense of security in the successful operation of this League to Enforce Peace.

For the time being the people who are afraid that the United States will make itself helpless to defend its rights against unjust aggression are unduly exercised. Any practical League of Nations will require the United States to maintain a potential military force sufficient to comply promptly with its obligations to contribute to an international army whenever called upon for League purposes. Such obligation may well be made the basis and reason for universal training of youth, in accord with the Australian or the Swiss system—a system that trains youths for a year physically and mentally and gives them a proper sense of duty and obligation to the state. There may be a difference of opinion as to whether we should have such a system; but there is nothing in the League to Enforce Peace and its principles which prevents its adoption; and either that or some other means of maintaining an adequate force to discharge our obligations under a League must be found. While we should lay broad the foundations for a League looking as far into the future as we may, we must trust to the future to work out the application of those principles, to amend the details of our machinery and to adapt it to the lessons of experience. We know that the real hope of reducing armament and keeping it down is the maintenance of a League which shall insure justice and apply in its aid the major force of the world. As the operation of that League is more and more acquiesced in, the possibility of the safe reduction of armaments in all countries will become apparent to all and will be realized.

Another question that has agitated a good many people is whether we should admit Germany to the League. That depends upon whether Germany makes herself fit for membership in the League. If she gets rid of the Hohenzollerns, if she establishes a real popular government, if she shows by her national policies that she has acted on the lessons which the war should teach her, in short if she brings forth works meet for repentance, then of course we ought to admit her and encourage her by putting her on an equality with other nations and use her influence and power to make the League more effective. The long-drawn-out payment of indemnities will keep her in a chastened mood and will keep alive in her mind the evils of militarism.

I shall not now discuss the difference in the obligations of the members of such a League as between the Great Powers and the lesser Powers. All should have a voice in the general policy of the League; but it is well worthy of consideration whether, with the burden of enforcing the obligations of the League by military force which the greater Powers must carry, they should not have the larger voice in executive control. As they are the only ones likely to be able to create the major force of the world, they may reasonably claim a right to more administrative power. The rights of the smaller nations will be protected in the Congress, in which they have a full voice, and by the impartial judgments of the judicial tribunals and the recommendations of the Commission of Conciliation. There is not the slightest likelihood that the mere executive control by the larger Powers would lead to oppression of the smaller Powers because, should selfishness disclose itself in one of the Great Powers, we could be confident of the wish of the other Great Powers to repress it.

One of the difficulties in the maintenance of a League of all nations will be the instability of the governments of its members if the League embraces all nations. On the whole, the Greater Powers are the more stable and the more responsible. It is well therefore that upon them shall fall the chief executive responsibility. While the principles of the League would prevent interference with the internal governments as a general rule, the utter instability of a government might authorize an attempt to stabilize it. That this can be done better by a disinterested League than by a single nation goes without saying.

The possibilities of many-sided world benefit from a League after it is well established and is working smoothly, it is hard to overestimate. For the present, as the result of this Congress of Nations to meet and settle the terms of peace, we may well be content to have a League established on broad lines, with principles firmly and clearly stated, and with constructive provisions for amendment as experience shall indicate their necessity.

I verily believe we are in sight of the Promised Land. I hope we may not be denied its enjoyment.

Notes

Address delivered at Convention of the League to Enforce Peace, Madison, Wisconsin, under the auspices of the University of Wisconsin, November 9, 1918.

1. Mr. Taft has expressed himself elsewhere on this topic as follows:

Certainly we do not wish to contend for a sovereignty that shall not be limited by international law. That law should prevail in a decent community of nations—I mean the law of good form, the law of universal brotherhood, the law of neighborly feeling, which is over and above the absolute rules of international law. All that this League proposes is that every nation shall enjoy complete sovereignty within the limitations of that international law and that good form among nations.

What is this League of Nations to do to uphold that sovereignty? It agrees to give sanction to law that regulates sovereignty. That sovereignty, regulated by law, is to be clinched through the organized action of all the nations of the world.

Any other view, any objection to that view, savors of what? It savors of the desire to use the sovereignty of our nation to achieve purposes that will be defeated by the restraints which the League offers. That is what it means. It is the German idea of sovereignty—the power to use that sovereignty to achieve your purpose even when that purpose transgresses international law or moral law.—*The Atlantic Congress for a League of Nations, New York, February 5, 1919.*

To recur again to the objections which run as a thread through all of Senator Poindexter's attacks upon the constitution of the League, namely, that the League minimizes the sovereignty of the United States and of every nation which joins it, there is a misconception in the mind of the Senator as to sovereignty that needs to be pointed out. No reasonable and patriotic and properly self-respecting citizen of the United States can claim that our sovereignty should be more than a right to freedom of action within the limitations of international law, international morality, and a due regard for the rights of other nations. The only sovereignty which we ought to claim is sovereignty regulated by these limitations. It is exactly analogous to the liberty that we enjoy as individuals, which is liberty curtailed and regulated by law in order that other citizens may enjoy the same liberty. It is an exercise of rights on my part consistent with the exercise of the same rights on the part of every other man. It is not complete liberty of action. Proper national sovereignty is similarly restricted. Now the League does not proceed to restrict that sovereignty further than, through the joint compulsion of all nations, to keep a would-be outlaw nation within the proper existing limitation.

The League is not a super-sovereign. It is only a partnership. Its power is in only a partnership. Its power is in joint agreement—not in the establishment of government. The Senator's objection is fundamental. If it were analyzed and logically developed it would be seen to be a reactionary doctrine that belongs to the German view of the state and its needs and rights. It is not consonant with any hope of settling international differences other than by the power of the sword. It leads directly to the proposal that "might makes right." It is based on a doctrine of supreme national selfishness. It is the pessimistic and despairing view of any possibility of restricting war. It contemplates with entire complacence the prospect of another war in ten or twenty years like that through which we have passed. It perverts the glorious idea of a national sovereignty and prevents its aiding the family of nations. It perverts our grand federal constitution rendering helpless—so far as aiding the outside world is concerned—a nation which, under the providence of God, has become the world's greatest Power.

Will the American people acquiesce in such a small view of our responsibilities toward mankind and of our governmental capacity to be helpful? We may be confident they will not.—*Address at Portland, Oregon, February 16, 1919.*

And then "sovereignty"—what is sovereignty? Well, I can give you the German view and I can give you the American view. The German view is that sovereignty is the power to overcome the sovereignty of other nations by force. That is all. What is the American idea of sovereignty? It is a sovereignty regulated by international law and international morality and international decency and international neighborly feeling. Do we wish any sovereignty greater than that? Sovereignty is analogous to the liberty of the individual. The latter is liberty regulated by law which protects that liberty: and sovereignty is the same thing applied to nations. We do not change that in this League of Nations. All we do is to furnish the means of determining peaceably and justly what those limitations are, and provide the means of maintaining them. Does that deprive us of any sovereignty?—*Address at San Francisco, February 19, 1919.*

[Marburg]

17

Workingmen and the League

The pressing imminence of the issue of a League is not as fully understood in this country as it is in Great Britain, in France and in Italy. The movement was initiated in the United States in 1915 by the formation of the American League to Enforce Peace; but the question then had more or less of an academic aspect because of the remoteness of peace, and, indeed, at that time, for us, the remoteness of the war. Associations were subsequently formed in Great Britain and in France. As the peoples of these countries became war-weary, as the working population felt the suffering and dreadful pinch of starvation and want, their souls were gripped with a determination to have no more war. The subject was given world-wide attention through the addresses of President Wilson. The Socialists had always included the abolition of war as a fundamental plank in their platform. While the great majority of the Socialists and the workingmen in the allied countries admitted the necessity of fighting this war through, they made a peremptory demand for a League of Nations to Enforce Peace after this war was over and after the unconditional surrender of militarism.

The League of Nations, therefore, in England, France and Italy has become the slogan of workingmen and Socialists and they will brook no hesitation on this subject by the representatives of their countries in the Peace Congress.

Note

Philadelphia Public Ledger, November 13, 1918.

18

A League of Nations Our National Policy

Speeches are made from time to time in the Senate on the plan of a League of Nations to Enforce Peace. Senators Poindexter and Reed have pronounced judgment upon the plan as dangerous to the Republic and contrary to the established traditions of the nation. With deference, this judgment is not up to date. It fails to note that the war, our participation and avowed purpose in it and the treaty which is to end it have so changed our relation to Europe and the world that such traditions have ceased to be applicable. These traditions were shown to be outworn by the fact that we could not keep out of the war. We were driven into it because of our relations as close neighbors to the European belligerents. Having been thus driven into war, are we to make a separate peace with Germany, merely securing a guaranty from her that in the future we shall be immune, as a neutral, from submarine attack upon our commerce? This would be the logical outcome of the attitude of the opposing Senators. Are we not rather to take part in framing the articles of a general treaty as to Alsace-Lorraine, Poland, the Trentino, the Czecho-Slavs, the Jugo-Slavs, Russia, Armenia and in respect to the numerous other questions that must be constructively answered in the treaty?

Certainly the American people have no doubt that we are to have a full share in the settlement of all these issues. No other inference can be drawn from the messages of the President, acquiesced in by all. If we sit at the international council table and make this general treaty, it is idle to talk of our taking no further part in European world politics. If we enter into this treaty rearranging the map of Europe and the world in the interest of the rule of, by and for the various peoples of the world, and to secure them the blessings of permanent peace, we have got to see it through. We can't make such a treaty and run away from it as our abandoned child. We must share, with those with whom we act in making it, the responsibility of securing and maintaining its full and beneficent operation. If we make a treaty to fill the outlines of President Wilson's message of January 8, as amended by the Allies, we shall have the job of its execution lasting a number of years. It will not execute itself.

We have put our hand to the plow and we cannot turn back. The opposing Senators do not see the problems which confront us.

The imagination of Senators has been strained to conceive a situation in which the United States shall have had a judgment against her, in the international court, of vital character which she resists, and the united military forces of the world combine to destroy her. If the judgment against her is just, she ought to obey it. If it is not, why assume that it will be rendered at all or that, if rendered, all nations would join in a world war to enforce it? Indeed, may not our imagination, if we let it run riot, as easily conceive such a union of military forces of the world against the United States without a league and its machinery as with them?

Thus far the opponents of the League on the Senate floor have been from both parties. If President Wilson returns to his first view of the need for such a League of Nations to Enforce Peace and succeeds in securing the concurrence of our European allies in this view, we may assume that the Democratic party will support him in his policy. The League of Nations to maintain peace will likewise have the passionate support of all the peoples of our Allies and of neutral nations. It will have the earnest support of organized labor in this country. It will arouse the enthusiasm of the peace-loving people of this country, who are vastly in the majority. The Republican members of the Senate will do well to consider whether it would be wise for them to furnish to Mr. Wilson and the Democratic party an issue upon which the Administration would be most likely to win, and one which would dwarf all others upon which the Republicans now base their hope of success. Of course, this is no reason for yielding in the face of fundamental principle, but it may well weigh heavily when objection to the League is based on hypotheses, strained and improbable.

Note

Article in the *Philadelphia Public Ledger,* December 1, 1918.

19

Why a League of Nations Is Necessary

My feeling about the League of Nations to Enforce Peace is that the stars in their courses are fighting to make it inevitable.

We are in a League of Nations to Enforce Peace, we have been enforcing peace, and we are in a place where we cannot escape it.

We went into this war because we were driven into it. We had to be driven because of the Washington policy and entangling alliance doctrine; and we stayed out of it a long time after, as we look at it now, we ought to have gone in. We were forced in to defend our rights on the seas. That was why those men who feared entangling alliances were willing to waive their objection or reached the conclusion that we were not departing from that policy: our rights on the seas had really been invaded by murderous submarine attacks on neutral ships and on enemy merchant ships, bearing our citizens. And they had a right, under international law, to be there.

When we got into the war Mr. Wilson stated—and I never heard any objection from anybody—that our purpose in this war was to make the world safe for democracy. Not the United States, the *world*. It was to suppress militarism. Where? Not in the United States. Not in Europe. In the world. To say that we are not to take our part in world politics is to ignore just exactly where we are, what our position is—a position we cannot escape from.

We have made an armistice, we have imposed terms on Germany with respect to that armistice; but we made that armistice on a basis of a treaty which was to deal in a general way with fields that were outlined in the message of January 8, 1918, as amended by the Allies before the armistice was submitted to the Germans. One amendment referred to the freedom of the seas, the Entente Allies reserving the right to deal with that subject as they were advised. The other concerned the meaning of the word "restoration," which was made entirely free from doubt with reference to indemnities.

That is the basis of the treaty; those are the fields to be covered in the treaty. And now it is a matter of good faith, as I understand, between the parties.

How are you going to regulate the question of how much armament each nation shall have? How maintain the limit fixed upon? Of course, everybody understands that the armament we are especially interested in is Germany's armament. We are going to see to it that that is only such "as domestic safety shall require."

Are we just going to leave that requirement in the treaty and make no provision for enforcing it or maintaining it? Is that the way we are to deal with Germany? Under such conditions, what will happen if Germany unites with German Austria to make a very considerable power and retains her military spirit? Shall we not rather create an agency which shall see to it that this Covenant is effective?

Then there is Russia, controlled by the Bolsheviki. I do not know what we are going to do about Russia. I know what we ought to have done. We ought to have sent two hundred thousand men in there originally, and with additional forces from our Allies we could have stamped out Bolshevism. When a man says you encumber the earth and that the only way to have happiness on earth is to kill you—the only way you can deal with him is to kill him. That is all there is about it; and the idea of dealing with Bolshevism in any other way is an iridescent dream. We will have to stamp it out. That will have to be done by the Allies, and we will have to maintain a force for that purpose.

The countries we propose to set up have got to be held in leading strings. You cannot do that except by a League of Nations that notifies them—every one of them: "This war was fought for your liberty and that democracy might be safe, and we do not propose to have you start a conflagration and bring about another war that we have sacrificed millions and billions and endured all sorts of suffering to avoid."

We created a republic in Cuba. We surrounded it with all possible safeguards, and then we had to send a force down there to compose a revolution of gentlemen on the outs who wanted to get in and gentlemen on the ins who did not want to get out. That is the trouble we will find in these new republics.

I say this with deference, but if there is not a League of Nations created in Paris the whole thing is a failure—and I do not think they are going to make a failure at Paris.

It is perfectly easy to suggest objections to a plan like this. Take the Constitution of the United States. When it was adopted, the prophecies in respect to it were quite as formidable as certain distinguished Senators hold the difficulties in the operation of the League to be. And you can imagine cases now with reference to the operation of the Constitution that would lead to such a disturbance as to destroy the Government. We had one but survived it. We had to camp outside the Constitution until we did, and then we got back under it again.

In the disputed election between Hayes and Tilden we had to create an extra-constitutional body to settle that question, but we were self-governing people and we did it.

What seems to me important is to get nations into the habit of settling their differences otherwise than by war. You can't get rid of war until some substitute is offered to prevent injustice and to enable you to get justice. Of course, we have produced that in our constitutional system. Every state has the right to go into the Supreme Court to ask justice against every other state. In many cases there is no law which governs the behavior of states except international law, and that is administered by the Supreme Court of the United States in such cases.

I do not care what you call it, you have got to have a court, you have got to have a committee of conciliation, you have got to have force, you have got to fix rules of international law. You cannot get away from these.

20

Lesser League of Nations

Subjects for consideration by the conference at Versailles will naturally divide themselves into two great classes. The first will embrace those terms exacted of Germany and the other conquered nations to prevent them from again beginning war now or in the near future; the indemnities to be assessed against them for damage inflicted on France, Belgium, Serbia and the other Allies; the redistribution of their territories and carving out of them the new republics to be set up; together with the machinery for securing those terms and their maintenance. The second class of subjects for discussion and settlement will be less exigent and have more of a world-wide character. Such will be the definition of freedom of the seas, open diplomacy, the prevention of discriminating economic barriers and the machinery for a general League of Nations to Enforce Peace.

This league may well consist of only the Allied nations, England, France, Italy, Japan and the United States. These are now the only "great" Powers for practical purposes. They cannot achieve the end of this war without such a league. How, if at all, this league shall be expanded to include other or all nations may be properly inquired into by a Congress of

Nations of the World, continuing the sessions of the Versailles conference. The greater league would thus be a growth from the smaller league into which the Allied Powers will find themselves forced by the necessities of the situation. This is the best method of developing political institutions. It is the Anglo-Saxon way. They are framed and set in operation to meet immediate needs and then are expanded as their adaptation to larger usefulness makes itself clear.

A question as to the first or smaller league will at once demand answer from us. That is, whether we shall join it. The reactionaries, of whom there seem to be several in our Senate, will insist that we should keep our skirts clear of it and leave it to the other four Great Powers. After we have signed and approved the treaty, in their view, we should rid ourselves of any responsibility for its enforcement or the maintenance of the just, equitable and democratic status which its signatories seek to establish. This is the counsel of cowardice and atavism. It breaks the word of promise to the oppressed peoples of Europe. It would take out of the executive council of such a league the only member of it to which the peoples of the new republics and the rest of Europe would look with confidence for purely disinterested counsel and action. After our magniloquent declarations of purpose in this war, after our high-sounding announcement of the equitable bases of settlement of the war upon which the armistice and the treaty to follow are conditioned, what a lame and impotent conclusion it would be for our President to come back to this country, leaving, as an arbiter of half the world, a League of Nations in which we were to have no voice and over whose actions we were to have no control!

Could we thus selfishly retire to our isolated seclusion and repudiate the responsibility that our participation in the war and in the terms of peace must thrust upon us as the most powerful and most impartial member of the family of nations? It is inconceivable that President Wilson, after what he has written and said to the world, would consent to play such a humiliating part. If, on the contrary, he is consistent with himself, if he stands up to the character he has assumed before to the plain people of Europe and the world, and signs a treaty by which the United States becomes a responsible factor in the world's progress, the men of small vision in the Senate and Congress will be swept from their opposition by a public opinion they cannot withstand.

Such a general league must always be of the highest benefit to every small nation. It would offer protection against any oppression by a greater nation, and it would give relief from the burden of armament. Full reliance could be had on the fairness of the league, because a conspiracy by all the Great Powers, including the United States, to oppress a small Power is unthinkable. Therefore, every small nation would ultimately seek admission. It would then willingly submit to reasonable restrictions on its own representative weight in the league to which, as an initiating constituent member, it might make vociferous objection.

Note

Article in the *Philadelphia Public Ledger,* December 9, 1918.

21

Disarmament of Nations and Freedom of the Seas

The original program of the League to Enforce Peace contained no clause with reference to disarmament of nations. This was not because the projectors of the league did not deem disarmament of the utmost importance in the ultimate maintenance of permanent peace but because they deemed real disarmament possible only as the result of the successful operation of the league. The league could only serve its purpose by furnishing to the nations the protection that the nations secured by armament. It was to be substituted for armament. Until it proved its usefulness as such, the armed nations could not be expected to part with their own insurance.

In a league of nations to Enforce the Versailles Treaty the Allied Powers must retain armament to constitute a police force to secure peace between the new nations of Middle and Eastern Europe and Asia Minor. This will justify the United States in maintaining a potential army by a system of universal training. It accords with Secretary Daniels's recommendations that we continue the peace plan of increasing our navy.

As the smaller league of peace proves its adequate protection against war the motive of economy will prompt compliance with Mr. Wilson's armament clause in the fourteen points by a proportionate decrease in all armaments, and a mutual agreement will become possible and practical. Meantime we must be patient. Reforms of this kind do not come at once and should not be expected to. We take an important step, and its success leads to another forward movement.

There is nothing in England's position respecting her fleet that should discourage the friends of the League of Nations to Enforce Peace. The exaggerated language of a Winston Churchill should not discourage us. It is the language of an advocate in a heated political campaign. We must admit the justice of England's position—that she cannot give up her fleet in the absence of the test of a new league of nations. She cannot know whether the League will be sufficient protection to her against attack. Her isolated position requires her to protect herself against starvation in time of war. She is dependent on other countries for food and raw materials. These can only reach her by the sea. She must keep open the access by sea in time of war. Only by her fleet can she do this. Not until the operation of the League of Nations demonstrates that this danger in war is minimized can she be expected to reduce her fleet.

So far as freedom of the seas in time of peace is concerned, wherever the British flag floats there is and always has been freedom of the seas.

Note

Article in the *Philadelphia Public Ledger,* December 11, 1918.

22

The League of Nations and the German Colonies I

No one can overestimate the weight in winning this war of the morale of the Allies born of the righteousness of their cause. They said, and the world believed them, that they were engaged in this war for no selfish purpose. They were enlisted in the terrible struggle to end the hideous immorality and unmorality of militarism, to restore stolen goods and to further the establishment of governments in accordance with the will of those governed.

France sought Alsace-Lorraine as a measure of justice. Italy sought the Trentino and Trieste on the same ground. The United States and Great Britain sought the acquisition of no new territory. Great Britain has indicated that she does not desire the return of Helgoland, that island off the mouth of the Elbe which Lord Salisbury sold to Germany and which has proved so formidable a naval outpost of the German empire in this war.

The question as to the German colonies, however, has raised a doubt among some whether Great Britain will adhere religiously to the attitude of seeking no additional territory. Germany has colonies in East and West Africa of large extent. She has a colony of large area in the neighborhood of Australia, part of the island of New Guinea. The Australians, the New Zealanders and the South Africans among the English colonists object to the return of these colonies to Germany, because Germany's ownership of them has been a threat to Australia and New Zealand and has required special defenses by them.

It is to be inferred from the clearly proved outrageous treatment by Germany of her colonists that the Peace Conference in Versailles will conclude that none of her colonies should be returned to Germany. They have not been administered for the benefit of the backward peoples in the colonies. The treatment of these peoples is of a piece with the atrocious conduct of the Germans in this war.

Under the principles laid down in the fourteen points, therefore, the only question which the conferees can take up is how shall these colonies be administered. That they are not now capable of self-government goes without saying. The Australians and New Zealanders would doubtless wish that the German colony in New Guinea should be taken over by Great Britain. The South African English colonists will probably seek the same result.

It would be too bad for Britain to yield to the urgings of her daughters in this regard. She cannot afford to do it. It will arouse at once the attack that she is exhibiting the same land-grabbing propensities which have been charged to her in the past.

There is no argument making more strongly for the establishment and maintenance of a league of nations in connection with this treaty than the need of a proper method of providing for these German colonies. They should be governed by an agency of the league of nations charged with the duty of educating the natives, leading them on in the paths of civilization and extending self-government to them as rapidly as their fitness will permit. They will thus prove to the world the equitable and just motives and aims of the nations who frame the provisions of this epoch-making treaty.

Note

Article in the *Philadelphia Public Ledger,* December 16, 1918.

23

The League of Nations and Religious Liberty

The earnest effort of the Jews of the United States to induce our executive to remedy the intolerable condition of their co-religionists in the backward countries of Europe has often been met and defeated by the argument that our government cannot interfere with the domestic affairs of another nation. This argument has little if any application to the present situation. There is much evidence accumulating to show that the pogroms and abuses of the Jews continue in the countries where they have heretofore existed, and that the chaotic and lawless condition in these countries has offered an opportunity for the cruel gratification of race and religious prejudice. On the whole, it is not too much to say that the people of the Jewish race have suffered more in this war, as noncombatants, than any other people, unless it be the Serbians and the Armenians.

In Poland and in Galicia the true story of their agonies and losses is heartrending. The five nations who are to draft the treaty at Versailles are setting up governments in Poland, in the Ukraine and in the Baltic provinces. In all of these the Jewish population is a substantial percentage of the whole. In their sad story we find the Jews in the Middle Ages seeking refuge from the oppression and cruelty of Western Europe and rushing to the great empire of Poland, then stretching from the Baltic to the Black Sea, to take advantage of a charter of religious tolerance and opportunity granted by one of the liberal Polish kings. The irony of fate, however, ended the Polish kingdom and a large part of it was turned over to Russia, which ground the Jews under its tyrannous heel. This is why half of the thirteen millions of Jews living in the world were at the beginning of this war to be found in the Russian pale in which Jews were permitted to live, to which they were limited, and which was practically coterminous with the territory which Russia had taken from old Poland.

One of the great projects of this Congress of Powers at Versailles is to set up independent governments in these territories of the Russian Jewish pale. We shall be derelict in our duty if we do not require, as part of the fundamental law of these new republics, that the Jews shall have as great religious freedom as they have in the United States. But we must do more. We must have a league of nations to see to it that such fundamental law exacted by the treaty shall be enforced. We find full precedent for such a provision in the law in the treaty made by the Congress of Berlin, in which Bulgaria and Romania were established as independent countries. Romania, which had long been a heinous sinner against the Jews, was forced by the Berlin Congress to accept, as part of its constitution, a declaration that there should be complete religious freedom and that no citizen should be discriminated against on account of his religion in any respect. The Romanian government had the audacity, after incorporating the guaranty in its fundamental law, to declare and hold that Jews who had lived in Romania for two or three hundred years, father and son, were aliens. In this way the protection of the Jews provided for in the treaty of Berlin was denied, and this was after Romania had secured recognition as a government on an additional promise of fair treatment of the Jews.

Let us have no farcical result in working out this treaty of Versailles. Could we find a stronger argument for the continuance of our league of nations than this ignominious failure of that congress of 1879, under the presidency of Bismarck, to carry out its declared purpose? If there be any

24

President Wilson and the League of Nations

President Wilson says that the statement of the *Chicago Tribune* that, before sailing, he approved the plan of the League to Enforce Peace is untrue and that he never directly or indirectly endorsed the plan. It is not believed that any one, for the American League, ever claimed that he did. From what he has said, however, he has given the world reason to believe that he favored action by a league of nations to achieve results only to be brought about along the lines of the American League to Enforce Peace. He has, because of his addresses and messages on the subject, come to be regarded as the foremost champion of a league of nations to maintain peace after this war. It is the confident belief of the people of France that he has attended the conference in order to secure such a league which prompts their enthusiastic and affectionate acclaim. He will do well to bear this in mind. He must not give the word of promise to the ear and break it to the hope. He has spoken so much on the objects of this war, he has laid down in a didactic form so many principles in their application to all the peoples in the sphere of the war, he has pictured with such eloquence the idealistic results for the freedom, justice and peace of the large and small nations affected by the war, that if he now fails to propose and secure in the treaty practical machinery for a real league of nations, which shall enforce peace, he will properly be held responsible for a lame and impotent conclusion before the world and its expectant peoples.

Mr. Wilson is master of an inspiring style of promise, in which he encourages hopes and ideals and awakens the enthusiasm of popular expectancy without committing himself to constructive suggestions for a definite method of achievement. In dealing with the peoples of the world, who are looking to him as a savior from future war and a preserver of peace and democracy, this habit of mind and expression is now to be subjected to the severest test in his career. He has in his keeping not alone his own reputation for good faith, but that of the great people for whom he is the spokesman.

Let us see what this League of Nations, whose formation, he says, is absolutely indispensable to the maintenance of peace, is. Let us study it from his speeches.

On May 27, 1916, Mr. Wilson delivered a written address at the dinner of the League to Enforce Peace in Washington. He expressly declined to discuss the program of the League, whose guest he was, but he clearly specified certain objects and laid down principles of international action which accorded with the objects and principles of the league. He said the people of the United States would wish "a universal association of the nations to maintain an inviolate security of the highway of the seas for the common and unhindered use of all nations of the world and to prevent any war begun either contrary to treaty covenants or without warning and full submission of the causes to the opinion of the world—a virtual guarantee of territorial integrity and political independence." He further said at this dinner that "the world was even then upon the eve of a great consummation, when some common force will be brought into existence which shall safeguard right as the first and most fundamental interest of all peoples and all governments, when coercion shall be summoned not to the service of political ambition or selfish hostility, but to the service of a common order, a common justice and a common peace."

He delivered these words to a society whose plan included for its proposed league of nations a congress of Powers to improve international law, an international court and an international council of conciliation, to which all international differences were to be submitted, and, finally, a common and combined police force of the nations together with combined economic boycott to prevent the advent of war before there has been full submission of the dispute to such tribunals. It was impossible for those who heard the President against this background to escape the conviction that he was in general and almost specific accord not only with the purposes but with the method of the league. How could the just results which he sought be obtained without international tribunals? How could a league of nations act through a common force without obligation of its members to respond with contributors to such a common force when war was begun without submission?

Since that speech much has happened. But the President has continued to refer to a league of nations and to the major force of the world as a means of securing peace and justice.

In the fourteen points of the message of January 8, 1918, we find references to a League of Nations and its guarantee as follows:

In the second point it is said that the high seas may be closed only "by international action for the enforcement of international covenants."

In the third point establishment of equality of trade conditions is to be required "among all nations consenting to the peace and associating themselves for its maintenance."

In the fourth point adequate guarantees are to be "given and taken that national armaments will be reduced to the lowest point consistent with domestic safety."

In the eleventh point it is provided that "international guarantees of the political and economic independence and territorial integrity of the several Balkan States should be entered into."

By the twelfth it is enjoined that "the Dardanelles should be permanently opened as a free passage to the ships and commerce of all nations under international guarantees."

In the thirteenth point it is required that Poland shall be secured "a free passage to the seas," and her "political and economic independence and territorial integrity should be guaranteed by international covenants."

In the fourteenth point it is said that a "general association of nations must be formed under specific covenants for the purpose of political independence and territorial integrity to great and small States alike."

In his address of September 27, 1918, he said: "There can be no leagues or alliances or special covenants and understandings *within* the general and common family of the League of Nations. There can be no special, selfish economic combinations within the League and no employment of any form of economic boycott or exclusion, except as the power of economic penalty by exclusion from the markets of the world may be vested in the League of Nations itself as a means of discipline and control."

He signaled the entry of the United States into the war by his message of April 2, 1917, in which he said we were to fight "for a universal dominion of right by such concert of free peoples as shall bring peace and safety to all nations and make this world itself at last free."

Other passages of similar import might be cited, but these are enough to show that those who read them had a right to believe the President was committing himself to a league of nations, bound by covenants of its members to maintain justice, freedom and peace among nations large and small and to do this by force; i.e., by the combined armies and navies of the members of the League. The maintenance of justice necessarily carries with it the conception of a court to administer it: to hear the differences submitted, pronounce judgment and enforce it through the executive agencies of the League.

This is the general plan of the League to Enforce Peace. Mr. Wilson's plan is more ambitious in that the members of the League are mutually to guarantee the political and territorial integrity of all the signatories of the treaty. By this the United States would bind itself to preserve by arms the boundaries and independence of Poland, of the Balkans, of the Czecho-Slavs and all the new republics to be born of this treaty, as Great Britain did those of Belgium.

We cannot suppose that, after giving these assurances to the peoples of Europe, President Wilson will be content with a treaty of mere good intentions and with declarations obligating no nation to do anything to maintain justice, freedom and peace, but leaving it to the uncertain moral sanction of the conscience of each nation to find out what justice is and then to do it.

Note

Article in the *Philadelphia Public Ledger,* December 23, 1918.

25

Senator Lodge on the League of Nations

Senator Lodge's speech in the senate on the twenty-first of this month was the best yet made on the aims of the Allies and the elements of a satisfactory treaty of peace. It was comprehensive and accurate, lucid and forcible, felicitous in phrase and elevated in tone. It was in the senator's best style, and that is a high standard.

Its great merit is in its broad vision of the real purposes of the United States and her present obligation. The senator summarizes certain objections to the general League of Nations. These are, as lawyers would say, *obiter dicta* in this speech, because he now asks a postponement of that subject matter, not its rejection on its merits.

There are those who minimize the burden the United States should assume in execution of this peace; they deny that she should share it with her Allies. Mr. Lodge is not one of those. He is not a little American. He does not recur to the farewell address of Washington and the phrase, "entangling alliances," enjoined by Jefferson in order to employ them narrowly to limit the responsibilities of the United States, now that it has become the most powerful nation in the world.

In his address he said:

> We went to war to save civilization. For this mighty purpose we have sacrificed thousands of American lives and spent billions of American treasure. We cannot, therefore, leave the work half done. We are as much bound, not merely by interests and every consideration for a safe future, but by honor and self-respect, to see that the terms of peace are carried out, as we were to fulfill our great determination that the armies of Germany should be defeated in the field. We cannot halt or turn back now. We must do our share to carry out the peace as we have done our share to win the war, of which the peace is an integral part. We must do our share in the occupation of German territory which will be held as security for the indemnities to be paid by Germany. We cannot escape doing our part in aiding the peoples to whom we have helped to give freedom and independence in establishing themselves with ordered governments, for in no other way can we erect the barriers which are essential to prevent another outbreak by Germany upon the world. We cannot leave the Jugo-Slavs, the Czecho-Slovaks and the Poles, the Lithuanians and the other states which we hope to see formed and marching upon the path of progress and development, unaided and alone.

He says that the United States is obliged to aid Russia in rising from the chaos and disorder which has come upon her to the place which she ought to occupy in the family of nations; that the object of the Russian Bolsheviki has been to destroy their fellow citizens and every element which was necessary to a social fabric under which men could live and prosper while they themselves profit in money and in power from the ruin they have wrought; that they indulged in murder and massacre, destroyed property and all the instruments of industry, and the unhappy and ignorant people of Russia, in whose name they undertook to act, are today suffering from famine and disease, and are in a worse condition than they were in the days of the Romanoffs; that if Russian anarchy should be permitted to spread through western civilization, that civilization would fall; that we cannot leave Russia lying helpless and breathing out infection on the world; and that it would be discreditable to the United States if we failed to recognize our duty to her.

The Senator's speech was delivered to establish the necessity for postponing the consideration by the conference of five of the fourteen points of the President's message of January 8, referring to secret diplomacy, to freedom of navigation and the seas, to the removal of economic barriers, to the reduction of armament, and to the central League of Nations.

It must be admitted the Senator's argument for a postponement of these questions to an adjourned conference has weight. It may be that in the immediate settlement of them is to be found a means of solving difficulties in agreement upon specific terms of peace, of which neither the Senator nor we are advised.

A stipulation that the five Allies dictating this treaty should not make any treaty as between themselves inconsistent with the purpose of the great treaty and should make no secret treaties at all, may well strengthen mutual confidence in the good faith of all in the main treaty.

The general reduction of armaments of all nations does not immediately concern the peace in the sphere of war, provided Germany's teeth are effectively drawn.

The provision against economic barriers is a general question of world trade, the immediate settlement of which does not, on the surface, seem essential to the adjustment of the purposes of the nations in winning this war. The sub-currents of selfish purpose in respect to trade, however, may require a preliminary settlement of such a general principle as the best basis for adjusting special interests.

The freedom of the seas in time of war is a very general issue, postponement of which to the adjourned conference would hardly interfere with a satisfactory peace settlement for the present.

What should be emphasized, however, and what Senator Lodge brings out with force of argument that cannot be met, is the fact that we now have a league of nations—the United States, England, France, Italy and Japan—whose obligations in respect to securing the results of the war in Europe are equal. They are dictating this peace. The treaty will not enforce itself.

Unless we stamp out the poisonous infection of Russian Bolshevism and prevent its spread throughout the countries of Europe, we shall only substitute anarchy, chaos and plundering, murderous violence for imperial despotism.

26

The League: Why and How

It is possible that we need not include all the nations in the League in order to perform the task that we have set for ourselves; but it is essential that we should have a league of the Great Nations to enforce peace, if the treaty of peace is to accomplish any of the objects that we and the Allies have had in the war.

Now, the expression league of nations is used to indicate something, and I think it is just as well to define it so that we may know what we are talking about. Of course it serves some purposes to have a slogan which you do not have to define. It gives you an opportunity to make a campaign without reference to details. You shout it to the crowd, and when anybody presents objections you can say that that is not the kind of a league of nations you favor. Therefore I think it best to define what we mean. I say we; I mean a party of dreamers, mayhap, who got together, after the war began, to formulate something. Way back in an administration that is now forgotten—I did not wish to bring it up again, but I only refer to it as a reminiscence and a date—treaties of peace were negotiated with England and with France by the United States. They provided for arbitration of all justiciable issues between the contracting parties. We thought we had made a good deal of progress in negotiating and signing those treaties, and the Secretary of State and the Ambassadors who signed were photographed and there was a general feeling that something had been done that was of historical interest. Well, that is the only interest it has now; because when they got to the Senate, that august body truncated them and amended them and qualified them in such a way that their own father could not recognize them.

There was no danger of war between the United States and either France or England; we had proven the lack of danger by a hundred years of peace. And since the treaties had really been framed as models, when they came back thus crippled and maimed, they were not very useful. So I put them on the shelf and let the dust accumulate on them in the hope that the Senators might change their minds, or that the people might change the Senate; instead of which they changed me. Now those treaties were an improvement on previous treaties. The previous treaties, of which there were many (there is no trouble in getting treaties of arbitration; you can get them by the bushel when they do not clinch anything), had provided that the contracting nations would arbitrate every question except one that concerned vital interests, honor or territorial integrity, leaving it, of course, to either party to determine what concerned its vital interests or its honor. Well, as no nation would ever go to war for anything but what did, in its opinion, concern its vital interests or its honor, the treaties ought to have read, and properly and freely rendered did read, "We agree to arbitrate every question which is not likely to lead to war." Therefore the assistance such treaties gave in the matter of peace was not perceptible.

So we adopted this form by which we agreed to arbitrate every justiciable question. It is necessary to know what justiciable means. Old Noah Webster said that the word had become obsolete. Well, since his time it has been revived, notably in the decisions and opinions of the Supreme Court. It is used by Mr. Justice Bradley, by Chief Justice Fuller and by Mr. Justice Brewer, and it means a controversy that can be settled in court on principles of law; one capable of settlement by the disposition of justice.

Those of us who have been engaged in promoting the settlement of difficulties by arbitration were of course overcome with disappointment when the war broke out. We knew that armament was heavy; but we thought it would be a brake on the people, who must realize from the armament itself first, how destructive war would be, and second, how enormously expensive it would be. Nevertheless, within a week after the first of August, 1914, Europe was at war. And then those of us who had suffered this disappointment gathered ourselves together to see if we could not get some plan to discourage war, some plan which we could induce the nations to adopt after this war was over, after this dreadful destruction had come to an end, and when men would be longing for some means of promoting and making peace permanent. We met at the Century Club and afterwards at the Independence Hall, and organized the League to Enforce Peace.

When the war began the people of this country were anxious to keep out of it. The President's proclamation of neutrality was received by them with approval. We did not realize then what was at stake. We thought we could be neutral and keep within the lines of international law and avoid being drawn into the struggle. We were neutral and we did keep within the lines of international law; but we found it was impossible to avoid being drawn into the struggle. Of course we say we were drawn into it, as we were, by the blindness and cruelty of Germany's submarine policy. But what did that grow out of? It grew out of the circumstance that in war, as it is now carried on, it is impossible for a nation, which furnishes to the world what we furnish, to remain neutral. We were the market to which all the nations engaged in this war resorted for food, munitions and war equipment. Until the British navy swept the German navy from the seas, we furnished to both sides with impartiality what they came to buy. The fortunes of war having limited us to the Allies as our customers, that which was inevitable came about: Germany came to realize that our resources were going to enable the Allies to win the war. We were within our rights under international law in doing what we did. But it was found that we were so close to Europe, so much involved by our trade with all of Europe, that it was practically impossible for us to exercise our rights as international tradesmen without in effect so strengthening one side that that side was bound to look upon us as the means by which they could carry on the war; and its enemy was bound to take the same view. Accordingly Germany determined to resort to the murderous policy of the submarines, in which she was willing to sacrifice the rights of innocent noncombatants and citizens of the United States in order to frighten us out of exercising our international rights upon the seas. That is what drove us into the war; and any future European war will probably bring about the same result. It shows how deeply interested we are, even from a selfish standpoint, in suppressing European war or war anywhere that is likely to spread. The world is now so closely knit together, oceans today being means of union rather than of separation, that in future wars there will be no great neutral.

When we got into this war we found that its issues were infinitely greater than that which drove us in. Our vision broadened. We discovered that our purposes in the war must be as broad as the purpose of the enemy we were fighting, that we must utterly crush him in order to cure his lust for power and to defeat that which was divulged as no less than a purpose to rule the world. Germany had, for forty years, been preparing for this war. Bismarck had taught her the value of military force. By wonderful successes in three wars, in each of which Germany, or Prussia, acquired territory and by all of which Germany was solidified, the German people became convinced that they were supermen, became convinced that they had learned the secret of applying scientific principles to the military art. They were taught in their schools that the highest development of national greatness was military force. They were taught to worship the supremacy of the German State. Having applied this system of efficiency and thoroughness and these scientific principles to the military art, they proceeded to extend them to every field of human activity. That thoroughness, that system, that efficiency, which they called "kultur," enabled them to win in agriculture, manufacture, business, transportation, and every field of applied science.

It also added to the size of their heads, already enlarged by military successes. They prospered under that false and wicked philosophy. Materialism forced itself into their schools and dominated their general view; and while growing ever more materialistic they began to use the conception of God as a partner in the enterprise. They said that He needed them in supporting His philosophy, that it was their design, under His direction, to spread this kultur by force in order to help Him make civilization a success. No consideration of decency, humanity, honor or morality must be allowed to interfere. That was the doctrine; you can see it in the lectures from their university platforms. The whole people were saturated with this dreadful principle, namely, that the victories of the state must be achieved at all hazards and without regard to those ordinary considerations that re-strain individuals in society. And that led to their atrocious conduct of the war. They became obsessed with a madness. When we got into the war we began to realize—what our Allies had realized before—that the only thing that could rid the world of this danger was complete defeat of the German people. We were fighting the German people, not the Hohenzollerns alone; for until we cured the German people of this obsession, until we cured them of this disease which was in their heads, we had not achieved the purposes of the war that had forced itself on us. We could only do this by a surgical operation on their heads to be performed with a club. We have been using that club and now we have got to keep our grip on it for some time until they show, by bringing forth works meet for repentance, that the cure has been effected.

That is the purpose of the war. How are we going to achieve it? We have got through the first act, a very important one; but others remain. The armistice was made as the basis of a future treaty which was to cover the subject matter and to achieve the purposes outlined in President Wilson's message of January 8, 1918, as modified and qualified by the Allies' insistence upon indemnities and by the refusal on their part to yield to the clause with respect to freedom of the seas, which they said was too indefinite.

We shall have to use some agency like the League of Nations in dealing with Constantinople, which will have to be internationalized, because the Bosporus, the Dardanelles, and the Sea of Marmora constitute a throat through which the countries on the Black Sea obtain access to the Mediter-ranean. Constantinople must therefore not be presided over by any nation having a selfish motive to close that passage.

Then we come to Russia, what are we going to do about Russia? Russia had the Romanoffs, but as between a one man despot and a mob I prefer the one man. The Bolsheviki are the lowest proletarians led by a few profes-sionals and if you can get a worse combination than that, I do not know what it is. They proceed on the theory that anybody with thrift, anybody with enterprise, anybody who dresses well and tries to help his family to a higher level, is an enemy of society. In order to be rid of them they get the country into a condition where there is not enough food to go round, di-vide the people into classes—the rich, or rather those who were rich, the bourgeoisie, the intellectuals and the proletariat—feed the lowest element of the proletariat, starve the other classes, and then, if the latter do not disappear rapidly enough, imprison the leaders and shoot them *en masse* without trial. This is simple, if it does not commend itself in any other way; and that minority—for they are a minority of the proletariat—will ultimately become a majority if they just keep it up. The Bolsheviki are, in fact, deadly enemies of society. They are not democrats; they are not republicans; they are not in favor of popular rule. They called a constituent assembly and then drove the delegates out of the assembly chamber. On what ground? On the ground that a majority of those elected were bourgeoisie; they were respectable; and they could not brook having a respectable majority in power. Therefore they took forcible possession of the country and through the Soviet they are maintaining a tyranny the like of which has never been seen in history. They have far exceeded the tyranny of the French Revolution, without any justification. Unless we suppress that, unless those nations that are responsible for this loosening of the social ties see to it that that poison is stamped out, they have not done their work, they have not achieved their purpose. We must (when I say we, I mean the Allies), by some means, and force is the only means, give to these poor people of Russia an opportunity themselves to set up government by majority; and we cannot do that unless we maintain a combined force of the Allies. That is an essential part of it, and that is one of the provisions of our League.

Then there are half a dozen republics, perhaps more, which we are to launch. Their peoples have not had any experience in self-government. Self-government, which has been defined by President Wilson as character, is a great boon to people who are able to practice it. It needs training, self-restraint. We do not realize that in this country. We seem to think that it is a panacea which we can apply to the troubles of Hottentots or anybody else. The same is true of our idea of liberty. We talk about liberty, but we really don't understand its value, because it comes to us as the air we breathe. It is hard to make people understand the benefits which they are enjoying under this government and to realize that our liberty has been the result of sacrifices and blood and struggle for a thousand years by our Anglo-Saxon ancestors. And so it is with self-government. We had to take our liberty by forcibly separating ourselves from England; but she had herself enabled us to learn self-government even before we separated. This country has since become the great exemplar of self-government by the power of popular self-restraint. At no time is this self-restraint more in evidence than in the period between the presidential conventions and the second day after the election. Each party holds a convention and makes a platform. The platform explains with elaborate detail, with eloquence and with perfect fairness, what a horrible thing it will be to let in the other party or to continue the other party in power. Candidates are nominated and subjected to a scrutiny which belittles the power of the microscope. I know something about it. And then the orators, the torch-light procession, and the party activity! The visitor from Mars, interested only in the developments attending these great mass meetings and heated discussions, says: "Well, I will stay here until the election, because, with all this feeling, with people dividing into such equal forces and determined to win, there is certain to be an explosion then." The election comes and it is as quiet as a May morning. Each voter, man or woman, goes into the booth and votes as he or she wishes, or he votes as she wishes or she votes as he wishes. The votes are counted and the result is announced, perhaps that night, perhaps the next day or the next afternoon. But when the result is known, every man and woman is aware who it is that is certain, if he lives, to carry on and guide the destinies of this country in the executive branch of the government. Everybody acquiesces, and men, women and children follow the pursuits of the day as usual. Now, that is self-government. The minority acquiesce. They may think of the next election, but they make no trouble. Why? Because they realize that the majority, when they come into power, will administer the government as a trust for all the people, and that the rights of all will be preserved equally. That is what makes self-government possible. In Central America you find a very different state of affairs. There, whenever they have an election, the minority take to the woods, with their guns, and try to shoot themselves into a majority. Those are the two extremes. But any people, who have not had the training in popular self-restraint that we have had—this understanding of the responsibility of the majority for all the people—are likely to stumble and fall. We have tried it in the Philippines and in Cuba. We gave Cuba self-government. After three years they had an election which caused a revolution. Mr. Roosevelt sent me down there to stop it and launch the Republic once more. Well, I could not stop it except by sending for the army and navy of the United States. That step had a wholesome, conciliating, quieting effect. We were not called upon to fight. We took over the island and held it for two years. We passed a lot of good statutes, among them an election law, held a fair election under it and then turned over the government to those elected. We had launched her once more. If she ever requires it, we will do the same thing over again and launch her again, and then again, until she gets strong enough—I hope she is now—to stand alone. And now, instead of setting up one Cuba we are setting up half a dozen. We are carving them out of the dominion of the empires that we have been engaged in fighting. We are putting them where the racial resentment, combined with memory of the tyranny practiced, will prompt them to be impatient and headstrong in dealing with those empires. And the people of those empires will harbor the resentment which always comes against persons that have broken away from one's control. We are setting up these governments for two reasons: first, because we are in favor of giving people a chance to choose their own government; and second, because we are hemming in Germany, taking away the territories she ought not to have so that she may never again raise her head in pursuit of world power.

In order to do this we have got to arrange the machinery that shall maintain peace. The old powerful empires were much more likely to maintain peace than are these numerous new governments left to themselves. Unless we exercise the power of the father over these new children of ours they will prove unruly and bring about the very war that we are trying to prevent by creating them. I do not know any mathematical demonstration that is clearer than that. The danger is that these nations do not know their rights. They have the frailties of human nature, and it is an unaccustomed business for them. They are ambitious. Each one is dealing, without experience, with liberty and independence and self-development. Our liberty is liberty regulated by law. And when you say liberty regulated by law, you mean liberty regulated and limited by the rights of others so that all may enjoy the same liberty and equal rights. Just so nations must have independence limited and regulated by law—by international law; and we have got to devise and maintain the machinery that shall make it possible.

This treaty is going to be as long as the moral law. There never was a treaty so complicated as this will be. No matter what the character of the contract, even though drawn by the ablest lawyer who ever drew a contract, if it has many provisions, if it is complicated, it will need interpretation in application. But how interpret a contract authoritatively? That is a justiciable matter. That is what we have courts for; and it is impossible for this treaty to be executed unless you have a court, appointed by the same power that made the treaty, to interpret the treaty. It will be especially needed when the new events arise that are certain to arise in the lives of these new nations. If you know any way by which those questions can be satisfactorily decided other than by a court with authority to decide them, I shall be glad to hear of it. And there you have the first plank in the platform of the League to Enforce Peace.

Next, there will be questions of policy which do not come under the head of justiciable questions. You have got to have somebody representing the League to negotiate and adjust compromises of that kind. This League that is meeting in Paris is a ponderous body. Premiers and Presidents cannot be there all the time. They have got to leave an agency there and that agency must represent the League in the matter of settling differences which arise between the nations they are creating and the nations out of which they are created. And so you have the second provision as to a commission of conciliation. These new nations are going to manifest all the faults and the weaknesses of children. It is inevitable. And the thing that makes children better and leads them on is discipline. You do not always have to use the broad hand, but it is helpful to have it in the family. Therefore we need a combined force, which can be counted on when needed, to convince these creations of this treaty, these governments, and these people, that there is a power having the means of enforcing the judgments and the compromises that will be reached under the court or the commission. This is the third or force plank of the League platform.

Then the Congress of Powers is bound to enlarge and, in a way, codify and make more definite the principles of international law, and this is the fourth plank of the platform of the League to Enforce Peace.

Now, having that League before us as a necessity, the question arises, shall we go on to the larger League? Shall we invite in the other nations of the world to form a league that shall assume the responsibility of this treaty and also endeavor to make war less probable in the world at large? Shall we introduce a league which shall work not only to keep peace in that sphere but also to keep peace between the very Powers that make this league, and between all the other Powers of the world? The question whether that shall be done now or later is a question that can be determined on the ground. Even if it is not determined now, the step that is taken by creating this smaller league to achieve its purpose of maintaining peace, where peace is more doubtful and where the problems are so much more difficult than in a normal world at peace, will be a long step towards the possibility of a general League of Nations. Heretofore this has been an academic question. People have been interested in its discussion, but the war seemed remote and peace seemed remote. Now the question is live; it is before us; since the President will bring back with him this treaty with a provision for a league of nations in it.

If the President does come home with a treaty like this, then it behooves us all to unite in support of it; if there be difficulties in it, to suggest how the difficulties may be overcome; but to appreciate the purposes of that League, to appreciate the fact that the world is longing for it and the oppressed and suffering peoples of the Allies are longing for the machinery that shall prevent a recurrence of the dread disaster through which they have passed. We should look at it from a progressive standpoint, should realize that something has happened since the war began, that the assumption that everything which has occurred in the past is going to recur, that there is no hope of change, is the doctrine of pessimism and fatalism. This war has been fundamental in its character. It has shaken the foundations of society. And people who look forward, who look for better things, are not discouraged because something like that which is now proposed has been tried before and failed. They refuse to assume that it will therefore fail again. Progress is not made without some risk. We never enter into new experiments without realizing that there may be a failure. But is that a reason why we should not go forward? Eloquence is all right, platforms are all right, declarations of ideals are all right, provided they are accompanied by willingness to make sacrifices and run risks to accomplish the ideals. But they must not be treated as things of substance, their mere declaration an end in itself, imposing no obligations on those who have uttered them to go on and do the things they extol.

I have heard it said that this League of Nations takes away sovereignty.

Mr. Taft: That is a very apt question. I think it is wise to begin with the Great Powers. When you organize a club and you want clubable members you make your selections with care. There are a lot of nations that are irresponsible. If you call them all into a convention at once, they will insist on having equal voice with the most responsible and powerful nations, and I am not in favor of that. I am in favor of a practical arrangement; and this peace creates the opportunity for it. These five nations are an initiating nucleus that is most valuable in creating a real league of all nations which are responsible nations. If we call a convention of all then every one will want to be heard and they will object if they are not given full representation. Now you have got to make a practical arrangement. Every nation ought to be heard in a congress that lays down the rules of law. What the proportion of representation should be is a matter of expediency and justice. You cannot fix it according to population alone, because China would then have four times as many votes as the United States. There ought to be a proportionate representation on some fixed basis, depending on importance and power, and perhaps on the average intelligence of the people; but you can fix that when you have a managing committee that passes on qualifications for admission. Such a league is going to be a great boon for the small nations. It is going to give them protection; and therefore it is going to be such an advantage that they will be glad to come in under reasonable conditions. But if you consult them all at once they will not be able to agree. We have had experience in that matter. In arranging the framework of an international court of admiralty prize, a court to deal with captures at sea, we were able to agree upon the membership because there were a lot of nations which had no navies and no merchantmen and which were therefore not concerned about naval prizes. But just as soon as we tried to establish a world-court, passing on general disputes between nations, then every nation wanted a judge on that court. That would have made the court worse than a town meeting, and it became impossible.

I am not in favor of letting in Germany for a long time. She must show herself worthy. She is a criminal before the bar of justice. When you arrest a criminal and find a pistol on him you take it away. That is why, in this matter of reduction of armament, we have the right to say to Germany, "We will draw your teeth," and that is what we have been doing. I do not know whether you share my feeling, but nothing has occurred since the armistice that has given me more satisfaction than the delivery of those great war vessels at the Firth of Forth, and of those submarines at the mouth of the Thames. The punishment was richly deserved.

Note

Address delivered at Montclair, New Jersey, December 30, 1918, under the auspices of the College Women's Club.

27

From an Article in the *Public Ledger*, January 1, 1919

The League of Nations, to be useful, must command the respect of the
world as upholding right and justice. The United States is the least interested of all the nations of the League in the terms of peace from a selfish
standpoint. Our membership in it is, therefore, of the highest value. It will
give confidence to the peoples of Europe in the purity and sincerity of the
League's intentions to secure the good of all. President Wilson's trip has
shown clearly the weight the United States has in this respect. It is not too
much to say that he is stronger today with the people of Great Britain,
France and Italy than are the respective Premiers of these countries. The
longing of these peoples for a league of nations to maintain peace and his
championing of such a league have had much to do with bringing about
this result. It has secured the support of Lloyd George and Clémenceau for
the League. This phase of the situation imposes the heaviest obligation on
the United States to retain an active part in the execution of all the provisions of the treaty.

28

Representation in the League

An objection made to the general idea of a League of Nations is the impossibility of adjusting properly and satisfactorily the representation of the small and large nations in the governmental agencies of the League. Every one is aware of this difficulty. It was one upon which the proposal for a world court halted before the war. The Study Committee of the League to Enforce Peace, believes the solution is to be found in giving representation, where representation is necessary, according to responsibility.

The functions of the League may conveniently be divided into the legislative, the judicial, the mediating and the executive. The congress of all the world Powers, great and small, will consider and determine general principles of international law and policy for the guidance of the judicial and executive branches. It may well codify international law and give it that definite legislative sanction the absence of which has led some jurists to deny that it is law at all. In such a congress the nations should have representation in accord with their world importance, measured by power, population and responsible character.

The great advantage of having a small league of the great Powers formed first for the immediate necessities of maintaining the terms of this peace and constituting the initiating nucleus of a larger world league is that the small league could work out the equitable representation of the smaller nations as they apply for admission. The protection the greater league will assure them will induce them to seek the boon of membership.

The great Powers of the small league as the trustees for all, made so by circumstances, may then fairly adjust the representation which each incoming member of the great league should have.

The judicial branch or court of the League should not be a representative body at all. It should be a tribunal made up of great international jurists, selected for their high character, judicial and impartial bent of mind, their learning in jurisprudence and their ability. They should be permanent judges, made independent in tenure and compensation. Citizenship in countries parties to the controversy should disqualify members of the court in the particular case. They should have jurisdiction only to hear pure questions of law and fact.

No political question should come before them. They should interpret treaties and declare and apply the international law as now established or as qualified and enacted by the congress of Powers. The difficulty as to representation should not, therefore, arise as to the constitution of the court. Of course, to give confidence in its broad view of the world law, care should be taken to select judges from different countries with different systems of law, and thus give the tribunal a world character.

The commission of conciliation, which is a negotiating, mediating body, should have the representative feature. The small nations are too many to have members of it permanently; but every nation having a real interest in the issue to be settled should be represented on it for the time being, and its representative should take part in the mediation, hearing and recommendation of settlement.

In its practical working the great Powers will furnish the police force of the League, and their representatives should exercise the executive function. The safety and security of the lesser nations who cannot be expected to share the burden of military contribution will be found in the judgments of the impartial international court, in the recommendation of the commission of conciliation and the principles of international justice ordained in a congress of the world's nations. Moreover, without representatives in the executive, they may well confide in the friendly and just attitude of the united executive council of great Powers in carrying out the judgments of the League court and in dealing with the compromises recommended by the League commission of conciliation. The great Powers in the executive council will have no united interest adverse to small nations as a group or individually. On the contrary, they will watch one another in dealing with every small nation. The resultant action will be dictated by the common purpose of the League.

We are not now considering the representation of the United States in the branches of the League. As one of the great Powers, it will have an influential voice in all of them. We are only suggesting a method of giving the small nations the protection they should have and a representation when practical and needed.

Note

Article in the *Philadelphia Public Ledger,* January 3, 1919.

29

Criticism Should Be Constructive

Objections to a general League of Nations are numerous. Senator Borah makes merry over it. The funny column of the *Evening Sun* is filled with hypotheses of its operation and its absurd results. Mr. Lodge and Mr. Knox treat the proposal with more deference. Mr. Lodge, in a speech at the dinner of the League to Enforce Peace in May 1916, advocated the use of force to support an international tribunal's judgment. Since that time he has changed his mind, but in his last speech he appreciates the seriousness of the proposal sufficiently to discuss in more detail the plan of the League. Mr. Knox has favored treaties of universal arbitration of justiciable questions and therefore has also a past to observe.

The force and weight of objections to the League should be gathered first from the attitude of mind of the objector. If he is content to dispose of the matter on the ground that the idea is an old one and has never been realized, we are not likely to have useful help from him. One who does not hope that the great war has changed the feeling of the peoples of the world toward war so that they are willing to bind themselves to a world policy of peace as they never were before will certainly not entertain the plea of the

League with patience. He must be waked up before he will give it his consideration. One who has no sense of responsibility about future world peace, but is anxious to return to domestic business and politics, is equally beyond reach.

It is only from those who appreciate our great opportunity in the dreadful results of this war to arouse all peoples to the wisdom of uniting the major force of the world to prevent their recurrence that we can have sympathetic discussion and constructive thought. The proposal of a league of nations should not be flouted because the members of the Senate are justifiably indignant over the way in which the President has ignored them and ignored Congress in this matter. When he returns with a treaty providing for some kind of a league of nations to maintain peace, the people are unlikely to be interested in the personal soreness of the Senate or to accept that as any factor in judging the treaty. The Democrats of the Senate, with only one or two exceptions, will approve what the President submits. If the Republicans who object to the League are numerous enough to defeat the treaty they will have to decide whether their objection is really so weighty and sincere that they wish to furnish it as an issue to the President and his party in the next campaign. The pressure of the popular desire will be to have immediate peace. The party which delays that must have a strong case.

The League of Nations is very strong with the peoples of Europe. It is growing stronger here. Organized labor has approved it. It is going to attract the mass of wage-earners and the plain people as it has abroad. With the President and the Democratic party behind it, Republican objectors who manifest no constructive desire to create machinery to keep the peace, but depend wholly as of old on armament and troops to settle difficulties, will not be heard with favor. The contemptuous skepticism of the Senate cloakroom, the cheap sarcasms of "the old diplomatic and senatorial band," the manifest spirit of "how not to do it," will be very poor weapons with which to combat an idealistic campaign for a definite plan for permanent peace and democracy.

The next presidential campaign promises well for the Republican party if that party, through its congressional representatives, does nothing to change the present trend. But if enough Republican senators attempt to defeat or hold up the treaty of peace because it makes the United States a member of a League of Nations to maintain peace they will seriously endanger the chance of Republican success.

The Senators who discuss any plan for a League should show their interest, not by knocking it out with one blow, but by suggesting changes in it which would be more practical than the ideals proposed and would still serve the general purpose. They should make their consideration hopeful and optimistic by searching for alternative details of method which might avoid the objections they conceive. If any of the critics of the League in the Senate, or out of it, have given such evidence of their sympathetic interest in the project and its purpose, it has not been brought to our knowledge. The whole tone of the objectors has been pessimistic. Running through all their attacks is the cynical assumption that the great war has made no difference in the attitude and duty of the peoples of the world toward war and peace, except that for the time it has injured the power of Germany to make further trouble. They, in effect, advocate the retirement of the United States to its shell of isolation, to reappear again only when the war-making proclivities of any nation, Germany, or any other country, shall threaten the interests of the United States. This is the gospel of despair and national selfishness.

The possibility of a breach of national faith may be pointed out as a weakness of the League. If so, it is inherent in every treaty, the value and utility of which must ultimately rest in the honor of the nations making it. The more responsible the nations the greater their power of performance, the keener their appreciation of their honor, the clearer their perception of the value to themselves and the world of maintaining the treaty, the greater the certainty that the treaty will live and effect its purpose.

Note

Article in the *Philadelphia Public Ledger,* January 5, 1919.

30

Roosevelt's Contribution to League of Nations

The last editorial of Colonel Roosevelt on the League of Nations, posthumously published, is one of the most important he ever wrote. It is important in its useful suggestions and limitations as well as in the spirit of constructive statesmanship which prompted it and shines through it.

The idea of a League of Nations is not a new one, as Senator Knox pointed out in his Senate speech. Among others, Sully, the great minister of France, proposed it. Tennyson with his poetic vision and pen fixed it forever in memory. In more recent times Theodore Roosevelt, in his speech accepting the Nobel peace prize, revived the thought and gave it more definite character by emphasizing the feature of an international police force which could impose international justice.

During the war, men of action, intensely absorbed in the great and critical task of developing all the energies of the Allies to win in a contest so fraught with the fate of the world, found it difficult to be patient with the discussion of a plan for peace which could only be realized after the war was won, and under which they saw lurking a tendency to a peace by negotiation and without victory. Roosevelt, Clémenceau and Lloyd

George shared this feeling. As might be expected, it found freer expression from the American leader, in his unofficial status, than from the other two. Colonel Roosevelt's nature recoiled from association with an idea he found supported by men without a country who exalt internationalism and deprecate nationalism. With them the League of Nations seems to mean the dilution of that intense and moving love of country, the source of all real effective progress, into a nervous, colorless, flabby and transcendental brotherhood of man. Universal brotherhood should, of course, be an increasing influence in the world and is, but it will never be useful if it means the loss of patriotism. The relation of one to the other should be as love of home and family is to the love of country. The one strengthens the other. The emasculated supporters of internationalism as an antidote for love of country are inclined to regard the home and family as reactionary. Those institutions find no sympathetic protection among the Bolsheviki, foreign or domestic.

Moreover, men of the dynamic type, like Roosevelt, had a suspicion that all pacifists were pressing a league of nations as a stalking horse for compromising the vital principles at stake in the war. Hence their coldness toward the subject and their criticism of any definite plan. But proceeding in due order, these men of action now find themselves confronted by a situation that demands an organization of world force to secure the just fruits of the war. Now they look upon a league of the Great Powers, who won the war, as an existing fact, and they face the problem of how the manifold and complicated purposes of the treaty, after they have been defined and the treaty signed, shall be effectively carried out and maintained. As practical men they now take up the League of Nations and study it in the earnest desire to make it work.

In this way Theodore Roosevelt, having long ago proposed a league in his Nobel prize address, was brought around by logic of events to a sincere effort to frame a plan which would avoid the numerous objections that have been suggested by himself and others and still make progress toward the ideal he held out at Christiania. He studied all the plans proposed, considered their possible weaknesses and defects and busied his ingenious mind with finding alternatives which would be practical and still achieve the main purpose. He had in his mind the thought that under the general obligations of the League, when force had to be threatened or used, a great

Power like the United States should act as a policeman in the western hemisphere, while the great Powers of Europe should in the first instance keep the peace of the world in the Balkans and in Eastern Europe.

It was clearer to him than it seems to be to others who do not see the real need of a league and who are not so anxious, therefore, to make it useful to the world, that the European nations will only be too glad to recognize our Monroe Doctrine as a policy in the interest of world peace. Why should they not, when the principles and operation of the League are really directed to the creation of a Monroe Doctrine of the world?

What Colonel Roosevelt always insisted on was that the United States should not promise in a treaty to do things which it could not or would not perform. Certainly, every one must sympathize with this common-sense restriction upon unwise and transcendental enthusiasm. He feared there were issues not to be settled on principles of law and thus called non-justiciable, which might, nevertheless, be submitted to a court and decided against the will of a party to the treaty. His suggestion is that each nation might state those issues and after discussion have them specifically incorporated in the treaty as nonjusticiable.

He feared, too, that the United States might be committed to an obligation not to maintain military preparedness sufficient to protect itself against unjust aggression. He protested against reduction of armament which was on the theory that the League of Nations would form a substitute for reasonable defense, at least until its efficacy for such a purpose had been fully demonstrated by actual test of time. Certainly, many who earnestly support a League concur in such a view and believe with him that universal military training of the Swiss type may well be instituted in this country, both as an insurance against unjust aggression and as a proper preparation for such contribution to the world's police force as the United States may be called upon to make. Incidentally it will constitute an important factor in the education of our youth in the duties of life.

For these reasons the proponents of the League of Nations to enforce peace may rejoice in this posthumous aid that Theodore Roosevelt gives to the League. He has the greatest personal following in this country, and his words go far.

His attitude toward the problems involved in the League may well furnish an example to the doubters and opponents. Let them treat the

31

The League of Nations, What It Means
and Why It Must Be

The original program of the League to Enforce Peace adopted at Philadelphia June 17, 1915,[1] was enlarged and made more ambitious at a meeting of the governing body of the League on November 24, 1918. It then declared that the *initiating nucleus* of the membership of the League should be the nations associated as belligerents in winning the war.

It declared further:

First, that the judgments of the international court on justiciable questions should be enforced;

Second, that the League should determine what action, if any, should be taken in respect to recommendations of the Council of Conciliation in which the parties concerned did not acquiesce;

Third, that provision should be made for an administrative organization of the League to conduct affairs of common interest and for the protection and care of backward regions and international places and other matters jointly administered before and during the war, and that such administrative organization should be so framed as to insure stability and progress, preventing defeat of the forces of healthy growth and changes, and providing a way by which progress could be secured and the needed change effected without recourse to war;

Fourth, that a representative Congress of Nations should formulate and codify rules of international law, inspect the work of the League's administrative bodies, and consider any matter affecting the tranquillity of the world or the progress or the betterment of human relations;

Fifth, that the League should have an executive council to speak with authority in the name of the nations represented and to act in case the peace of the world is endangered.

It further declared that the representation of the different nations in the organs of the League should be in proportion to the responsibilities and obligations that they assume, and that rules of international law should not be defeated for lack of unanimity.

It will thus be seen that the American association has become more ambitious in its aims since its first declarations. Under the first declaration it did not propose to enforce judgments of the court or in any way to deal with the recommendations of compromise, the exercise of force by the League being directed only against a nation beginning war before submission to the Court or the Council.

In England, after the organization of the American League, a British League of Free Nations Association was formed, proposing a Court and a Commission of Conciliation, the use of force to execute the decisions of the Court, and the joint suppression, by all means at their disposal, of any attempt by any State to disturb the peace of the world by acts of war.[2]

It looked to the immediate organization of a League of Great Britain and her then allies, with a view to the ultimate formation of a League of Nations on a wider basis, including states then neutral or hostile. It excluded the German peoples until they should bring forth works meet for repentance and become a democracy.

It contained a provision for action by the League as trustee and guardian of uncivilized races and undeveloped territories. It proposed as a substitute for national armaments an international force to guarantee order in the world, and proposed a further function for the Council of the League in supervising, limiting, and controlling the military and naval forces and the armament industries of the world.

Late in 1918 a French Association for the Society of Nations[3] recommended that the Society of Nations should be open to every nation who would agree to respect the right of peoples to determine their own destiny, and to resort only to judicial solutions for the settlement of their disputes; that the use of force be reserved exclusively to the international society itself as the supreme sanction in case one of the member states should resist its decisions; that the Allies should form their association immediately and should work it out as completely as possible in the direction of sanctions of every kind—moral, judicial, economic, and in the last resort military—as well as in that of promulgating general rules of law.

The French Society further provided that the Society of Nations thus immediately formed should control and conduct the negotiations for the coming peace.

It will thus be seen that the League of Nations, as conceived by its proponents in three of the four great nations that have won this war, has substantially the same structure. It includes a court to decide justiciable questions, a Council of Conciliation to consider other or nonjusticiable questions and to recommend a compromise. It calls for the organization of the combined economic and military forces of the world to enforce the judgments of the courts, and to deal with a defiance of the recommendations of the mediating council as the executive body of the League shall deem wise.

The American, English, and French plans all show a purpose to create a smaller League of the allied nations fighting this war, who are, so to speak, to be charter members of a larger League, which they are to form by inviting other nations into it as they show themselves fitted to exercise the privileges of the League, to enjoy its protection and to meet their obligations as members. The American plan refers to these allied nations who won the war as the initiating nucleus of the larger League.

Each plan looks to the enforcement of judgments and leaves open to the League the question of what shall be done with reference to compromises recommended and not acquiesced in. Each one looks to a congress of nations to declare and codify international law.

One of them provides for the reduction of armament; the others omit it. It does not appear in the American plan. I may say that this was not because the ultimate reduction of armament was not regarded as important, but because it was thought that this feature of a League of Nations might meet serious objection until the League should be shown to be an effective substitute for the insurance which reasonable preparation for self-defense gives against unjust foreign aggression.

What are the objections to a League of Nations developed in this way and thus constituted? The first and chief objection is that the United States ought not to bind itself to make war upon the decree of an executive council in which it has but one vote out of four or five.

What authority and duty does the executive council have in the League? It will be its duty to see that judgments are executed.

Why should we object if called upon to declare war and make our contribution to the police force to maintain peace by enforcing a judgment of an impartial court? Such a judgment is not the result of the vote of other powers than our own. It is merely a decision on principles of international law as between two contending nations.

We have heard a great deal during this campaign of international justice. Why should we favor international justice and then refuse to furnish the machinery by which that justice can be declared and enforced? What risk do we run?

With reference to the enforcement of recommendations of compromise, the executive council should consider whether it is a case in which peace would be promoted more by economic or military enforcement than merely by international public opinion.

If, in such a case, it is thought that a majority of the executive council should not control the right to call for military execution of the compromise, such action might be limited to a unanimous decision of the executive council. This would prevent the imposition of the burden of war, by the determination of the League members, upon any nation without its consent. Or the enforcement of such a compromise, if determined on by a majority of the executive council, might be left to that majority.

Senator Knox seems to anticipate that the United States will be drawn into war against its will by a majority vote of a convention of heterogeneous nations.

No such result could follow from the organization of a League as indicated above. The assumption that the votes of Haiti, or San Salvador, or

Uruguay could create a majority forcing the United States into a war against its interest and will, under a practical League of Nations, is wholly unfounded. It would be left to the vote of an executive council of the Great Powers, and even then the United States, under the modifications above suggested, could not be drawn into war against its will.

Objectors who rely on the Constitution seem to assume that the League plans contemplate a permanent international police force, constantly under command of a Marshal Foch, who may order the international army to enforce a judgment or a compromise without the preliminaries of declarations of war by the League members. This is wholly unwarranted and no plan justifies it. When force has to be used, war will be begun and carried on jointly in the usual way.

Notes

An address delivered before the National Geographic Society, in Washington, D.C., January 17, 1919.

1. The program is printed in full on pages 3–4.

2. The first important group formed in England for advancing the idea of a League of Nations was the Bryce group. Others which followed were the League of Nations Society, the Fabian Society group and the Union of Democratic Control. The London International Allied Labor and Socialist Conference February 22, 1918, likewise put out a most important program. Following the formation of the League of Free Nations Association, to which Mr. Taft refers, that body and the League of Nations Society merged into the League of Nations Union. [Marburg]

3. In France we had, antedating the French Association for the Society of Nations, two very active groups, The League of the Rights of Man and League for a Society of Nations. [Marburg]

32

League of Nations and President Wilson's Advisers

The reports of correspondents to whom has been attributed the privilege of peeping into the presidential mind give rise to some concern among the sincere advocates of a League of Nations to Enforce Peace. The failure of the President to indicate any definite structure for the League, as the champion of which he is now hailed by the world with such acclaim, creates an uneasy suspicion that he has not thought out any definite plan of his own. In his frequent references to the League, he has stated what it will not be rather than what it will be. His attitude is that of one seeking a plan which will encounter no objections either in the congress at Paris or in the congress at Washington. In the formulation of a new political institution the sincere and successful builder works by the affirmative method primarily. He has before him always the object to be achieved, and he frames the cooperating parts of his plan with that first in view. He should be trying to do something. He should not be trying merely to fulfill a promise to do something by coming as near to it as he can without meeting criticism. No reform worth having was ever put through without a fight. Faith not only in the value of the ideal but faith in a practical plan needed to realize the ideal is required to bring real results.

The element of the plan of a present League of Nations, which must distinguish it from past efforts to secure peace by agreement of nations, is the organization of the forces of lawful nations to compel justice from lawless nations. The President loves to dwell on the moral sanction of justice which is to prevail after this war. Let us agree with him that it will be stronger than before the war and that in and of itself it will help to make war less probable. But if that is the only sanction the League of Nations is going to furnish for the judgments of its court and for the suppression of lawless violence by recalcitrant nations, it will be a failure and a laughing stock—at least the influence of such moral force will be as great without the League as with it.

It is unfortunate that the President, with his apparent lack of any definite plan for a league should not be able to find a single earnest supporter of a real league of nations to secure peace in the commission which he has taken with him.

Secretary Lansing has heretofore always been opposed to a league of nations to enforce peace. His confidential adviser, James Brown Scott, has always opposed it and vigorously urged merely an international court, whose judgments are to be enforced by the obligations of honor and moral suasion. Mr. White has had the traditional attitude of the old diplomatic hand toward such an innovation. Few know, if any, what Mr. House's real attitude is or that of General Bliss. The commission is now engaged in examining forty different plans, we are told, with the hope, by the selective method, of hitting upon something as innocuous to Senate predilections as possible. A reported interview with Mr. White makes conformity to the Senate's views his objective. Has the cold attitude of the commission toward an effective league been changed by the eagerness of the common peoples of the Allies for it and by the enthusiasm with which the President's eloquent periods concerning the League have been greeted? Let us hope so.

Lloyd George and Clémenceau are practical men. They have declared for a league. They will wish to create something which will be a real instrument to do the things that have to be done by the treaty. They have men about them, Lord Robert Cecil, M. Leon Bourgeois and others, who, as earnest advocates of a league, have been framing plans and studying details under the official authority of their respective governments. May we not hope that in this way there will be offered to the President by Great Britain and France the constitution of a league which will have vigor and clinching efficacy and which, after full consideration and needed qualification, he will accept? A mere reliance on moral force and good intentions to maintain peace among the new and old nations of Central and Eastern Europe and to resist and suppress the pacifistic ideals of the Bolsheviki, and the massacres and destruction wrought by them, will make the congress a dangerous and discouraging farce. It will be retreat and not advance.

Note

Article in the *Philadelphia Public Ledger,* January 20, 1919.

33

"The League of Nations Is Here"

The expression at the Peace Conference of President Poincaré and Premier Clémenceau in reference to the League of Nations and the published rules of the Congress are reassuring to those who look to the growth of an effective and real league out of the situation. The French leaders see clearly, and say with emphasis, that we have a league of nations now, and that it must be maintained in order to achieve the purpose of the war. The circumstances of the struggle forced the Allies into an interallied council and then into a common command of the armies under Foch. But for that the war might not have been won.

The rules of the Congress recognize that the five great nations, Great Britain, France, Italy, Japan and the United States, are the ones which have an interest in all the questions coming before the Congress as guardians of the welfare of the world, made so by the logic of their winning the war. They are thus established as the initiating nucleus of a world union, as the charter members of a league of nations.

It is to be noted that the League of Nations is the first subject to be considered by the Congress. This seems to be at variance with the views of

James M. Beck and Senators Lodge and Knox. Mr. Beck argues that, as our fathers waited five years after winning independence before making a constitution, the nations ought to be equally deliberate in discussing and framing a constitution for the world. Most people agree, after reading the description by Hamilton and Madison of conditions existing in the interval between our independence and the convention of 1787, that it would have been much better if the convention could have been called earlier. Of course it may be said that the bad state of affairs during the interval was necessary to bring the people to see the necessity for a stronger government. But surely Mr. Beck would not wish a recurrence of the quarrels of nations and another war to convince the peoples of the world of the necessity and advantage of world unity to suppress war and maintain peace. It is now, just after this horrible war when its agonies, its sufferings, its lessons, its inhuman character, all are fresh in the minds of men, that they will be willing to go farther in making the needed and proper concessions involved in a useful and real league of nations. Delay will dull their eagerness to adopt the machinery essential to organized protection against war.

But another fact which Mr. Beck and Mr. Knox seem to ignore is that a treaty of peace cannot be made at Paris, by which the peace of Europe can be secured and maintained without a league of nations. These gentlemen may well be challenged to tell us what arrangements they would suggest to the five nations engaged in forming this treaty for peace and in making it work, unless it be a continuing league of those five nations to maintain it.

How can the objects and purposes of the fourteen points, especially those directed to rearranging the map of Eastern and Central Europe and Asia Minor, be achieved and carried to peaceful realization except through a league of nations embracing the five great powers? No one opposed to the league of nations idea has essayed to answer this very practical question. The Paris conference is confronted with it and must answer it suggestively by making the League of Nations the first subject for discussion. Premier Clémenceau said:

"The League of Nations is here. It is for you to make it live." Senator Lodge in his speech fully recognized the existence of the League of great nations in the war and the necessity for its continuance. Indeed it is probable that if Senator Knox and Mr. Beck were cross-examined, their admissions would show them to be not very far removed from the view that something substantially equivalent to a league of great nations must be definitely formed by this Congress with agreed-upon means of enforcing the stipulated peace.

The Associated Press informs us that a league of nations is in the forming, but that the super-sovereignty of an international police force is to be rejected as part of it. This negation is not very helpful. Except in Tennyson's poetic vision and in the plans of impracticables, no such suggestion as super-sovereignty has been advanced. . . .

Most opponents of the League idea have assumed that the so-called international police is to be a permanent body under an international commander and subject to orders without invoking consent of the nations contributing to the force. This is a misconception. A potential international police force will be erected by an agreement of the Great Nations to furnish forces when necessary to accomplish a legitimate purpose of the League. In most instances, no actual force will need to be raised. The existence of an agreement and confidence that the nations will comply with it is all that will be needed. Nations who have judgments against them in a court of the nations will generally perform them. It will only be where defiances of such judgments will lead to a dangerous war that the League force need be raised.

Of course, during the interval after the conclusion of peace, the possibility of differences and the danger of Bolshevism may require a retention of some of the war army strength of the Allies to see the treaty through to its effective execution. But after the return of normal times the strength of the League to secure compliance with the treaty obligations and justice will not be in its serried columns, but in its potential power under the joint agreement.

In the convenient division of the world into zones, in which the respective Great Powers shall undertake the responsibility of seeing to it that members of the League conform to the rules laid down by the treaty, it will be unnecessary for any nation to send forces to a distant quarter. The United States can properly take care of the Western Hemisphere and need not maintain in normal times a military establishment more extensive than she ought to maintain for domestic use and the proper maintenance of the Monroe Doctrine without such a league. They may be well supplied, not by a professional army, but by a system of universal training on democratic principles like that in Switzerland or New Zealand. If this be conscription, its opponents may make the most of it. It will help our boys in discipline of character and in a most useful educational way. It will provide for the prompt display of democratic power to achieve justice. The picture painted by Senator Borah of the army of the United States needed for the purposes of the League is the result of a lively imagination, but does not find support in the real need of the League.

After the League of the Great Powers has been established for the purpose of executing the plans of the new treaty, it will be time enough to take in all other responsible Powers. The lesser League will grow naturally into a larger League. Experience will test the practical character of the lesser League and in this wise and in due course the world League will come into being. But meanwhile as a necessary condition precedent to the success of the treaty of peace, it must provide for a League of the Great Nations.

Note

Article in the *Philadelphia Public Ledger,* January 23, 1919.

34

The League's "Bite"

Those who are looking for something real in a league of Nations to preserve peace, in creating sanctions for international law, justice and equity, may well feel concerned over the developments in Paris. Such persons have based their hopes on the psychological effect of the horrors of the war upon all nations, which should make them willing to concede much to achieve the main object of the war. They have counted on securing a covenant between the members of the League to unite, whenever necessity may arise, with the powerful members of the League to compel compliance with judgments of the League and to suppress recalcitrant members faithless to the principles of the League and to their obligations. They can hardly be blamed for so doing, in view of President Wilson's words, as follows:

> I pray God that if this contest have no other result, it will at least have the result of creating an international tribunal and producing some sort of joint guaranty of peace on the part of the great nations of the world. . . . Now, let us suppose that we have formed a family of nations and that family of nations says: "The world is not going to have any

more wars of this sort without at least first going through certain processes to show whether there is anything in the case or not." If you say, "We shall not have any war," you have got to have the force to make the "shall" bite. And the rest of the world, if America takes part in this thing, will have the right to expect from her that she can contribute her element of force to the general understanding. Surely that is not a militaristic idea. That is a very practical ideal.

The endorsement of these views by Mr. Lloyd George was as follows: "The best security for peace will be that nations will band themselves together to punish the peace-breaker."

Mr. Asquith's comment on the President's views was as follows: "The President held out to his hearers the prospect of an era when the civilization of mankind, banded together for the purpose, will make it their joint and several duty to repress by their united authority and, if need be, by their combined naval and military forces, any wanton or aggressive invasion of the peace of the world. It is a fine ideal, which must arouse all our sympathies."

From these statements of this ideal it is a descending climax now to hear that no member of the League is to bind itself to unite its forces with any other in enforcing the judgments of the league court or in punishing the peace-breaker. We are now to depend on moral force or the exercise of an economic boycott, it may be, and on the general public opinion of the world. If a nation which is interested in a judgment in its behalf desires, it is to be given the right to go to war to enforce it. We have still the wonderful and eloquent preaching of the ideal of a League of Nations while we see its strength and "bite," to use Mr. Wilson's expression, fading into merely moral aspirations and moral sanctions.

This is doubtless in part due to the difficulties that the nations now sitting around the council board in Paris are having in maintaining their armies. After four years of war the pressure of the men engaged in it to be released from their military duty is so strong that the nations cannot resist it. That is probably the explanation of the very weak policy adopted in respect to the Bolsheviki. The Congress certainly would not have run the risk of exposing its members to just criticism had they not felt deeply the difficulty confronting them in sending an adequate force to Russia to stamp out the contagion, to rescue the Czecho-Slavs and to give Russia a chance. The error that our administration made during the war was in resisting the urgent appeal of our Allies to send a large force into Russia, through Vladivostok and Archangel, to create an eastern front. Such a force would have largely obviated the Bolsheviki complication. The Czecho-Slovaks, whom we have promised to help, are in a perilous situation, while our own little handful of men are fighting an aimless fight against great odds near Archangel.

Should they who have expected real "bite," to repeat Mr. Wilson's expression, in the League of Nations, be discouraged? Institutions like the League of Nations, which represent an advance in civilization, are created by the necessity of the situation. . . .

It is, of course, difficult to comment on plans for the League as they are outlined in the cabled reports of correspondents. They seem to be anxious to convince everybody that, while the League of Nations is a beautiful idea and inspires emotion when urged as President Wilson urged it in the congress at Saturday's session, nevertheless, its covenants are not going to involve any trouble or obligation or burden for the United States, but will permit complete freedom of action or withholding of action when war shall come again.

Lord Robert Cecil is reported to have suggested a court to which all justiciable questions are to be submitted, while nonjusticiable questions leading to trouble are to go to a council of conciliation. This is accompanied, however, by the notable proviso that every nation may determine for itself whether the question threatening war is justiciable or not. This is equivalent to saying that every nation may keep out of the court of the League if it chooses, no matter what the issue. The court is thus to be constituted to decide questions which both quarreling nations are willing to submit to it. It is thus as effective as the present voluntary arbitration of the Hague tribunal and no more. If, now, every proposal with anything of a "bite" in it is to be weakened to ineffectiveness, the common peoples of France, England, Italy and the United States, who have been looking upon the League as a real machine, with the "bite" in it to prevent future wars, may well feel that there has been much thundering in the index about the League of Nations without tangible result. If the League is only to be an agreement to confer over any breach of peace by the nations, and will not even bind nations to submit legal differences to a court, the man in the street will not put much faith in fine words in the future.

Note

Article in the *Philadelphia Public Ledger,* January 29, 1919.

35

The League of Nations and the
German Colonies 2

It was to be expected that selfish desire to take advantage of the victory over Germany would appear in the congress at Paris; but it should not be gratified. The strength of the Allies was in the justice of their cause. German lies and propaganda concealed the facts and at first misled many. As the war progressed, Germany's sole responsibility for the war and the grinning skeleton of her vicious purposes were revealed. They were confirmed by her atrocious conduct of the war. The claim of the Allies that theirs was only a defensive struggle to save the world from the German monster of militarism, in which they were prompted by no spirit of conquest or self-aggrandizement, gained credence among all nations. Declarations of war against Germany as the enemy of mankind followed from every quarter of the globe. Her isolation from all the world save from her allies, who were under her iron heel, became a greater and greater factor in lowering the morale of her people. The material influence of the moral righteousness of the cause of the Allies is one of the inspiring circumstances in the history of the Great War.

This feature of the victory should not be allowed to lose its beneficent force by a yielding to selfish claims of participants in the peace pact. The restoration of Alsace-Lorraine to France or even of the coal mines of the neighboring Saar district is only justice. The German outrageous destruction of the mines at Lens and elsewhere makes the transfer of the Saar district only an equitable indemnity. The same view justifies the delivery to Italy of Italia Irridenta. But no such principle applies in respect to the German colonies.

All will applaud and support the conclusion that Germany has forfeited ownership of her colonies. She has grossly mistreated the backward peoples living in them, and in whose interest they should be administered. How are they to be governed? It is agreed that their peoples are now incapable of self-government; that to attempt to extend it to them would be only less hurtful to them than German domination. Who then shall govern them? As a member of the conference, Australia asks the transfer of the South Pacific colonies to it or to Great Britain, while British South Africa presses for British control over the former German dependencies in her neighborhood.

These pretensions are advanced on two grounds. First, that in the past the proximity of German possessions has been a continual threat to them, and, second, that their sacrifices in the war entitle them to take these territories over as an indemnity. As to the first, the exclusion of German control should remove any danger. As to the second, it is contrary to principles upon which, under the armistice terms, the treaty was to be framed. It involves in its essence the proposal that these countries and their backward peoples are to be traded as a commodity to compensate the two British dominions for sacrifices in war They are thus to be treated as something of value belonging to Germany and are to be used as a substitute for money indemnity.

President Wilson insists that they should be administered by the League of Nations for the benefit of their peoples. In this he is clearly right. Where his proposal lacks strength, however, is in his suggestion that the League shall administer them through the British dominions as "mandatories." Theoretically this means that the League shall supervise while the respective dominions actually govern. Previous experience shows that such arrangements are a source of much friction and interfere with effectiveness. The Algeciras method of dealing with Tangier and Morocco was like this and was not satisfactory. Moreover, the dealing by Australia and by South Africa with native races is not likely to be as just and equitable as that of their mother country.

Why should not the League itself establish and maintain a proper government of these countries? We could be in this way much more certain of right treatment of the backward peoples than under the "mandatories." No danger to their British colonial neighbors could arise from a government of the League.

Why then does Mr. Wilson suggest this plan which really hides territorial acquisition and complete possession and control under a thin cloak of League supervision? It is because he has not given any life to his ideal of a league. If he gave it flesh and bones in real and definite machinery and power, the purpose he has as to these German colonies might be successfully worked out. As it is, these colonies will in fact meet the fate of Bosnia and Herzegovina under Austria, which was complete absorption. It would seem to be better for the backward peoples who are the wards of the Peace Congress to give them directly and openly to Great Britain, who will govern them more sympathetically and wisely than will her own colonial daughters.

The President is being further embarrassed by the proposal that the United States shall administer Constantinople, Palestine and Armenia as a mandatory of the League. He does not wish to entangle the United States in the complications of the near Eastern question, and no wonder! Had he and his colleagues planned a real League of Nations and not a mere figure of rhetoric, or noble conception without body, the international agency to discharge this important function would be at hand.

Will not these troublesome experiences with the very first problems, simpler indeed than many yet to come, convince the Congress that a real league of nations with a "bite" in it is indispensable in achieving their purpose?

Is it too much to hope that the history of the framing of the Constitution of the United States may repeat itself in the present Congress and the proposed League of Nations? When the members of the convention met there were no definite plans of government except one which Hamilton had formulated and which was not adopted. Few thought they would be successful in framing a real nation. Hamilton and a few other constructive statesmen were the only ones who were not faint-hearted. As their delibera-tions proceeded, as the necessities of the situation developed, proposals which at first were thought to be chimerical and impossible seemed to be-come more practical and necessary, and out of it all we got our wonderful fundamental instrument of government. May not the League in the same way become a living thing?

Note

Article in the *Philadelphia Public Ledger,* February 3, 1919.

36

From an Address at the Atlantic Congress for a
League of Nations, New York, February 5, 1919

You will only get the ideal court when the members are independent, their
only qualifications being their probity, their ability, their learning and their
experience.

They will not represent anybody, but simple justice, on that court.
They are to apply pure principles of law and exercise their acumen to determine facts impartially in the disposition of the legal questions which come
before them. Therefore it is not representative. But, appointees should be
distributed with reference to bringing in knowledge of all law throughout
the world, just as our own Supreme Court is distributed, not by any law,
but through the discretion of the Executive, so that the different parts of
the country, with different methods of administration of law, may be
brought in.

37

Ireland and the League

The resolution proposed in the House of Representatives to urge upon the President in Paris that he take steps to secure a government in Ireland independent of the government of Great Britain is ill-timed. It can only embarrass him in securing an agreement between the Great Powers who are dictating the terms of peace to Germany and rearranging the map of Middle and Eastern Europe.

The relation of Ireland to Great Britain is a British domestic question, and cannot properly be made other by the intervention of the United States. Hope of a satisfactory peace in which the whole world is interested would have to be abandoned if the Great Powers were to look into and discuss the internal affairs of one another. The relations of the government of France to Algiers, to Tunis, to Morocco and her African interests, the relation of Japan to Formosa, that of the United States to the Philippines, to the Indian tribes or to the colored voters of the States of the South, might all be thus added to the bewildering issues that now claim the attention of the delegates at the Paris conference. This treaty is to close the war with Germany and her Allies, and England's relation to Ireland is not germane to that war and has no connection with it.

Irishmen must know that the wrongs of Ireland in the past have sunk deep in the minds and memories of the people of the United States. Whenever there has been a movement to remedy these wrongs, whenever the issue of home rule has been raised, it has awakened the strongest sympathy in the hearts and souls of Americans, whether of Irish blood or not. Americans have had immense satisfaction in learning that the land laws of Ireland have been so improved and changed that now there is a large increase in the number of small farms owned in fee simple by the farmers.

Sir Horace Plunkett, an Irishman, has led Irish farmers into associations by which they have learned to improve their agriculture and dairy farming, to unite in the disposition of their product and get rid of the heavy toll of the middlemen, so that today it is not too much to say that rural Ireland is in better economic condition than any other agricultural part of the British Islands. This has been directly due to the legislation of Parliament, the leadership of such men as Plunkett, and the capacity for organization developed among the farmers.

The political blundering of the English government and what, to many of us, seems the unreasonable obstinacy of the Protestant half of Ulster have prevented that home rule to which most Americans believe that Ireland is entitled. If she could have been made a Dominion like Canada, with hardly more than nominal union to Great Britain, except in international matters, Ireland would certainly have been satisfied before Sinn Feinism was fanned into flame by the delay in home rule.

Self-determination is not a certain solvent of political difficulty. Self-determination means a rule of the majority; but the question what the unit shall be, of which the majority is to rule, still remains. This is affected by considerations of geography, language, race, religion and other factors of solidarity or variety in the mental attitudes of the people concerned. Geography forbids a separation of Ulster from Ireland, especially in view of the fact that Ulster has been represented in Parliament by half home rule and half unionist members of Parliament. On the other hand, the geographical relation of Ireland to Great Britain makes the former a necessary outpost against hostile attack, while the difference in race and the traditional lack of sympathy justify the greatest autonomy in Ireland consistent with British protection.

It is remarkable that Great Britain, which has been wonderfully successful in dealing with colonial dependencies of all kinds, should have been so unsuccessful in Ireland. This has been true, even since her statesmen have been sincerely and earnestly anxious to be just to Ireland, and to eliminate completely from her Irish policy the motive which so long disgraced it, that of exploiting Ireland and her people for the profit of England. In Irish affairs, English statesmen are always a length behind. They are always willing to give, when it is too late, that which would have satisfied Irishmen at an earlier stage.

Whatever the merits of the issue now, it is not within the field of jurisdiction of the Paris conference, and those who press it there, whatever their motive, are not helping the successful outcome of that fateful congress. Pressure for the proposed resolution is due, first, to the sincere sentiment for it of men of Irish blood in this country; second, to the desire of reckless politicians to win political support by its advocacy; and third, to the timidity of others who, though really opposed to it as unwise, are afraid of the personal political consequences of their opposition. Nor should we omit from the elements pressing for its adoption a class of persons anxious to make the conference at Paris a failure. It is to be hoped that the resolution will be tabled.

Note

Article in the *Philadelphia Public Ledger,* February 13, 1919.

38

The Great Covenant of Paris

The League to Enforce Peace, of which this is a congress called for Oregon, Washington and Idaho, is a voluntary association of men and women of the United States organized early in 1915 to spread propaganda in favor of a plan for world cooperation to maintain peace, by enforced settlement of differences likely to lead to war, on principles of justice and fairness. Its promoters had long been interested in promoting arbitration between nations. They thought that the end of this world-destructive war would find the peoples of the various countries in a frame of mind in which they would gladly accept any reasonable international cooperation to prevent war. Accordingly the League adopted a platform in which it recommended that the United States enter a League of Nations, in which the members of the League should stipulate that all differences arising between them of a justiciable character should be submitted to a court and those of a non-justiciable character to a council of conciliation; that every member of the League should agree to refrain from going to war until after judgment by the court or recommendation by the council of conciliation; and that any member who violated this obligation by attacking any other member should be overwhelmed by the economic pressure of all the members of the League and the joint military forces of the League, if need be. Similar associations were formed in England and France, with similar platforms, except that they provided for a forcible execution of the judgments and a dealing with the recommendations of the councils of conciliation by the League.

There has been until now no means of knowing exactly what is meant by a league of nations except by reference to the platforms of these voluntary associations. The governments of England and France created commissions for the special purpose of studying the proper framework of a league of nations, but the result of their studies was not given to the public. Our government had declined to create such a commission. On Friday last, however, the committee to whom the great Paris congress had delegated the work of preparing a plan for a league of nations, of which President Wilson was the chairman, made a report which was concurred in by the representatives of all of the fourteen nations at the conference. Now therefore we have an authoritative statement of the constitution of a league of nations and an official basis for its discussion.

This constitution is indeed wider in the scope of its purpose than was the platform of our League to Enforce Peace. The platform of our League was a mere skeleton. It had prepared a tentative draft of a treaty to give it body and constructive details, but that tentative draft was never given to the public, because it was thought wiser by governmental authority to withhold it. The sole object of the League to Enforce Peace platform was to promote peace and avoid war by instrumentalities for administering justice between nations and by enforcing submission to such instrumentalities. It did not even contain a provision with respect to the limitation of armament. The purpose of the constitution reported at Paris, which we may properly call "the great covenant of Paris," is much wider. It is to organize a real and permanent league, whose first object is to provide for the just settlement of differences between nations and the prevention of war, and for this purpose to limit armaments. Its second object is to exercise executive functions in the administration of international trusts like the government of backward peoples whom this war has released from the sovereignty of the Germans and the other Central Powers. Its third object is to promote cooperation between the nations, with a view to the betterment of the condition of labor in all the nations and for joint action in respect to other useful matters now dealt with by international bureaus, like the postal union. This provides a constant series of functions for the League to perform and gives it substance.

The League is to be formed by a covenant which recites in its preamble its general purpose, and then states in twenty-six different articles the agreements included in the covenant.

The present membership of the League is to consist of the fourteen nations who are to be signatories to the covenant and to sign the treaty of peace. The most numerous acting governmental branch of the League is a body of delegates to meet once a year or oftener if necessary, to consist of at least one representative and not more than three from each nation, with but one vote for each state. This body of delegates is to pass upon the question of membership of other nations applying to be admitted. Before a nation shall be admitted it must show itself able and willing to conform to the covenant and must receive the vote of two-thirds of the members of the League. This is drawn to keep Germany out until she is fit. The body of delegates also has the function of taking the place of the executive council as a tribunal of conciliation and compromise when either party to the controversy demands it. The most important agency of the League is the executive council, which consists of representatives of the five Great Powers and of four other members to be selected by the body of delegates. This council has numerous executive duties for the League and in most respects is the League, and it performs an important function in mediation and settlement of differences. There is a permanent secretariat of the League, which is to be established at the seat of the League, there to perform the duties indicated by its name. A permanent military commission is to advise the council on questions of the limitation of armament and upon military and naval matters. The League is given a definite diplomatic status by securing to its representatives the immunity and privileges of ambassadors and extra-territoriality for the buildings and home in which it has its headquarters.

States members of the League, having a difference, may submit it by agreement to arbitration. The members of the League covenant that if they become parties to an arbitration they will abide the award of the arbitrators. If either party objects to arbitration, then the difference is to be submitted to the executive council for mediation or recommendation. If the council succeeds in securing an agreement it is to be published. If not, then the council may report a recommendation. If it is unanimous, excluding representatives of interested parties, then the council must take measures to carry the recommendation into effect. Should the executive council divide, the majority is required to publish its recommendations with reasons and the minority may do so, without further action.

Every member of the League agrees not to resort to any war until three months after the difference between it and its opponent has been submitted to arbitration and an award made, or to the executive council and a recommendation made, and not then if the party against whom war is threatened complies with the award or the recommendation. If any member of the League begins war prematurely and in violation of its agreement, such breach of its covenant is an act of war against all other members of the League and is to be met by universal boycott of all the members of the League against the recalcitrant member. Not only is this boycott to be conducted by members of the League, but they are required to prevent non-members of the League also from having any commercial or personal relations with the outlaw member and its nationals or citizens. The boycott is to include a complete severance of all trade, financial and personal relations between the citizens of the respective countries, and a sundering of all diplomatic and consular relations. The executive council is to recommend to the members of the League the effective military or naval forces which they should severally contribute to the armed forces of the League to be used to protect the covenants of the League. The members of the League are to divide the loss incident to the boycott falling on some members and not on others, and mutually to support one another in resisting any special measure of hostility brought by the outlaw state against any one or more of them. The League members are bound to afford passage through their territory for the force of any member or members who are cooperating to protect the covenants of the League. The participation in the boycott is obligatory upon all members of the League. The contribution of needed military force from the several members of the League, while fixed by the council, is not obligatory. The result is, however, to create a state of war between the recalcitrant member and all the members of the League at their option, much like that existing between certain South American countries and Germany during the late war.

The Paris Covenant does not immediately provide a permanent international court. It directs that the executive council shall formulate plans for its establishment, and that, when established, it shall be competent to determine any matter which the parties recognize as proper to submit to it. Its jurisdiction, therefore, even when created, will be dependent on the voluntary submission by the parties.

When a difference arises between a non-member and a member or between two non-members, they are to be invited to accept temporary membership of the League for the purpose of settling the dispute, in accordance with the procedure just described. If the non-member refuses to accept the obligations of the League, it is to be treated as a member of the League would be treated which violated its covenant. This attitude toward non-members is in pursuance of a declaration of the constitution that the League is interested in the maintenance of universal peace and holds any threatened breach of it as a matter of its concern as to which it may take action.

Three classes of countries with peoples not ready for self-government are committed to the trusteeship of the League, which administers them through competent governments as mandatories of the League.

A permanent mandatory commission is established, which is to require annual reports of the mandatories and to see that the restrictions contained in the constitution or in the special charters which are issued by the executive council to mandatories have been observed.

Amendments to the covenant are to be made only upon a unanimous vote of the executive council and a two-thirds vote of the delegates.

This summary of the constitution of the League shows very clearly that the nations that agreed to it intended to give the League real power. This power rests on the covenants of the members of the League and on their agreed cooperation in the universal boycott and in their voluntary cooperation by the use of military force to punish any covenant-breaking member.

This Paris covenant has been made by the five nations who are to prescribe the terms of the treaty of peace. It has been made in view of the necessities of that treaty and the machinery required for its execution. This is a very fortunate circumstance in the creation of the League and its growth into a League of all Nations. A convention of all the nations would never have agreed on anything as practical as this. Though the ultimate object of the League is the protection of the interest of weaker nations, such nations are most likely to be obstructive in their insistence upon excessive representation. This League is growing up as an institution forced by the necessities of the situation. It is a wholesome and natural process in the establishment of needed and permanent institutions. Out of a clear sky in normal times it would be a matter of the utmost difficulty to form such a League of Nations. Here the condition which confronts the world and those responsible for its welfare calls for immediate action. Out of that immediate action comes this League, adapted to present uses and admirably available as a foundation for a world league.

On the whole, the short program of the League to Enforce Peace, adopted in June 1915, differs but little from the nub of this, except that military contribution is not expressly obligatory and that in this either party to a difference may avoid a court and an award and seek a council of conciliation in the executive body of the League where unanimity of recommendation is required. The proposal to use compulsion to secure submission rather than execution of judgment or recommendation came from the program of the League to Enforce Peace, and was adopted by General Smuts in a remarkable brochure submitted by him December 16, 1918. It is understood that the President was much impressed with the paper of General Smuts and with his plan as well. We may be certain the constitution as now adopted was largely taken from his recommendation. He argued for the joint obligation of League members to use force, which was only partly adopted, as I have pointed out. He, too, recommended required submission of the justiciable questions to a court and of nonjusticiable questions to a conciliation council as the League to Enforce Peace had done. But the Smuts plan was much more comprehensive than that of the League to Enforce Peace. From that plan came the mandatory system of administering backward countries and internationalizing cities as wards of the League through competent and existing governments as agents answerable to the League. From that plan came the union of all present international bureaus under the League, as well as the permanent secretariat. He advocated international labor reforms through the League, and this function is left to be developed under the League. He, too, brought non-members of the League under its influence and action.

The giving to the Great Powers five votes in an executive council of nine is one of the most important features of the constitution and is indispensable to any practical working of it. They are the responsible members who are to do the work. The minor states of the League enjoy its protection, but will not be willing to expend money or effort in maintaining its authority. They should not be permitted to arrogate to themselves equal authority with the Great Powers and thus seriously interfere with the League's efficient operations. This is a sufficient safeguard against a too early admission of Germany.

The treaty of peace to be framed is to deal with Middle and Eastern Europe, the Near East and the German colonies. The plan is to create ten or a dozen new states, more than half of them independent republics and the remainder under some sort of suzerainty of the League. These new states are to be founded not only in the interest of the peoples who form them, but also to constitute bulwarks against a revival of German power. Finland, the Baltic provinces, Poland, the Czecho-Slovak state, the Ukraine, the Jugo-Slav state are all to be republics to curb and make impossible a revival of Germany's dream of Middle Europe and of an empire reaching from Hamburg to the Persian gulf. They are to prevent the extension of Germany's influence in Russia, where her commercial schemes have had in the past a controlling influence. These new nations must be rendered stable and must be kept at peace with each other and at peace with the countries out of which they have been carved. They will cherish resentments against their former owners because of the oppression which they suffered at their hands and the latter will feel bitter toward them because their independent existence will remind them of their deserved humiliation and defeat. Moreover, their peoples have never been used to self-government and we must expect internal disorders, due to that lack of self-restraint that practice in self-government gives. They are to be six or seven Cubas and must remain under the kindly assistance of the nations who dictate this peace until their stability is secured.

The League of Nations which existed during the war, and by which the war was won, continues in the conference at Paris and must be continued, after the signing of the treaty, with machinery to secure the peaceful settlement of the myriad questions and differences that will arise between the new countries and the old in the ultimate establishment of their relations. The fixing and the maintenance of the boundaries in the Balkans, always a most difficult question, and the determination of the rights of new neighbors will be a continuous source of adjudication and adjustment if peace is to be enjoyed instead of a continual state of war. In responding to these necessities this League has been constituted. No one could look into the problems before the nations conferring at Paris without realizing that a league with judicial and adjustment machinery and provision for the enforcement of judgments and settlements was an absolute requirement. As the conferees proceed to consider the details of the treaty and the need for speedy and enforced settlements and measures repressive of war, they may conclude that the provisions contained in this constitution are not fully adapted to the present needs. If so, special articles can be added to the constitution to meet such exigencies. Indeed one may reasonably predict that within the elastic provisions of this constitution new means will be developed to increase the effectiveness of the League as a peacemaker.

On the whole, we should thank God that such a great advance toward the suppression of war and the promotion of permanent peace has been made as in the agreement upon this constitution, with every reasonable prospect of its embodiment into the permanent treaty at Paris. Is it possible that such a vital feature of the treaty, upon which fourteen states through their representatives at Paris agree, is to be defeated by the lack of the necessary two-thirds vote in our Senate? I cannot think so. When President Wilson returns to present the result of his visit to Europe it must be that the American people will welcome him with approval and congratulations upon the success of the congress in which he has taken so prominent a part.

In the President's addresses and messages during the war and since, he has promised to the long-harassed peoples of the Allied nations that the United States would press for a League of Nations which should secure permanent peace when this war ended. Thus he revived the morale of the war-weary soldiers and workers of our Allies. These promises were not repudiated by any American when they were made. They were echoed in all the appeals to the American people and they found ready response among them and no protest. The nation is thus pledged to the idea of a League of

Nations to render peace permanent. Good faith requires that what other nations are willing to undergo to secure the peace of the world we should ourselves be willing to undergo.

Only now, after the reaction that the end of the war brings and after impatience at the delays in reaching peace conditions, do we hear on the floor of the Senate the criticisms of the President's promise of a league of nations. If uttered during the war they would have been out of tune with the overflowing spirit of the American people and their determination to win this war and end the possibility of any such war in the future. Now for the first time do we hear the claim that we did not go into this war for the benefit of the world, but for our own selfish purposes.

Senator Poindexter attacks the eighth article of the constitution of the League on disarmament as follows: "The provision is unconstitutional and an impairment of the sovereignty and independence of this country."

Congress under the constitution determines what our armament shall be; and therefore, even if we made an agreement, Congress would retain the constitutional power of violating that agreement and increasing the armament beyond the limit set; but that does not prevent the treaty-making power from entering into the obligation. It is not a transfer of sovereignty—it is only an agreement to limit our fortifications and our means of attack in consideration of other nations doing the same thing. The most famous agreement that we have made on this point is the agreement we have with Great Britain, by which we bind ourselves not to fortify the water boundary between Canada and the United States, or to place war vessels on the lakes. That agreement is of one hundred years' standing, and has been praised by every statesman who has referred to it. It was first made by correspondence between two secretaries of state and afterwards was embodied in a treaty. Does Senator Poindexter claim that this was unconstitutional and destroyed the sovereignty of the United States? The Senator says we cannot agree with another nation to take over and govern the exclusive right of manufacturing munitions and instruments of war. Why not, if other nations agree to do the same thing and to limit their production in the same way? The trouble with Senator Poindexter's conception of this government is that it hasn't the powers of other great nations to help along the world by a joint agreement that shall prevent the dangerous increase of armament on the part of any nation. In assuming to exalt the sovereignty of the nation as above everything, he falls into the error of minimizing its power to do anything to help the preservation of peace.

Senator Poindexter objects to article XVIII, in which the League is to supervise the traffic of arms in countries where it is deemed necessary, for the public welfare, to restrict the traffic. No one who is not a searcher for objections could apply that article to the United States. It of course refers to countries of backward peoples who cannot be trusted with firearms, and whose use of them the world may well restrict to maintain its safety.

The most extreme position of Senator Poindexter is that the United States cannot consent to arbitration of issues between it and other countries because it might affect the vital interests of the nation. There have been scores of arbitrations between the United States and other countries, many of them of very great concern. The question of the payment of the Alabama claims related to a principle of international law and international safety that was of the highest importance. The arbitration of the Alaskan boundary was another. The arbitration of our rights in the Bering Sea and in the seal herd of the Pribilof islands was another. On this arbitration we submitted to the decision of an impartial tribunal the question whether we had the rights or not which we claimed. The assumption that either the court of arbitration or the executive council of the League by unanimous judgment would seek to take away the sovereignty or the liberty or the independence of the United States is utterly gratuitous. It is so extreme a view that it ought not to be given any weight as an objection to machinery for the peaceful adjustment of differences by decision of international courts.

Note

Address at Portland, Oregon, February 16, 1919.

39

To Business Men

We have been discussing the question for four years as to how the world could make anything out of this war that would be useful for its further progress. Four years ago we adopted a plan in the League to Enforce Peace which provided for the cooperation of nations in attempting to stop the spread of war. We thought that if there was anything silly, anything cruel, it was war, and that the nations could not be said to be forward-looking or intelligent or businesslike, or even to have common sense, if they permitted the condition of affairs to continue which made possible such a war as we have just had. That was an academic question when we raised it—academic in the sense that people were thinking rather of how the war could be ended than what we should do after it ended.

Then we got into the war ourselves. We were a long time in getting in. As we look back upon it now, I think we regret that we did not get in earlier. I am offering no criticism that we did not, because our hindsight is always a great deal better than our foresight; but what I would like to say to you gentlemen, business men of San Francisco, is this: use your fore-sight now rather than your hindsight hereafter in respect to this particular question that we are bringing before you. I do not want you to be in the attitude of the man who rides with his back to the engine and does not see anything until he gets by it. And that is what you are likely to do unless you take this thing to heart and understand what the necessity of it is and what it means.

If, in ten or twenty years, we are called into another war, that war will be world suicide. The instrumentalities now capable of being used in war are far more destructive than they were when this war began; we have discovered explosives and poisonous gases which can destroy a whole community.

Are we going deliberately to allow that condition to continue which will make such a war possible? Are we going to sit down here in San Francisco and think that we are so many thousand miles away from Paris that we are not concerned in that matter?

That is what we thought for three years of this war, and then we were drawn into it. And even when we were drawn into it we did not realize it: it was still remote. I know what I am talking about. I was going around the country. Those in Washington and those in responsible positions began to realize what it meant. But it was a long time before the real spirit of earnestness entered into the people of the United States; and it spread west with a good deal of slowness. Finally it became the solidest public opinion that America ever had.

Now comes the reaction from the efforts made to win the war and we are looking around to get on a peace basis. We feel that the war is over and that Germany, under this armistice, cannot again come to the front as it did. Therefore we will let the world wag as it will and we will not concern ourselves about finishing a task in such a way as to make another war impossible.

I want to stir you up, men of business! The labor men are getting stirred up; they are receiving communications from their brethren over there and they are beginning to understand it. Now, I want you to study this thing, and take it to your hearts and souls, and understand that no one has a deeper interest in getting this League of Nations than you have.

The American people are intelligent, but the difficulty is to challenge their attention. They have got their minds on something else. That something else is the question of domestic readjustment, and this deliberation at Paris and the telegrams concerning it, though they fill the front page of the newspapers, do not bring home to you the issues that are in Paris. The question is whether you are up to date; whether you sympathize with the forward-looking men that are trying to take a great step forward in civilization and end war or make it so remotely possible that you can say that the prospect is that it is ended; whether you are going to agree with men who believe that the sovereignty and the Constitution of the United States lend themselves to going forward with other nations; or whether you agree that they are to be perverted to defeat the plans of the world framed to benefit mankind.

Is it possible that we cannot agree to settle our differences peaceably and refrain from appealing to the arbitrament of war, which seldom results in justice but always in the victory of the strongest? Sometimes the strongest is right; sometimes it is wrong. Now let us adopt some means of settling differences that shall lean on justice as a guide, and not on force.

Our President, representing this country, and the thirteen nations there in Paris have agreed upon a League of Nations.

I wish you would study that covenant; I wish you would work out what it means. It is a well-conceived plan. It does not involve as much compulsory force as our League to Enforce Peace has recommended, but it comes very near it; and it carries with it an arrangement for amendment and for an elasticity that, as experience goes on, will enable the League to adopt other methods.

Those nations that are gathered at Paris are in the presence of a very serious problem. Study it; analyze it; see whether they can get along without a League; see whether they can get along without the instrumentality for deciding questions justly by a tribunal of judges; see whether they can get along without a council of conciliation to adjust and readjust matters between the many new states there created.

We are interested in that problem. Our soldiers are over there to see that this peace is carried through. We are going to be involved in any mixup that comes from an attempt to settle this war without having the instrumentality for making that settlement effective. It is not a remote thing. It is at your door. We have got the responsibility for this peace along with all the other nations. These nations have realized that responsibility and have established the League of Nations, founded now with fourteen members, with a view of enlarging it afterwards and letting in others as they shall show themselves fit.

The covenant provides a way for the nations constantly to confer, to get closer together, to bring about a better understanding and to resort to joint action, when necessary, to secure justice.

Can we avoid that? Are we going to retire into our shells and say, "We are all right; we have resources within ourselves; we can live against the boycott; we can go on chasing the dollar comfortably and keep our people prosperous. What is the use? Why should we bother ourselves about other nations?" That is what we thought before this war, but we thought wrong.

Now, merely on selfish grounds, in order to avoid the disasters that may come to us in another war, we ought to do everything we can in the way of reasonable contribution to the general safety—and, certainly, all that is asked of us here is reasonable contribution. We are asked to join in a boycott, to unite with the other members of the League to say to any outlaw or recalcitrant nation that threatens to bring on war, "When you do, we will suspend all contracts and the payment of all monies which may be owing to your citizens; all the food, all the products, manufactures and raw materials, we are sending you will be stopped. We will withdraw our ambassadors and consular agents." And when all the world says that to a nation, that nation will occupy a position grand and gloomy, but peculiar.

We agree among ourselves that if there is any special loss to individual nations, all the other nations of the League will share that loss. The boycott may prove to be expensive. It may prove troublesome to some of our merchants who have dealings with the outlaw nation. But we can indemnify them, and doubtless the country would be entirely willing to do so.

So far as forcing this country into war is concerned, there is nothing in the constitution of the League that does this. Such a provision is found in the program of the League to Enforce Peace, and I should be glad to have it in the covenant. France wanted it. She is at the point of danger and she thinks she needs an obligation on the part of the other nations to come to her assistance; but the other nations did not agree to go so far. All they did was to provide that the executive council should recommend the number of forces that each country should contribute to make the League effective, and any neighbor of the outlaw nation is bound to allow the League's soldiers to go over its territory. The agreement does unite us with other nations; it does say that we shall live up to our ideals in dealing justly with other nations and respect their sovereignty; but that is all it entails.

We are told in a set of lurid speeches that we are surrendering our sovereignty and violating the Constitution. My friends, I recommend you to read the speeches that were made after the Constitution of the United States was framed, the speeches of George Mason and Patrick Henry and Samuel Adams, and of all those patriots who were vociferous in denunciation of the Constitution of the United States. You will find nothing in the present speeches in the Senate more startling.

Accompanying a forward movement there are always some who are looking backward. You always have those who see the difficulties without seeing the advantages. In the enthusiasm of debate they exaggerate difficulties; whereas, after the thing is done, they are very willing to forget it, and others have not time to look back to see how lacking in foresight these men were.

Note

Address before the Commonwealth Club of California, at San Francisco, February 19, 1919.

40

From an Address at San Francisco, February 19, 1919

In addition to its functions in respect to peace and war and the administration of territories containing backward peoples formerly administered by the defeated Central Powers, there are to be gathered, to act under the auspices of the League, all existing international bureaus like the postal union and all future international bureaus, including a new international bureau of labor under which it is proposed that, by international agreement, more humane conditions in respect to labor of men, women and children may be effected.

They give the Paris covenant wider scope and are greatly to be commended. They give the League substance and constant operation in some of its functions which will greatly promote the unity of nations. Out of this nucleus will come closer understanding and greater mutual interest suggesting new fields of international action for the betterment of mankind.

The administration of the German colonies with backward peoples in Africa and in the Pacific and the government of countries like Palestine,

Syria, Armenia, Mesopotamia and the Caucasus, not yet ready for self-government, is a problem forced upon the League because these countries cannot be trusted to the suzerainty or government of the defeated Powers. Their previous conduct toward them has forfeited all right, if any ever existed, to have them restored.

We agree to limit our armament in consideration of the other parties to this treaty limiting their armament, thus reducing the necessity for our maintaining an armament beyond that stipulated. The limitation upon our armament is not arbitrarily fixed by somebody else. It is to be fixed upon the recommendation of the executive council and agreed to by us. As our armament potentially threatens the other countries if used in a sinister way, so their armament potentially threatens us, and so by joint agreement we reduce the mutual threat by common proportionate reduction. To hold this beyond our power would be to hold that there is no possibility of curbing competitive armament, which, if it is to go on—and it will go on unless restrained—will invite world suicide.

41

From an Address at Salt Lake City, February 22, 1919

When they object to certain features of this covenant let them tell us what they would substitute for them in order to accomplish the same purpose. Have you heard any constructive suggestions from them? They do not enter into the consideration of this League in the proper spirit. The President has been struggling over there, with his colleagues in that conference, to work out the most difficult problem that has ever been presented to a congress. They have criticized him for going over. I am glad he went, because he got into the atmosphere of the conference, and there on the ground it was brought home to him what a tremendous problem it is for those nations, in conference, to settle; and there he learned, as he never had before, the necessity for a league of nations.

Why should we enter into the League? Well, I want to give you three commanding reasons: In the first place, we fought this war to secure permanent peace. That is what we promised our people when we came here and elsewhere, through our speakers, pleading for the Liberty Loan. They offered to you what? They offered to you the prospect of victory; and with the victory the defeat of militarism; and with the defeat of militarism, safety for democracy; and as a basis for safety for democracy, permanent peace. Those were the great objects proclaimed when we roused our people to action. Those were the objects proclaimed to our boys as they went over: "Go," we said, "we follow you with our hearts; we offer to make every necessary sacrifice because the struggle is worthy of every sacrifice."

Did we mean that, or didn't we mean it? That is the question. If we meant it, are we going to abandon the task and run away just at the moment when we can clinch it? Are we going to say to other nations: "No, we will not run any further risk. We have done all we ought to do. We will let you try to maintain the peace without us." Is that what we promised when we went in? Is that what we gave those peoples to expect when we sent the messages of our President across the seas? What did those messages contain? They contained a promise that we would fight this war through to victory, to the defeat of militarism, to making the world safe for democracy, to permanent peace. By what—by what, my friends? By a league of nations. That is what we said. That is what the President said; and he said it in a number of notes. The premiers on the other side said, "We agree to a league of nations." Now, what was the effect of those promises? It was to stiffen the morale of the plain people of those countries. At other conventions we have had present, as speakers, members of labor commissions and socialist commissions that were sent over by our government to talk with labor and socialist groups on the other side. What for? To offset the insidious conspiracies of German socialist and labor groups, aimed to defeat, to destroy the morale of those suffering peoples in France and Italy and England, who had been three long years in the war with the end nowhere in sight. When we came in with the promise of an army, their morale improved; though when our soldiers failed to come soon in great numbers, it began to weaken again. Then we followed with a promise to send more, and with the promise that we would give them a league of nations in order to make the peace permanent when it was won. These labor delegates testified to us that what maintained the morale of those people to fight the war through—soldiers, working men, all—was the promise of a league of nations in which the United States would take part. No one, at that time, when the President was promising this league of nations, no one said nay, in the Senate or elsewhere. Why not? Because the spirit of the people was aroused. They were willing to go the whole length in order to achieve this purpose; and there could not be a higher or a more glorious purpose. I do not mean to say that we did not enter this war with the idea that our interests were affected; but I do say there never was a war fought through in which a nation was less motived by desire for gain of power, for gain of money, for gain of territory, for the acquisition of anything but permanent peace, than this war.

Some say: "Let them have a league of European nations and leave the United States out." That is a great mistake. Who would constitute such a league? England, France and Italy—three nations. You would have an Entente Alliance; that is all—a balance of power with all the disappointing results that we have had in previous balances of power. The United States is indispensable to make that league go as a general league of nations, for the reason that it is the most disinterested member, the purest type of democracy, and its presence in the League will repudiate and refute any suggestion that it is an intrigue for autocratic action. Our presence will give to the League a potential strength and prestige which it will not have without us. So it is our duty to join, if we want to see the thing through, if we want to be square with those who fought this war for three years for us. We did not know they were fighting the war for us; but we found it out. They made enormous sacrifices before we went in. Are we going to say to them now: "We will not help further; our Constitution forbids; our policy against entangling alliances forbids. Oh, yes, we want to help you, but really, . . ."? How do you like that? How would you like to play that role in a partnership? I say that the men who advocate our staying out of the League by reason of a policy against entangling alliances laid down by Washington, for a small nation struggling for existence, whereas today we are one of the most powerful nations in the world—I say that these men belittle the United States and its people.

It is alleged that our entry into a league of nations would imperil the Monroe Doctrine. Now, what is the origin and nature of this doctrine? It was announced in a message of President Monroe to Congress in 1823 under the following circumstances. Many of the Spanish colonies had, from time to time, declared their independence and the United States had recognized them as independent governments. The Holy Alliance, formed to perpetuate the "Divine Right of Kings," and consisting of Russia, Austria and Prussia, had threatened to help Spain recover these colonies. Mr.

Canning, the British foreign minister, had urged upon our minister at London, Mr. Rush, the necessity for action to prevent this step and proposed that the United States and Great Britain unite in a protest against any such attempt. Thomas Jefferson and James Madison, both of whom were consulted by Mr. Monroe, thought the suggestion of Great Britain should be accepted and that there should be such an agreement to prevent the Holy Alliance from interfering with governments in this hemisphere. John Quincy Adams, who was Secretary of State, opposed the suggestion of a joint declaration. He felt that we should make the announcement alone, and his view prevailed. The message, probably drafted by Adams, opposed any extension of the monarchical system by interference with independent republics on this side of the water, and, having in mind Russia's attempt to push down her boundary in the old territory of Oregon, asserted that there was no longer room for future colonization by European governments in the Western Hemisphere.[1] That is the Monroe Doctrine as originally proclaimed. Later on, occasion gave rise to the extension of the doctrine in two instances. On one occasion some filibusters, who had gotten temporary control of Yucatan, offered to sell it to President Polk. When he said to them, "I do not want Yucatan," they threatened to sell it to France or England. To this threat Polk responded, "No, you will not; we will not permit it." It was Polk who introduced that new feature of the Doctrine. Again, in my administration, a resolution was introduced in the Senate demanding to know the circumstances under which certain lands on the shores of Magdalena Bay in Southern California were being taken over by a syndicate. It was reported that the Japanese were trying to get a base there. On investigation the State Department found the facts to be the following. A syndicate, which had acquired some thousands of acres on Magdalena Bay as an investment, were disappointed in their venture and attempted to unload. The attorney, in whose hands they had placed the matter, tried unsuccessfully to sell the property to a Japanese company, and thereupon told the "cock and bull" story about a Japanese corporation trying to acquire the land with a view to turning it over to the Japanese Government. But the Senate passed a resolution to the effect that outside nations could not be allowed to acquire strategic points near the United States and thus endanger its interests. I do not object to this extension of the Monroe Doctrine. On the contrary I think it is a good thing. But the

thing, and signing the treaty will only give to the United States the protection of the League in its traditional attitude.

When the Monroe Doctrine was declared by the United States, many American statesmen thought that it would certainly involve us in constant wars. For nearly a century, however, it has been peacefully and successfully maintained. Not a shot has been fired by the United States, not a soldier of the United States has been killed or injured in support of it. Its mere announcement, coupled with our known determination to enforce it, has dispensed with the necessity for the exercise of force.

It is a mistake to suppose that, under the League covenant, the armies of the United States are to be called into distant countries. We must expect the Executive Council to be reasonable in its recommendations in this respect not only because it will wish to be just but because it will want to act promptly in suppressing disturbance and the threat of war, and it can do this best by calling upon nations which are close at hand and which can do the work of the League most conveniently and economically. Moreover, with the unanimity required of the Council by a proper construction of the covenant, the presence of our representative in that Council will naturally make certain only a proper assignment of the League's work to the United States. The assumption that membership in the League will involve us in frequent wars is directly contrary to its purpose and natural operation. Its potential primitive force will prevent the coming of war.

Finally comes the question, my friends, whether we are willing to run the risk involved in joining the League. How much risk is there? I have tried to show that the risk is the danger of a boycott, the cost of a boycott, divided up between all the nations of the League, the risk involved in consenting to limit armament, after we have learned and consented to that limit, and the agreement to pay the expenses of a secretariat of the League jointly with other nations. As a consideration, we secure the strength of the union of nations in common action and a common purpose to suppress war and make peace permanent.

I appeal to the women who hear me: Do they want war again? Are they not willing that we should make concessions now in order that we may avoid war ten and twenty years hence? Do they wish their children and their grandchildren subjected to the suffering that we have seen England and France and Italy undergo? Is not this the time when enduring peace is to be born—when everybody is impressed with the dreadful character of war, and the necessity for avoiding it, when all the nations are willing to make concessions? Isn't now the time to take our share of the responsibility and say to our brothers: "We realize that the sea no longer separates us but is become a bond of union. We know that if a war comes to you, our neighbor, it will come to us, and we are ready to stand with you in order to keep off that scourge of nations. In the love of our brother we will do our share as men and women conscious of the responsibility to help along mankind, a responsibility which God has given this nation in giving it great power."

Note

1. The language of Monroe's message is:

The occasion has been judged proper for asserting, as a principle in which the rights and interests of the United States are involved, that the American continents, by the free and independent condition which they have assumed and maintained, are henceforth not to be considered as subjects for future colonization by any European power.

We should consider any attempt on their part to extend their system to any portion of this hemisphere as dangerous to our peace and safety. With the existing colonies or dependencies of any European power we have not interfered and shall not interfere. But with the governments who have declared their independence and maintained it, and whose independence we have, on great consideration and on just principles, acknowledged, we could not view any interposition for the purpose of oppressing them, or controlling in any other manner their destiny, by any European power, in any other light than as the manifestation of an unfriendly disposition toward the United States.

[Marburg]

42

League of Nations as Barrier
to Any Great Wars in Future

The practical working of this covenant will be to suppress and avoid most wars. Of course, hypotheses can be imagined that will break down any constitution, even that of the United States, or any plan of the kind I have described; but this plan has a real bite in it, a real mutual obligation for union of the lawful economic and military forces of the world to police the world and prevent the recurrence of such another awful war as that from which we have just emerged. I have said, "From which we have just emerged." That is a wrong term to use. I should use the expression "Which we are now trying to end in such a way as to achieve its purpose and make the peace a stable and permanent one."

You have heard Mr. Morgenthau describe, with trenchant accuracy, the conditions that now prevail in the sphere of war in Europe, and the danger there is from the spread of Bolshevism and from a reaction to autocracy as a desperate antidote for Bolshevism. Some who oppose the covenant most are blind to the critical conditions now existing in Europe, are blind to the absolute necessity for a league such as this covenant creates.

. . . From time immemorial a most frequent subject matter of treaties is an agreement to submit differences to arbitration. The earliest treaties made by the United States with England and the Barbary States, and with other countries, contained a clause providing for such arbitration.

Since that time we have had numbers of treaties of arbitration, among them general treaties of arbitration. These latter excepted some classes of questions, it is true, but they were general treaties, notwithstanding, in that the character of the differences could not be anticipated. Not by the wildest stretch of the imagination can such an agreement be construed to be a delegation of governmental powers or a parting with sovereignty. It is no more a curtailment of sovereignty than is the obligation of a man to abide the judgment of an impartial court, or the award of an agreed arbitration, an infringement on his liberty secured by the Constitution.

. . . This covenant does not create a super-sovereignty—it is only a loose obligation among the nations of the world by which they agree to unite together in a policy of submitting their differences to arbitration and mediation, to withhold war until those efforts have proved unsuccessful and to boycott any nation which violates the covenant to comply with this obligation. It provides a method for reaching an agreement as to a limit of armament and an obligation to keep within that limit of armament until conditions shall require a change by a new agreement. The agreement on the part of one balances the agreement on the part of others in securing a general reduction of armament. It does not impair our just sovereignty in the slightest—it is only an arrangement for the maintenance of our sovereignty within its proper limits: to wit, a sovereignty regulated by international law and international morality and international justice, with a somewhat rude machinery created by the agreement of nations to prevent one sovereignty from being used to impose its unjust will on other sovereignties. Certainly we, with our national ideals, can have no desire to secure any greater sovereignty than this.

The argument that to enter this covenant is a departure from the time-honored policy of avoiding entangling alliances with Europe is an argument that is blind to the changed circumstances in our present situation. The war itself ended that policy. *Res ipsa loquitur.* We attempted to carry it out. We stayed out of the war three years when we ought to have been in it, as we now see.

We were driven into it because, with the dependence of all the world upon our resources of food, raw material and manufacture, with our close-ness, under modern conditions of transportation and communication, to Europe, it was impossible for us to maintain the theory of an isolation that did not in fact exist. It will be equally impossible for us to keep out of another general European war. We are, therefore, just as much interested in stop-ping such a war as if we were in Europe. This war was our war. The settle-ment of the war is our settlement. The maintenance of the terms of that settlement is our business, as it is the business of the other nations. To say that we should avoid it is to say that we should be recreant to our duty to ourselves and to the world and blind to the progress of events. To say that it mixes us up with kings is amusing when we consider the dominance of democracy in Europe.

The superlative expressions contained in the denunciations of Mr. Fess and Mr. Reed and Mr. Borah and Mr. Poindexter as to the dangerous working of this covenant find no basis in a clear understanding of its provi-sions. The contention that we are to be bound by the decision of the Exec-utive Council on a critical issue of war or peace, of arbitration or no arbitration, of limit of armament or no armament, finds no justification in the covenant itself.

The Executive Council is an executive body only to recommend mea-sures to be adopted by the nations in the matter of the reduction of arma-ment and in the matter of the furnishing of military forces and in other lines of action. The obligation is upon the governments through their usual constitutional agencies (which, in our case, is Congress) to perform the obligations they have assumed. Our obligations are: first, to submit differ-ences to arbitration or mediation; second, not to make war until three months after an award or a report of a proper settlement and not then if the losing nation complies; third, to lay an embargo or boycott against a covenant-breaking nation; fourth, to keep within an armament Congress agrees to. These are the "bite" of the League.

The fundamental weakness of the attitude of Senator Poindexter and Senator Reed and Senator Borah is that they confine their arguments to pointing out the dangers of this Covenant to the United States, which, as I think I have shown, are comparatively slight, while they utterly fail to tender any constructive suggestions to the conference for a method by which peace can be maintained and the just results of the war can be secured. They are merely destructive critics and are not in search of a solution of the difficulty that we, in common with the other nations at the Paris conference, have to meet and solve. Such criticisms are not helpful. They are apparently prompted by a desire to find fault rather than by the duty of suggesting a remedy.

General Smuts, who recommended the system of mandatories, thought that the League itself could not get up an organization sufficiently effective to conduct these governments, that therefore it ought to employ competent governments as agencies to carry on the governments of these dependencies for the benefits of the people in them and that they should make a report of their trusteeship at the end of each year. In his opinion the principles should be laid down in the treaty or be contained in a charter granted by the Executive Council, so as to make a rule of conduct for the agencies acting as mandatories.

Now, there is nothing in the League that requires any government to accept the position of a mandatory. The South Sea colonies and the Pacific colonies of Germany will doubtless come under England or under Australia. There are some Northern islands, perhaps, that may come under Japan as a mandatory. Then Palestine and Armenia and Constantinople may come under some other government. They would be glad to have the United States take that, but you will remember that the representatives of the United States said in the Council, that this was impossible, that they could not agree to it.

Now, if they took that attitude in the Council, how unreasonable it is to contend that they would have consented to a league which obliged a member to accept a mandate of this character. You will find nothing compulsory in this provision of the League.

Note

Address at the National Congress for a League of Nations at the Odeon, St. Louis, February 25, 1919.

43

The Paris Covenant for a League of Nations 2

We are here tonight in sight of a league of peace, of what I have ever regarded as the "promised land." Such a war as the last is a hideous blot on our Christian civilization. The inconsistency is as foul as was slavery under the Declaration of Independence. If Christian nations cannot now be brought into a united effort to suppress a recurrence of such a contest it will be a shame to modern society.

During my administration I attempted to secure treaties of universal arbitration between this country and France and England, by which all issues depending for their settlement upon legal principles were to be submitted to an international court for final decision. These treaties were emasculated by the Senate, yielding to the spirit which proceeds, unconsciously doubtless, but truly, from the conviction that the only thing that will secure to a nation the justice it wishes to secure is force; that agreements between nations to settle controversies justly and peaceably should never be given any weight in national policy; that in dealing between civilized nations we must assume that each nation is conspiring to deprive us of our independence and our prosperity; that there is no impartial tribunal to which we can entrust the decision of any question vitally affecting our interests or our honor; and that we can afford to make no agreement from which we may not immediately withdraw, and whose temporary operation to our detriment may not be expressly a ground for ending it. This is the doctrine of despair. It leads necessarily to the conclusion that our only recourse to avoid war is competitive armament, with its dreadful burdens and its constant temptation to resort to the war it seeks to avoid.

The most important covenant with reference to peace and war in the constitution of the League is that looking to a reduction of armament by all nations. The Executive Council, consisting of representatives of the United States, the British Empire, France, Italy, Japan, and of four other nations to be selected by the body of delegates, is to consider how much the armaments of the nations should be reduced, having regard to the safety of each of the nations and their obligations under the League. Having reached a conclusion as to the proportionate limits of each nation's armament, it submits its conclusion to each nation, which may or may not agree to the limit thus recommended; but when an agreement is reached it covenants to keep within that limit until, by application to the Executive Council, the limit may be raised. In other words, each nation agrees to its own limitation. Having so agreed, it must keep within it.

Our Constitution contains no inhibition, express or implied, against making such an agreement. On the contrary, for one hundred years we have maintained an agreement to limit armaments between this country and Canada. The evil of competition in armament as between us has been avoided by abstaining from armament altogether. Could there be a more complete precedent for this provision of the Paris Covenant?

The importance of providing for a reduction of armament every one recognizes. It is affirmed in the newly proposed Senate resolution. Can we not trust our Congress to fix a limitation which is safe for the country and to stick to it? If we cannot, no country can. Yet all the rest are anxious to do this and they are far more exposed than we.

The character of this obligation is affected by the time during which the covenants of the League remain binding. There is no stipulation as to how long this is. In my judgment there should be a period of ten years or a permission for any member of the League to withdraw from the covenant by giving a reasonable notice of one or two years of its intention to do so.

The members of the League and the non-members are required, the former by their covenant, the latter by an enforced obligation, to submit all differences between them, not capable of being settled by negotiation, to arbitration before a tribunal composed as the parties may agree. They are required to covenant to abide the award. Should either party deem the question one not proper for arbitration, then it is to be taken up by the Executive Council of the League. The Executive Council mediates between the parties and secures a voluntary settlement of the question if possible. If it fails, it makes a report. If the report is unanimous, the Executive Council is to recommend what shall be done to carry into effect its recommendation. If there is a dissenting vote, then the majority report is published, and also the minority report, if desired, and no further action is taken. If either party or the Executive Council itself desires, the mediating function is to be discharged by the Body of Delegates in which every member of the League has one vote. There is no direction as to what shall be done with reference to the recommendation of proper measures to be taken, and the whole matter is then left for such further action as the members of the League agree upon. There is no covenant by the defeated party that it will comply with the unanimous report of the Executive Council or the Body of Delegates.

And right here I wish to take up the objection made to the League that under this machinery we might be compelled to receive immigrants contrary to our national desire from Japan or China. We could and would refuse to submit the issue to arbitration. It would then go to mediation. In my judgment the Council, as a mediating body, should not take jurisdiction to consider such a difference. Immigration by international law is a domestic question completely within the control of the Government into which immigration is sought, unless the question of immigration is the subject of treaty stipulation between two countries. If, however, it be said that there is no limitation, in the Covenant, of the differences to be mediated, clearly we would run no risk of receiving from the large body of delegates of all the members of the League a unanimous report recommending a settlement by which Japanese immigrants shall be admitted to our shores, or Japanese applicants be admitted to citizenship, against our protest. But were it made, we are under no covenant to obey such recommendation. If it could be imagined that all of the other nations of the world would thus unite their military forces to compel us to receive Japanese immigrants under the covenant, why would they not do so without the covenant?

These articles compelling submission of differences either to arbitration or mediation are not complete machinery for settlement by peaceable means of all issues arising between nations. But they are a substantial step forward. They constitute an unambitious plan to settle as many questions as possible by arbitration or mediation. They illustrate the spirit of those who drafted this covenant and their sensible desire not to attempt more till after actual experience.

The next covenant is that the nations shall not begin war until three months after the arbitration award or the recommendation of compromise, and not then if the defendant nation against whom the award or recommendation has been made shall comply with it. This is the great restraint of war imposed by the Covenant upon members of the League and nonmembers. It is said that this would prevent our resistance to a border raid of Mexico or self-defense against any invasion—a most extreme construction. If a nation refuses submission at all, as it does when it begins an attack, the nation attacked is released instanter from its obligation to submit and is restored to the complete power of self-defense. Had this objection not been raised in the Senate one would not have deemed it necessary to answer so unwarranted a suggestion.

If the defendant nation does not comply with the award or unanimous report, then the plaintiff nation can begin war and carry out such complete remedy as the circumstances enable it to do. But if the defendant nation does comply with the award or unanimous report, then the plaintiff nation must be content with such compliance. It runs the risk of not getting all that it thought it ought to have or might have by war, but as it is asking affirmative relief it must be seeking some less vital interest than its political independence or territorial integrity, and the limitation is not one which can be dangerous to its sovereignty.

The third covenant, the penalizing covenant, is that if a nation begins war in violation of its covenant, then *ipso facto* that is an act of war against every member of the League and the members of the League are required definitely and distinctly to levy a boycott on the covenant-breaking nation and to cut off all commercial, trade, financial, personal and official relations between them and their citizens and it and its citizens. Indeed, the boycott is compound or secondary in that it is directed against any non-members of the League continuing to deal with the outlaw nation. This is an obligation operative at once on each member of the League. With us the Executive Council would report the violation of the covenant to the President and it would be reported to Congress. Congress would then, by reason of the covenant of the League, be under a legal and moral obligation to levy an embargo and prevent all intercourse of every kind between this nation and the covenant-breaking nation.

The extent of this penalty and its heavy, withering effect, when the hostile action includes all members of the League as well as all non-members, may be easily appreciated. The prospect of such an isolation would be likely to frighten any member of the League from a reckless violation of its covenant not to begin war. It is inconceivable that any small nation, dependent as it must be on larger nations for its trade and sustenance, indeed for its food and raw material, would for a moment court such a destructive ostracism as this would be.

Other covenants of the penalizing article impose on the members of the League the duty of sharing the expense of a boycott with any nation upon which it has fallen with uneven weight and of supporting such a nation in its resistance to any special measure directed against it by the outlaw nation. But there is no specific requirement as to the character of the support beyond the obligation of the boycott, the contribution of expenses and the obligation of each member of the League to permit the passage through its territory of forces of other members of the League co-operating with military forces against the outlaw nation.

If, however, the boycott does not prove sufficient, then the Executive Council is to recommend the number of the military and naval forces to be contributed by the members of the league to protect the covenants of the League in such a case. There is no specific covenant by which they agree to furnish a definite force, or, indeed, any force at all, to a league army. The use of the word "recommend" in describing the function of the Executive Council shows that the question whether such forces shall be contributed and what shall be their amount must ultimately address itself to the members of the League severally for their several decision and action. There is this radical and important difference, therefore, between the obligation to lay a boycott and the obligation to furnish military force, and doubtless this distinction was insisted upon and reached by a compromise. The term "recommendation" cannot be interpreted to impose any imperative obligation on those to whom the recommendation is directed.

By Article X, the high contracting parties undertake to respect and preserve against external aggression the political independence and territorial integrity of every member of the League, and when these are attacked or threatened the Executive Council is to advise as to the proper means to fulfill this obligation. The same acts or series of acts which make Article X applicable will be a breach of the covenant which creates an outlaw nation under Article XVI, so that all nations must begin a boycott against any nation thus breaking the territorial integrity or overthrowing the independence of a member of the League. Indeed Article X will usually not be applicable until a war shall be fought to the point of disclosing its specific purpose. Action under it will usually take the form of preventing, in a treaty of peace, the appropriation of territory or the interference with the sovereignty of the attacked and defeated nation. We have seen this in the construction put upon the Monroe Doctrine by Secretary Seward and President Roosevelt. The former, when Spain attacked Chile and that country appealed to the United States to protect it, advised Spain that under our policy we would not interfere to prevent the punishment by war of an American nation by a non-American nation, provided it did not extend to a permanent deprivation of its territory or an overthrow of its sovereignty. President Roosevelt, in the Venezuelan matter, also announced that the Monroe Doctrine did not prevent nations from proceeding by force to collect their debts provided oppressive measures were not used which would deprive the nation of its independence or territorial integrity. This furnishes an analogy for the proper construction of Article X.

The fact that the Executive Council is to advise what means shall be taken to fulfill the obligation shows that they are to be such as each nation shall deem proper and fair under the circumstances. Remoteness from the seat of trouble and the fact that the nearer presence of other nations should induce them to furnish the requisite military force would naturally be included among the factors considered. It thus seems to me clear that the question, both under Article XVIII, and under Article X, as to whether the United States shall declare war and what forces it shall furnish, are remitted to the voluntary action of the Congress of the United States under the

Constitution, regard being had to the matter of a fair division between all the nations of the burden to be borne under the League and the proper means to be adopted, whether the enjoined and inevitable boycott alone, or the advance of loans of money, or the declaration of war and the use of military force. This is as it should be. It fixes the obligation of action in such a way that American nations will attend to America, European nations will attend to Europe, and Asiatic nations to Asia, unless all deem the situation so threatening to the world and to their own interests that they should take a more active part. It seems to me that appropriate words might be added to the pact which would show distinctly this distribution of obligation. This would relieve those anxious to exclude European or Asiatic nations from forcible intervention in issues between American nations until requested to intervene by the United States, or by an executive council of the American nations formed for the purpose.

Objection is made that Great Britain might have more representatives in the Executive Council than other countries. This is an error. The British Empire, which, of course, includes its dominions, is limited to one delegate in the Executive Council. As regards the other central organ, known as the Body of Delegates, provision is made by which, upon a two-thirds vote of that body, new members may be admitted who are independent states or are self-governing dominions or colonies. Under this Canada and Australia and South Africa might be allowed to send delegates. I presume, too, the Philippines might be admitted. But the function of the Body of Delegates is not one which makes membership in it of great importance. When it acts as a mediating and compromising body, its reports must be unanimous to have any effect. And the addition of members is not likely to create greater probability of unanimity. More than this, the large number of countries who will become members will minimize any increase of British influence from the addition of such dominions and colonies, which are really admitted because they have different interests from their mother country. When analyzed, the suggestion that Great Britain will have any greater power than other member nations in shaping the policy of the League in really critical matters will be seen to have no foundation whatever.

A proposed resolution in the Senate recites that the Constitution of the League of Nations in the form now offered should not be accepted by the United States, although the sense of the Senate is that the nations of the world should unite to promote peace and general disarmament. The resolution further recites that the efforts of the United States should immediately be directed to the utmost expedition of the urgent business of negotiating peace terms with Germany satisfactory to the United States and the nations with whom the United States is associated in the war against the German Government, and that the proposal for a League of Nations to insure the permanent peace of the world should be taken up for careful and serious consideration later. It is said that this resolution will be supported by thirty-seven members of the new Senate, and thus prevent the confirmation of any treaty which includes the present proposed Covenant of Paris.

The President of the United States is the authority under the Federal Constitution which initiates the form of treaties and which at the outset determines what subject matter they shall include. Therefore, if it shall seem to the President of the United States, and to those acting with him with similar authority for other nations, that a treaty of peace cannot be concluded except with a covenant providing for a league of nations, in substance like that now proposed, as a condition precedent to the proper operation and effectiveness of the treaty itself, it will be the duty of the President and his fellow delegates to the Conference to insert such a covenant in the treaty. If accordingly such a covenant should be incorporated in a Treaty of Peace, signed by the representatives of the Powers and should be brought back by the President and submitted by him to the Senate, the question which will address itself to the proponents of this Senate resolution will be not whether they would prefer to consider a league of nations after a Treaty of Peace but whether they will feel justified in defeating or postponing a treaty because it contains a constitution of a league of nations deemed by the President necessary to the kind of peace which all seek.

. . . In the dark background is the threatening specter of Bolshevism, hard, cruel, murderous, uncompromising, destructive of Christian civilization, militant in pressing its hideous doctrines upon other peoples, and insidious in its propaganda among the lowest element in every country. Confronted with the chaos and the explosive dangers of Bolshevism throughout all the countries of Europe, a League of Nations must be established to settle controversies peaceably and to enforce the settlement.

Were the United States to withdraw, the League would be nothing but a return to the system of alliances and the balance of power. We would witness a speedy recurrence of war in which the United States would be as certainly involved as it was in this war. New inventions for the destruction of men and peoples would finally result in world suicide, while in the interval there would be a story of progressive competition in armaments, with all their heavy burdens upon peoples already burdened almost to the point of exhaustion. With such a prospect, and to avoid such results, the United States should not hesitate to take its place with the other responsible nations of the world and make the light concessions and assume the light burdens involved in membership in the League.

No critic of the League has offered a single constructive suggestion to meet the crisis that I have thus summarily touched upon. The resolution of the Senate does not suggest or refer in any way to machinery by which the function of the League of Nations in steadying Europe and maintaining the peace agreed upon in the treaty shall be secured. Well may the President, therefore, decline to comply with the suggestions of the proposed resolution. Well may he say when he returns with the treaty, of which the covenant shall be a most important and indispensable part, "If you would postpone peace, if you would defeat it, you can refuse to ratify the treaty. Amend it by striking out the Covenant and you will leave confusion worse confounded, with the objects of the war unattained and sacrificed and Europe and the world in chaos."

. . . Whatever nation secures the control of the seas will make the United States its ally, no matter how formal and careful its neutrality, because it will be the sole customer of the United States in food, raw material and war necessities. Modern war is carried on in the mines and the workshops and on the farm, as well as in the trenches. The former are indispensable to the latter. Hence the United States will certainly be drawn in, and hence its interests are inevitably involved in the preservation of European peace. These conditions and circumstances are so different from those in Washington's day and are so unlike anything which he could have anticipated that no words of his, having relation to selfish, offensive and defensive alliances, should be given any application to the present international status.

Objection is made that the Covenant destroys the Monroe Doctrine. The Monroe Doctrine was announced and adopted to keep European monarchies from overthrowing the independence of, and fastening their system upon, governments in this hemisphere. It has been asserted in various forms, some of them extreme—I presume that no one now would attempt to sustain the declarations of Secretary Olney in his correspondence with Lord Salisbury. But all will probably agree that the sum and substance of the Monroe Doctrine is that we do not propose in our own interest to allow European nations or Asiatic nations to acquire, beyond what they now have, through war or purchase or intrigue, territory, political power or strategical opportunity from the countries of this hemisphere. Article X of the Constitution of the League is intended to secure this to all signatory nations, except that it does not forbid purchase of territory.

In recent speeches in the Senate the Monroe Doctrine has been enlarged beyond what can be justified. Those who seek to set up a doctrine which would make the Western hemisphere a preserve in which we may impose our sovereign will on other countries in what we suppose to be their own interest—because, indeed, we have done that in the past—should not be sustained. Our conquests of Western territory made for civilization have increased our own usefulness and the happiness of those who now occupy that territory. But we have reached a stage in history when the world's progress should be determined and secured under just and peaceful conditions, and attempted progress through conquest by powerful nations should be prevented.

To suppose that, with the great trade relations between North America and Europe, we can isolate ourselves is to look backward, not forward. It does not face existing conditions.

The European nations desire our entrance into this League not that they may control America but to secure our aid in controlling Europe; and I venture to think that they would be relieved if the primary duty of keeping peace and policing this Western hemisphere were relegated to us and our Western colleagues. I object, however, to such a reservation as was contained in the Hague Conference against entangling alliances, because the recommendation was framed before this war and contained provisions as to the so-called policy against entangling alliances that are inconsistent with the present needs of this nation and of the rest of the world if a peaceful future is to be secured to both. I would favor, however, a recognition of the Monroe Doctrine as I have stated it above by specific words in the covenant, and with a further provision that the settlement of purely American questions should be remitted primarily to the American nations, with machinery like that of the present League, and that European nations should not intervene unless requested to do so by the American nations.

Objection is made to this League on constitutional grounds. . . . The Supreme Court has over and over again, through Mr. Chief Justice Marshall, indicated that the United States was a sovereign nation capable of dealing with other nations as such, and seized of all the powers inferable from sovereignty. It is said that the League will change the form of our government. But no function or discretion which it now exercises is taken from any branch of the government. It is asserted that the Covenant delegates to an outside tribunal, viz., the Executive Council, the power vested by the Constitution in Congress or the Senate. But the Executive Council has no power but to recommend to the nations of the League courses which those nations may accept or reject, save in the matter of increasing the limit of armament, to which, after full consideration, a nation shall have consented. In our case it would be Congress that had considered and consented to the limitation. Neither the Executive Council nor the Body of Delegates, in the machinery for the peaceful settling of differences, does other than recommend a compromise which the United States does not, under the League, covenant to obey. In all other respects these bodies are mere instruments for conference by representatives for devising plans which are submitted to the various governments of the League for their voluntary acceptance. No obligation of the United States under the League is fixed by action of either the Executive Council or the Body of Delegates.

Then it is said we have no right to agree to levy an embargo and a boycott. It is true that Congress determines what our commercial relations shall be with other countries of the world. It is true that if a boycott is to be levied Congress must levy it in the form of an embargo, as that which was levied by Congress in Jefferson's administration and sustained by the Supreme Court, with John Marshall at its head. It is also true that Congress might repudiate the obligation entered into by the treaty-making power and refuse to levy such an embargo. But none of these facts would invalidate or render unconstitutional a treaty by which the obligation of the United States was assumed.

In other words, the essence of sovereign power is that while the sovereign may make a contract it retains the power to repudiate it if it chooses to dishonor its promises. That does not render null the original obligation or lessen its binding moral force. The nations of Europe are willing to accept, as we must be willing to accept from them, mutual promises, the one in consideration of the other, in the confidence that neither will refuse to comply with such promises honorably entered into.

Finally, it is objected that we have no right to agree to arbitrate issues since we might, by arbitration, lose our territorial integrity or political independence. This is a marvelous stretch of imagination by the distinguished Senator who made it. In the face of Article X, which is an undertaking to respect the territorial integrity and political independence of every member of the League, how could a board of arbitration possibly reach such a result? Moreover, we are not compelled to arbitrate a dispute. If preferred, we can throw the matter into mediation and conciliation, and we do not covenant to obey the recommendation of compromise by the conciliating body.

We have agreed in treaties to arbitrate classes of questions long before the questions arise. Now, in the present treaty, the issue to be arbitrated would have to be formulated by our treaty-making power—the President and the Senate of the United States. The award would have to be executed by that branch of the government which executes awards, generally the Congress of the United States. If it involved payment of money, Congress would have to appropriate it. If it involved limitation of armament, Congress would have to limit it. If it involved any duty within the legislative power of Congress under the Constitution, Congress would have to perform it. If Congress sees fit to comply with the report of the compromise by the conciliating body, Congress will have to make such compliance.

The Covenant takes away the sovereignty of the United States only as any contract curtails the freedom of action which an individual has voluntarily surrendered for the purpose of the contract and to obtain the benefit of it. The Covenant creates no super-sovereignty. It merely creates contract obligations. It binds nations to stand together to secure compliance with those obligations. That is all. This does not differ from a contract between two nations. If we enter into an important contract with another nation to pay money or to do things of vital importance and we break it, then we expose ourselves to the just effort of that nation to attempt by force of arms to compel us to comply with our obligations. This covenant is only a limited and loose union of many nations to do the same thing. The assertion that we are giving up our sovereignty carries us logically and necessarily to the absurd result that we can not make a contract to do anything with another nation because it limits our freedom of action as a sovereign.

Sovereignty is freedom of action of nations. It is exactly analogous to the liberty of the individual regulated by law. The sovereignty that we should insist upon and the only sovereignty we have a right to insist upon is a sovereignty regulated by international law, international morality and international justice, a sovereignty enjoying the sacred rights which sovereignties of other nations may enjoy, a sovereignty consistent with the enjoyment of the same sovereignty by other nations. It is a sovereignty limited by the law of nations and limited by the obligation of contracts fully and freely entered into as in respect to matters which are usually the subject of contracts between nations.

Those persons who require more than this are really demanding the license—they term it necessary American sovereignty—to trample upon all tribunals and to assert their own unregulated desires. That is not in accord with American principles nor with the Constitution of the United States.

The President is now returning to Europe. As the representative of this nation he has joined in recommending, in this proposed covenant, a league of nations for consideration and adoption by the conference. He returned home to discharge other executive duties and this has given him an opportunity to follow the discussion of the question in the Senate of the United States and elsewhere. Some speeches, notably that of Senator Lodge, have been useful in taking up the League Covenant, article by article, criticising its language and expressing doubts either as to its meaning or as to its wisdom.

The President will differ, as many others differ, with Senator Lodge in respect to many of the criticisms, but in the constructive part of his speech he will find useful suggestions which he will be able to present to his colleagues in the conference. These suggestions should prove especially valuable in the work of revising the form of the Covenant and in making changes, to which the conference may readily consent, where Senator Lodge

44

Answer to Senator Knox's Indictment

My friend, Senator Knox, has presented a formidable indictment against the proposed Covenant of the League of Nations. A number of his colleagues seem to have accepted his views as to its meaning. He says that it is unconstitutional in that it turns over to the Executive Council of the League the power to declare and make war for us, to fix our armament and to involve us as a mandatory in all sorts of duties in the management of backward peoples. He says that it thus transfers the sovereignty of this nation to the governing body of the League, which he asserts the Executive Council to be.

When Senator Knox's attack upon the validity of the Covenant is analyzed, it will be seen to rest on an assumption that the Executive Council is given executive powers, which is unwarranted by the text of the instrument. The whole function of the Executive Council is to be the medium through which the League members are to exchange views, the advisory board to consider all matters arising in the field of the League's possible action and to advise the members as to what they ought, by joint action, to do.

The Council makes few if any orders binding on the members of the League. After a member of the League has agreed not to exceed a limit of armament, the Executive Council must consent to raising the limit. Where the Executive Council acts as a mediating and inquiring body to settle differences not arbitrated, its unanimous recommendation of a settlement must satisfy the nation seeking relief, if the defendant nation complies with the recommendation.

These are the only cases in which the United States as a member of the League would be bound by action of the Executive Council. All other obligations of the United States under the League are to be found in the covenants of the League, and not in any action of the Executive Council. When this is understood clearly, the whole structure of Senator Knox's indictment falls.

The Executive Council is a most necessary and useful body for coordinating the activities of the League, for initiating consideration by the members of the League of their proper joint and individual action, and for keeping all advised of the progress of events in the field of the League jurisdiction.

It is impossible, in the time I have, to follow through Senator Knox's argument in all the Articles of the League, but his treatment of Article XVI is a fair illustration of the reasons he advances for ascribing to the Executive Council super-sovereign power.

Article XVI is the penalizing section. Whenever a member of the League violates its covenant not to make war under Article XII, it is an act of war against the other members and they are to levy a boycott against the outlaw nation. There is in the Covenant no agreement to make war. An act of war does not produce a state of war unless the nation acted against chooses to declare and wage war on account of it. The Executive Council is given the duty of *recommending* what forces should be furnished by members of the League to protect the covenants of the League. The members are required to allow military forces of a member of the League, cooperating to protect the covenants, passage through their territory.

Of this article Senator Knox says: "If any of the high contracting parties breaks its covenant under Article XII, then we must fly to arms to protect the covenants." Again he says of it: "Whether or not we participate, and the amount of our participation in belligerent operations, is determined not by ourselves but by the Executive Council in which we have seemingly, at most, but one voice out of nine, no matter what we think of the controversy, no matter how we view the wisdom of a war over the cause, we are bound to go to war when and in the manner the Executive Council determines." He asserts that the power of the Executive Council is that of "recommending what effective military or naval forces each member of the League shall contribute to protect the covenants of the League, not only against League members but non-League members: *that is, as a practical matter, the power to declare war.*"

I submit in all fairness that there never was a more palpable *non sequitur* than this. I venture to think that were Senator Knox charged as Secretary of State with construing the obligation of the United States under this Covenant, he would on behalf of the United States summarily reject such a construction.

By what manner of reasoning can the word "recommend" be converted into a word of direction or command? Yet upon this interpretation of the meaning of the words "recommend," "advise" and words of like import, as they occur in many articles, depends his whole argument as to the powers of the Executive Council under the Covenant, and their supersovereign character.

Senator Knox contends that the plan of the League will create two Leagues—one of the Allies and one of the outcast nations. The Covenant provides for a protocol to invite in all nations responsible and fit for membership. Certainly Germany and the other enemy countries ought not now to be taken in, but they ought to be kept under control. The League wishes to prevent war in the world and realizes, of course, that excluded nations are quite as likely to make war as their own members.

The Covenant therefore declares the concern of the League in threatened war between nations whether members or not and asserts its right to take steps to prevent it. This declaration is made as the justification for Article XVII, by which a nation or nations not members of the League who threaten war are invited to become temporary members of the League in order to enable them to settle their disputes peaceably as permanent members covenant to do. These temporary members are visited with the same penalties for acts which would be, if committed by permanent members, breaches of their covenants not to begin war. Thus the scope of the League's action is extended to all nations.

This is the explanation and the purport of Articles XI and XVII. They involve the whole world in the covenants of the League not to make war. They operate to defeat the formation and warlike organization of a rival league of nations, composed of countries not admitted as permanent members to this league. They unite the rest of the world against such nations in any case of war threatened by them.

There is no supreme court to construe this Covenant and bind the members, and each nation, in determining its own obligations and action under it, must construe it for itself. Our duties under it are not to be declared and enforced against us by a hostile tribunal or by one actuated by different principles and spirit from our own. Its whole strength is to rest in an agreed interpretation by all. Its sanction must be in the good sense of the covenanting nations who know that, in order that it may hold together and serve its purpose, they must all be reasonable in their construction. What rules of interpretation should and must we therefore apply?

The President and Senate are to ratify this Covenant, if it be ratified, by virtue of their constitutional power to make treaties. This power, as the Supreme Court has held, enables them to bind the United States to a contract with another nation on any subject matter usually the subject matter of treaties between nations, subject to the limitation that the treaty may not change the form of government of the United States, and may not part with territory belonging to a State of the United States, without the consent of the State. The making of war, of embargoes, or armament, and of arbitration are frequently subject matter of treaties.

The President and Senate may not, however, confer on any body, constituted by a league of nations, the power and function to do anything for the United States which is vested by the Federal Constitution in Congress, the treaty-making power or any other branch of the United States Government.

It, therefore, follows that whenever the treaty-making power binds the United States to do anything, it must be done by the branch of that Government vested by the Constitution with that function. A treaty may bind the United States to make or not make war in any specific contingency; it may bind the United States to levy a boycott, to limit its armament to a fixed amount; it may bind the United States to submit a difference or a class of differences to arbitration. But the only way in which the United States can perform the agreement is for Congress to fulfill the promise to declare and make war; for Congress to perform the obligation to levy a boycott; for Congress to fix or reduce armament in accord with the contract; and for the President and Senate, as the treaty-making power, to formulate the issues to be arbitrated and agree with the opposing nation on the character of the court.

When the treaty provides that the obligation arises upon a breach of a covenant, and does not make the question of the breach conclusively determinable by any body or tribunal, then it is for Congress itself to decide in good faith whether or not the breach of the Covenant upon which the obligation arises, has in fact occurred, and finding that, it has to perform the obligation.

These plain limitations upon the Federal treaty-making power are known to nations of this conference, and any treaty of the United States is to be construed in the light of them. Following these necessary rules of construction, the provisions of the Covenant entirely and easily conform to the Constitution of the United States. They lose altogether that threatening and dangerous character and effect which Senator Knox and other critics would attach to them. They delegate to no body but to our own Federal constitutional agencies the duty of deciding in good faith what our obligations under the Covenant are, when they become immediate, the appropriate means and method by which they are to be performed, and the performance of them.

By the first article the action of the high contracting parties under the Covenant are to be "effected through the instrumentality of a meeting of a body of delegates representing the high contracting parties, of meetings at more frequent intervals of an Executive Council, and of a permanent international secretariat."

This means only that when the high contracting parties wish to take joint action, it is to be taken through such meetings. This does not vest these bodies with power except as it is especially described in the succeeding articles. The unusual phrase "Effected through the instrumentality of meetings" means what it says. It does not confer authority on the Body of

Delegates or the Executive Council, but only designates the way in which the high contracting parties shall, through their representatives, express their joint agreement and take action.

On this head, Lord Robert Cecil, who had much to do with formulating the Covenant, made an illuminating remark in his address following the report by the Committee of the Covenant to the Conference. He said:

> Secondly—We have laid down (and this is the very great principle of the delegates, except in very special cases, and for very special reasons which are set out in the Covenant) that all action must be unanimously agreed to in accordance with the general rule that governs international relations. That this will to some extent, in appearance at any rate, militate against the rapidity of action of the organs of the League is undoubted. In my judgment, that defect is far more than compensated by the confidence that it will inspire that no nation, whether small or great, need fear oppression from the organs of the League.

This interpretation by one of the most distinguished draftsmen of the League shows that all its language, reasonably construed, delegates no power to these bodies to act for the League and its members without their unanimous concurrence unless the words used make such delegation clear.

Senator Knox asserts that, as the recommendation for a reduction of armaments will be made with the consent of our representative on the Council, we shall be in honor bound to accept the limit and bind ourselves. It is difficult to follow this reasoning. The body which is to accept the limitation is the Congress of the United States. Why should the Congress of the United States be bound by a representative selected by the President to represent the United States in this function, in respect to a matter of great importance under the control of Congress?

That the United States should recognize the wisdom of a reduction of armament, under a world plan for it, seems manifest. The history of competitive armaments, with its dreadful sequel, is too fresh in the minds of the peoples of the world for them not to recognize the wisdom of an agreed reduction. If we are to have an agreed reduction, then there must be some limit to which the governments agree to submit. If the nations of Europe, with so many dangerous neighbors, are content to bind themselves to a limitation, why should we hesitate to help this world movement?

There is not the slightest probability that we will wish to exceed the limit proposed. Our national failing has been not to maintain enough armament. . . .

Senator Knox objects to the provision that no treaties made by members of the League shall have effect until after they have been registered in the office of the League. He says this is contrary to the Constitution, because treaties are to take effect when ratified by the Senate and proclaimed by the President.

This objection is not very formidable. All this requires is that the United States shall provide, in every one of its future treaties, that the treaty shall not take effect until it is registered in the Secretariat of the League. Certainly an agreement on the part of the United States and the nation with whom it is making a treaty as to conditions upon which it shall take effect is not in violation of the constitutional requirements to which Senator Knox refers. . . .

Senator Knox criticizes the League because it recognizes the possibility of war and proposes to use war to end war. Certainly there is no means of suppressing lawless violence but by lawful force, and any League which makes no provision for that method, and fails to recognize its validity, would be futile. He points out that the plan of the League is not war-proof, and that war may come in spite of it. Then he describes the kind of league which he would frame, a league which will involve the United States in quite as many wars and in just as great a transfer of its sovereignty as he charges this Covenant with doing.

He proposes to have compulsory arbitration, before an international court, of international differences, including questions of policy. His court would not settle all differences likely to lead to war, for questions of policy are just as likely to produce war as questions which are justiciable. Then he would declare war a crime and punish any nation engaged in it, other than in self-defense, as an international criminal. Would not punishing a nation as a criminal be likely to involve war? The court would have the right to call on powers constituting the league to enforce its decrees and awards by force and economic pressure. It would be difficult to conceive a league more completely transferring sovereignty to an outside body and giving it power to involve us in war than the plan of Senator Knox. It is far more drastic and ambitious, and derogates much more from national control than anything in this league. In contrast with it, the present league is modest.

The supporters of the present covenant do not claim it to be a perfect instrument. It does not profess to abolish war. It only adopts a somewhat crude machinery for making war improbable, and it furnishes a basis for the union of nations by which, if they are so minded, they can protect themselves against the recurrence of the disaster of such a war as that with which Europe has been devastated during the last four years. Experience under the League will doubtless suggest many improvements. But it is the first step that counts. Let us take it now when the whole world is yearning for it.

Note

Address at dinner of Economic Club of New York, March 11, 1919.

45

Paris Covenant Has Teeth

Many misconceptions of the effect of the Covenant of Paris have been set afloat by broadside denunciations of the League based on loose constructions of it entirely unwarranted by the text. The attitude of those who favor the Covenant has been misconstrued, increasing the confusion in the mind of the public in respect to the inestimable value of the instrument as it is. Were the alternatives presented to me of adopting the Covenant exactly as it is, or of postponing the coming of peace and continuing the state of war until the conference could reconvene and make other provisions for peace, I should, without the slightest fear as to the complete safety of my country under its provisions, vote for it as the greatest step in recorded history in the betterment of international relations for the benefit of the people of the world and for the benefit of my country.

I was president of the League to Enforce Peace and continue to be. Our plan was somewhat more ambitious in the method of settling differences peaceably, in that fewer might escape a binding peaceful settlement. The proposed covenant, however, makes provision for peaceful settlement of most differences. Both plans include a definite obligation on the part of all members of the League to use economic power to suppress an outlaw nation by withering world ostracism. Ours also provided for definite contributions of force to an army to be called upon if the boycott failed to effect its purpose. The present covenant does not, in my judgment, impose such a definite obligation on the members of the League, but its theory, doubtless sound, is that their voluntary action in their own interest will lead to the raising of sufficient force without a covenant. The proposed league has real teeth and a bite to it. It furnishes real machinery to organize the power of the peaceful nations of the world and translate it into economic and military action. This, by its very existence and certainty, will keep nations from war, will force them to the acceptance of a peaceable settlement, and will dispense with the necessity for the exercise of economic pressure or force.

Why, then, it is asked, if this is my view, have I animadverted upon the language of the League Covenant and suggested changes? I have done this not because I wished to change the structure of the League, its plan of action or its real character. I have done it for the purpose of removing objections to it created in the minds of conscientious Americans. There are many such anxious for a league of nations, anxious to make this peace permanent, whose fears have been roused by suggested constructions of the Covenant which its language does not justify. These fears can, without any considerable change of language or additions, be removed.

The language of the Covenant is in diplomatic phrases, is verbose and not direct. When, however, we examine the important treaties of history, including those negotiated by our own country, we find that this is characteristic of most of them. They are not drawn with the concise, direct words of a business contract, nor in the clear style of a domestic statute. When reduced to such a style, the Covenant becomes quite clear and presents to me no danger whatever of involving the United States in any obligation or burden which its people would not be, and ought not to be, glad to bear for the preservation of the peace of the world and their own.

Take, for instance, the Monroe Doctrine. The Monroe Doctrine in spirit and effect is a policy of the United States which forbids any non-American nation, by external aggression, by purchase or by intrigue, to acquire the territory in whole or in part, or the governmental power in whole or in part, of any country or nation in this Western Hemisphere. So far as external aggression is concerned, the policy is fully covered by Article X of the Covenant, which would enable the United States to use the whole power of the League, in addition to its own, to preserve the doctrine. So far as the acquisition of such territory or power by purchase or intrigue is concerned, the United States could at once bring the matter before the Body of Delegates, which will include representatives of all the nations of North, South and Central America. Unless the whole Body of Delegates, so constituted, unanimously rejects the Monroe Doctrine, the United States is completely at liberty to proceed to enforce it. Can it be supposed, by the wildest flight of imagination, that such a unanimous report could be obtained from a body including representatives of seventeen or eighteen countries of this Western Hemisphere? Though I have this view, I am entirely willing to see, and will be glad to see, a reservation introduced into the Covenant which shall be more explicit and more satisfying to those whose fears are roused.

From the plan of the Covenant, from the language of Lord Robert Cecil, one of its chief draftsmen, and from the general rules of construction of international agreements, I think that the action of the executive council, unless otherwise expressly provided, must be unanimous. This would necessitate the concurrence of a representative of the United States in such recommendations and other actions as it may, in the course of its duties in the League, have to take. The same is true of the Body of Delegates. But I would be entirely willing to have the rule of unanimity stated expressly; it would clarify a matter which troubles many.

Doubt has been expressed as to the time during which this Covenant is to run. There is now no express limitation. I would be glad to have a definite time limitation, say of ten years, for the League as a whole, and perhaps of five years for the obligation to restrict armament within a limit agreed to by the Congress of the United States. This would relieve many who reasonably fear perpetual obligations. My own view is that, unless this be done, the nations composing the League will construe this to be a covenant from which any one of them may withdraw after reasonable notice. I think it is wiser to give it a definite term than to have it a covenant from which any member may withdraw at will.

I do not mean to say there may not be other changes of a similar character that would aid in relieving unfounded objections. But I am distinctly opposed to a revision of the form of the League so as to change its nature. This is the League which, as amended in the conference, must be adopted unless we are to have an indefinite postponement of peace.

The suggestions of the impossible and radically different leagues which have been put forward as a better solution than the present one will not be particularly relevant or helpful. To provide for amendments and reservations, that do not change the structure of the League and its essence and do satisfy doubting, conscientious Americans in respect to the safety of the United States in the obligations assumed, is a high and important duty of the representatives of the United States in this conference. If they perform it, they will help materially to secure the ratification of the treaty.

Of course the securing of amendments after fourteen nations have fought their way by earnest discussion to an agreement in committee is not free from difficulty. European nations, anxious to have us join the League, will consent to reservations and limitations as to strictly American questions and policies; but it is not the easiest task to draw these in such form as to prevent their having wider effect. The solution of this problem will be facilitated by a consideration and study of the criticisms which are constructively directed to rendering this league unobjectionable. I regret to say that many of the speeches are so far afield and so entirely unwarranted by the present language of the Covenant that they are not helpful.

Note

Article in the *Philadelphia Public Ledger,* March 16, 1919.

imagination. The very object of the League is to prevent war, not to fight little wars, and the clearer the obligation to exert economic pressure and military force against the aggressor, the greater the improbability that wars will come. Instead of being a source of increased expense, the League will greatly reduce expenses to the government of the United States, first, in reducing armaments, and second, in reducing the number of the wars into which it is likely to be drawn.

If the provisions I have mentioned were limited to the members of the League they would lack comprehensiveness in preserving world peace, because it may be some time before two-thirds of the Body of Delegates shall conclude that it is wise to admit to permanent membership in the League countries like Germany, Austria, Turkey or Bulgaria, or countries with no sense of responsibility and so weak in police power and self-restraint as not to be able to perform the covenants of the League. To correct what otherwise would be a defect in the constitution of the League, there is a declaration that the League is interested in war between any countries whether members of the League or not, and will take such action as the peace of the world may require in order to prevent injury from such a war.

The four great steps to secure peace are, first, reduction of armament; second, union against conquest by arms; third, peaceful settlements of differences and a covenant not to begin war until every effort has been made to secure such peaceful settlement, together with a world boycott of the outlaw nation and the exercise of military compulsion, if necessary; and finally, fourth, the inhibition of all secret treaties and an enforcement of open diplomacy. Nothing like it has heretofore been attempted in the history of the world. The problem of German peace has forced it. . . .

We have fourteen nations, seven of them being the nations who won the war with Germany, agreeing through their representatives at Paris upon these steps. The question now is whether the Senate of the United States is to destroy the possibility of this advance in the civilization of the world by its vote against the action of the President and against what I verily believe to be the opinion of the majority of the people of the United States. I would unhesitatingly vote for the Covenant just as it was unanimously reported by the committee of representatives of the fourteen countries engaged in drafting the treaty. I am hopeful, however, that the fears of some, who conscientiously favor the treaty, as to certain possibilities of danger may be removed by more express limitation. The treaty is in process of amendment now and any clarifying amendments should be welcomed in order, if possible, to secure ratification. I believe the President and the Commission have a sense of duty in this regard and that we may look for amendments of this character.

What are the objections to the League? They are, first, that the United States has gotten along so well since the beginning without being drawn into the politics of the outside world that it ought to keep out of them and ought not to involve itself in a league of nations. This opinion, I think we may say, is confined to a small body of persons represented by Senators Borah, Reed and Poindexter. If there are others who take this position in the Senate, their names do not occur to me. All the other members of the Senate who have objected to this covenant have averred that they are in favor of a league of nations to secure peace. If they are, they are in favor of something that binds the United States to some kind of an obligation to help in the preservation of peace. A league of nations means something that binds one nation to another in respect to certain obligations. That is the etymological derivation of the word and that is its actual meaning. If they are therefore in favor of a league of nations, they have, by that fact, admitted the necessity of departing from the traditional policy of the United States to enter into no alliances with foreign nations, because a league is an alliance, and, as a league contains obligations, it must entangle the United States to the extent at least of the performance of those obligations.

We cannot avoid being affected by international quarrels in Europe. It is economical for us to unite with the other countries to maintain peace instead of waiting until we are driven into war and then making a superhuman effort to defend ourselves against a war that has meantime grown into enormous proportions because of our failure, and that of the other nations of the world to suppress it in its inception. . . .

The Executive Council has no power to fix the obligation. It does not determine conclusively for any member of the League any fact upon which the obligation of that member becomes immediate. Its duties are executive in the sense that it acquires all the necessary information, follows closely matters with which the League has to do and takes action in the sense of making a recommendation to the various Powers as to how the difficulties shall be met. It furnishes a means by which the Powers confer together in order that they may agree upon joint action; but in no sense is any power delegated to it to declare war, to wage war, to declare a boycott, to limit armament or to force arbitration.

The only two things which it does, things that can be said in any way to be binding on nations are, first, not to increase the limit of armament to which a nation has agreed to confine itself after full consideration, and, second (where jurisdiction is not taken from it by reference to the Body of Delegates) if it can act unanimously, to make a report of settlement of a difficulty such that if the defendant nation complies with it, the plaintiff nation may not begin war to get more. It may propose measures to the members of the League by which they can carry out its recommendations of settlement, but it does not decide upon those measures and it is left to the members of the League to agree whether they desire to use force to carry out recommendations or not. In every other respect its action is advisory and of a recommending character.

Still less can there be said to be sovereign authority delegated to the Body of Delegates. The Body of Delegates selects the four countries whose representatives are to enter the Executive Council. It elects, by two-thirds vote, new members to the League after they have shown themselves able to fulfill the covenants of the League. It may be substituted as a mediating body and a body to recommend settlement in place of the Executive Council. It may also advise the reconsideration by members of the League of treaties which have become inapplicable to international conditions and which may endanger the peace of the world. This is all.

It is impossible, therefore, for one looking through the Covenant, without a determined purpose to formulate objections to it, to find any transfer of sovereignty to the Executive Council or the Body of Delegates. The whole theory of the Covenant is that the nations are to act together under obligations of the Covenant, that they are to come to an agreement, through these two bodies, but that the action to be taken is to be determined by each nation on its conscience under its agreement, and that when the action is to be taken it is to be taken by that nation in accord with its constitution.

Note

From an address at the Methodist Church in Augusta, Georgia, March 23, 1919.

47

League of Nations Has Not Delayed Peace

The project of the League of Nations has, in the minds of its opponents, to bear the blame for many things. According to their view, if it had not been for the League of Nations, peace would now have been declared and everything would be smooth and easy in the sphere of the late war. It is their view that only the absurd insistence of idealists has postponed the settlement needed to produce normal times. The fact is entirely otherwise. The League of Nations was made the first subject of consideration by the conference because it could be more promptly and easily disposed of than other issues rearing their ugly heads among the Allies. These latter needed earnest and painful consideration in confidential interviews between the representatives of the leading powers. The full facts were not known to the conference and the issues were not ready for open discussion.

The delay in fixing the terms of the League would not have happened but for the need of settling the other questions. One of the most trouble-some of these is the amount of the indemnities which France and Belgium and Italy and England and Serbia should exact from the Central Powers. It is complicated with the question how much the Central Powers can pay.

Each premier has found himself embarrassed by promises to his people as to what the treaty must contain. In this regard, each one has found that his claims, based only on the viewpoint of himself and his countrymen, must be moderated.

Another burning question is that of the boundary of Italy on the Adriatic. Italy insists on having Fiume because the port has probably a majority of Italians in it. But it has always been the port of the Slav dependency of Hungary and it is surrounded by a country with which it has the closest business connection, a country which is overwhelmingly Slav.

It is the normal and appropriate seaport of the projected Jugo-Slav State. Sonnino, the Minister of Foreign Affairs of Italy, is reported to be uncompromising in his demand. Fiume has become a political issue in Italy. Orlando, a man of more judicial and conciliatory mind, is said to be embarrassed by Sonnino. Both are affected by the fact that the Italian elections are near at hand.

Then, as a background to the whole settlement, there is the question of the defense of France against another and sudden attack by Germany. Marshal Foch and the French military strategists see no complete protection unless France, in some way, controls the crossing of the Rhine. A proposal which has received great support in the French papers and which has been urged by France has been the creation of a buffer state called Rhineland. The objection to this is that Rhineland is really German. Its separation from Germany is not within the basis of the armistice. It has never within centuries been French. Its sympathies would all be with Germany. It would create a new Alsace-Lorraine, with the boot on the other leg. It would be a constant source of irritation in Germany and a persistent invitation to a new war by her when opportunity offered.

Lloyd George is seeking to make such a frontier unnecessary by a required limitation on conscription in Germany and an agreed limitation of armament among the Allied Powers. This, of course, would become a part of the machinery of the League of Nations for securing peace.

The question of Hungary, which is now being made prominent by the threat of Bolshevism or its actual appearance at Budapest and in the surrounding country, is also a difficult one. Unscrupulous leaders of Hungarian politics seem to have invited Bolshevism in order to fight a settlement which would limit Hungary to the Magyar country and the

Danubian plains. The Magyars are a masterful race, a race of aristocrats, who have arbitrarily oppressed the Slovaks in mountainous northern Hungary, the Rumanians in Transylvania and indeed the Germans where they have settled within the Hungarian kingdom. As they see their power passing, they have become desperate and war threatens again.

The specter of Bolshevism will not down. To charge this to delay due to seeking an agreement upon the League of Nations is ridiculously opposed to the facts. The outbreak in Hungary only demonstrates the necessity for a strong, firm league. The signing of a treaty which formally restores peace with Germany and Austria-Hungary will not give us peace unless there is guaranty in the power of the united Allies to compel peace. That power will be dissolved unless a league of allies, the nucleus of the League of Nations, shall be established, not only to suppress immediate disorder, but also to settle differences (a great number of which will at once arise between the new governments established and the old ones cut down) and to enforce the settlements peaceably arrived at.

The news that amendments are being considered in the League of Nations and that it is nearly ready for incorporation in the treaty itself demonstrates that it has not interfered at all with reaching terms of peace with Germany. The truth is, a league of nations is necessary to a satisfactory treaty. It helps and speeds it.

Note

Article in the *Philadelphia Public Ledger*, March 29, 1919.

48

"Open Diplomacy" Slow

The fluid conditions in the countries of the Central Powers lead all to press for a speedy peace treaty that shall stabilize them. But this very fluidity adds to the complexity of the problem and delays its solution. The Allies are also embarrassed by the unrest of their troops, who regarded the armistice as the end of the war and wish now to be released and to go home. Yet armies of occupation, and perhaps armies for further campaigns, are necessary. Then, between the seven Powers which fought the war, the peace terms are not easy to agree upon—the treatment Germany is to receive, the amount of indemnity she is to pay, the restrictions, if any, upon her competition in the world trade pending the slow industrial recovery of France and Belgium, the balancing considerations of the heavy indemnity and her opportunity for freedom in trade to enable her to pay it, the defensive frontier of France, the Italian frontier on the Adriatic shore, the boundaries of the new States, the definition of neighborhood rights, the Balkan boundaries, the autonomous units in Asia Minor, the disposition of the German colonies—all involve controversy, some of it of the most acute and irritating character.

We must bear in mind that the conference was delayed by the need to gather together, from fourteen nations from all over the world, men who are to frame the treaty. Special commissions had to be formed to get at the facts. Hearings had to be held for claimants. The British elections kept Lloyd George at home, and during that time made it impossible for him to join in those confidential interviews with other leaders and premiers so necessary in smoothing out difficulties and reaching understandings. While the making of the terms has been in the absence of the defeated powers, the interests of the conferees themselves are often acutely adverse. Then, too, the disinterested attitude of the United States leads its representatives to consider more carefully than those of the conferees seeking purely selfish objects the wisdom of restrictions upon Germany. Too great severity may defeat its own purpose.

The treaty is being negotiated by representatives of popular constituencies and not by kings. Explanation is easier to one man than to a people. Room has to be given for what is called in this country "buncombe." A show of fight must be made on hopeless issues for home consumption. "Open" diplomacy cannot move so swiftly as the old-fashioned kind.

Then, there is a more substantial reason for time in the deliberations: the negotiators must discuss and argue all of the conflicting issues over and over again until each one has deeply impressed on him the real point of view of every other. This often takes the form of heated criticism and even recrimination, apparently most discouraging to a prospect of agreement but necessary to clear the air. Such talk is not waste of time. It is the usual and the only way to reach a compromise.

The armistice in our Spanish war was signed on the 12th of August, 1898, and the treaty of Paris was not signed till December 12, a period of four months. This was in connection with a war which had only begun in the previous April. And it was a peace which involved the settlement of rather simple issues between only two nations.

The period between the armistice and the treaty of peace in the Franco-Prussian War was about the same and there, also, the issues were simple and limited to two countries.

The Congress of Vienna, convened to arrange the map of Europe after the Napoleonic wars, took a year for its deliberations, and the conferees had only kings and emperors to satisfy. We see, therefore, that the delegates

49

Russia, France, Danzig

One may admit that a great mistake was made in not sending large armies to Archangel and Vladivostok to establish an Eastern front in Russia during the war. Had this been done, Bolshevism could have been then repressed and an opportunity for a Russian constituent assembly and popular government could have been secured. But that is past history and the conference at Paris is dealing with present conditions. One of these is the difficulty of maintaining large armies at this juncture to enter upon a military crusade against Bolshevism in Russia. All the Allies hope to do is to prevent its spread into other countries. It will probably burn itself out in Russia because of its unfulfilled and impossible promises.

The issue with France as to proper provisions for her safety is not by any means so clear as these cocksure statesmen and correspondents would have their readers believe. . . .

The razing of fortresses on the German front, the enforced limit of German armament, the restriction upon German conscription, the appropriation of the German navy, the taking over of German guns and the united power of the League of Nations to defend France and restrain Germany will in the long run be far better protection to French territory and independence than what France now seeks at the instance of her military strategists.

The hesitation over Danzig is regarded as another damning proof of a weak yielding to German truculence. Danzig is a German city. The people object to Polish sovereignty. It is the only practical port of access to the sea for Poland. Can it be made a free port for full use by Poland without complete sovereignty? This is being argued in the conference. It is not a question which answers itself. One may differ with the statesmen, correspondents and critics and still not be guilty of basely betraying Poland or truckling to Germany. A similar question is presented, as to Fiume, between the Italians and the Jugo-Slavs.

Note

Article in the *Philadelphia Public Ledger,* April 7, 1919.

50

The Round Robin

The League of Nations is an organization which cannot disclose its advantages in the rapid manner an army or a military expedition can. Its operation is bound to be slow and cumbersome at first. Its influence on its members and on outside nations in avoiding war and promoting justice will grow as the real strength of the uniting and common covenants comes to be clearly perceived. Experience under the League will disclose defects and suggest useful changes to make it more practical and effective. But the agreement upon a covenant providing for reduction and limitation of armament, for union of nations to prevent conquest, for definite postponement of war till after every opportunity for peaceful settlement has been secured, and for spreading international agreements on the table before the world is a series of steps forward toward permanent peace which only "ready made" military correspondents can belittle.

If the cabled information as to the character of the amendments adopted is reliable, we may now confidently hope that the Senators who signed the Round Robin will be able to vote for the League as it is amended without being embarrassed in any degree by their signatures to that document. It will be remembered that they merely said that the Covenant in its then form was unacceptable to them, which of course does not prevent their consistently supporting the Covenant as at present amended. The further statement in the Round Robin was that they thought the peace treaty ought to be adopted at once and that the League should be postponed for further consideration. Of course such a view, which rested on the importance of having peace come at once without delaying it for the sake of framing a league of nations covenant, ceases to apply when the peace treaty has been signed, with the League of Nations Covenant as a part of it, and indeed as an indispensable condition to its effective enforcement. The Round Robin Senators may well say that the second objection is removed, because now to insist upon opposing or amending the League, which is web and woof of the peace treaty submitted to them, is to postpone peace rather than to expedite it.

Note

From an article in the *Philadelphia Public Ledger,* April 12, 1919.

51

Guaranties of Article X

It has been suggested that this Article X is in the interest of Great Britain, that it is designed to preserve the territorial integrity of her far-flung empire through the aid of the United States and other countries. There is no foundation for such a suggestion. Can any one point out in the history of the last fifty years any war against Great Britain by a foreign country to take away territory from her? No; war of that sort is not ordinarily begun against a nation as powerful as Great Britain. Wars are begun as Austria began the war against Serbia, namely, because Serbia was a weak nation and Austria a strong one; and this guaranty is for the benefit of the weaker nations whom it is to our interest to protect against a war of conquest that will ultimately involve the world, as the attack upon Serbia did.

Another objection made to this Article is that if Ireland were to rebel against England and seek to establish herself as an independent republic, England could invite, under this Article X, the other nations of the world to assist her in suppressing the rebellion. This is utterly unfounded, because Article X is only an undertaking to preserve territorial integrity and political independence against external aggression. Nations must take care of their own revolutions, and, if their conduct of government is such that revolutions occur and new nations are established out of old ones, there is nothing in Article X to prevent this happening.

Note

From an address at Kansas City, April 19, 1919.

52

Religious and Racial Freedom

News comes from Paris that the effort of a committee of the Jews to secure, in the constitution of the League, a declaration in favor of religious tolerance and the means of securing it has failed. This is not accurate. There is in the League Covenant a provision that in all countries which are to be governed by a mandatory of the League, the charter, under which the mandatory acts, shall require protection of religious freedom. This provision will apply in Constantinople, in Palestine, in Syria, in Armenia, in Mesopotamia and in the former colonies of Germany in Africa and the Pacific.

The Executive Council may add to such general provisions detailed guaranties and machinery to make the general declaration effective. The mandatories have to render yearly reports of their stewardship, so that violations of such guaranties may be brought before the organs of the League for remedy.

The failure of the application for a general declaration in respect to freedom of religion was doubtless due to the sensitiveness of the British colonies and, indeed, of the United States, toward the attempt of Japan to obtain a declaration in favor of social equality and against racial discrimination in any state of the League. The American representatives probably felt that such a declaration, however neutral in its effect in this country because our Constitution secures the equal protection of the law to all, would be successfully used to defeat the ratification of the League Covenant as part of the treaty. They were therefore obliged to sacrifice the clause securing religious tolerance.

But there still remains an opportunity to achieve every useful and practical end in regard to religious freedom. There exists no danger of pogroms and oppressive laws against the Jews in the United States or Britain or France or Italy. It exists only in certain states like Poland, Romania, the Ukraine and possibly in the Czecho-Slav and Jugo-Slav countries. Of these, Romania is the chief offender. Poland, under Paderewski, also shows obduracy in the matter. All these states are, so to speak, children of the League; they may well be required, as a condition of their national independence and the protection they are to enjoy from the League, to give pledges against racial and religious discrimination in their laws and in favor of complete religious freedom. Means should be retained by the League to enforce the pledges.

Pledges were required by the Congress of Berlin in 1879 from Bulgaria, Serbia and Romania that their fundamental laws would put Jews on an equality with all other citizens and protect them in the exercise of their religion. Bulgaria and Serbia faithfully complied, but Romania deliberately and dishonestly evaded, and dishonored, her solemn obligation. If now she is to receive Transylvania from Hungary by decree of the League, she may well be put under effective bond to give to her Jewish people that freedom and justice which she has faithlessly denied to them for forty years. Poland, too, which was long the only refuge for the oppressed and unhappy children of Israel, should be made, as the price of her restoration to nationality, to issue a new charter of religious liberty and civic equality to her Jewish citizens.

The Jews are not the only denomination who need protection. There are Unitarians and others who, in some of these new states, have suffered for their faith. It will be an important accomplishment if the League uses its power to remove this last vestige of medievalism.

Note

Article in the *Philadelphia Public Ledger,* April 24, 1919.

53

Secret Treaty Provisions That Are at the Root of the Crisis at the Paris Conference

Italian Claims to Fiume would, if granted, sow the seeds of trouble and discontent among the Jugo-Slavs.

The peace treaty with Austria-Hungary is delayed by the controversy over the disposition of the port of Fiume, near the head of the Adriatic. When the war broke out in 1914 the Entente Allies and Germany wooed Italy intensively to induce her to join their respective sides. The obligations of the Triple Alliance had not been made public, but it was understood that Italy was bound to lend her aid to Austria and Germany in case of a defensive war. Italy positively insisted that this was not such a war, and so maintained her neutrality for a time. Then she was induced by promises of the Entente Allies (Great Britain, France and Russia) to declare war on Austria and subsequently on Germany. Her course was criticized as one wholly influenced by greed of territory. The treaty by which she became an ally of France and Great Britain was secret, but enough was known to enable Italy's critics to aver that it was the consummation of a successful bid. Italy's defenders met these attacks by showing that she was entitled under the treaty of the Triple Alliance to be consulted before Austria attacked Serbia, and by revealing the bad faith of Germany and Austria in Italy's war with Turkey and their secret aid to the Sultan. This aroused sympathy with Italy, and it was assumed that the heart cry of the Irredentists for a restoration of Italy's territory everywhere had been satisfied by an agreement that Trentino and Trieste should become hers.

It now appears that the Dalmatian coast was also included in territory promised to Italy. As to Fiume, Italians perhaps form a majority of the inhabitants, but it is, and has been for years, a Croatian city. It is, and has been always, the port by which the solidly Slav population in the country behind the city reach the sea.

Italy seeks to push the principle of self-determination too far. The unit of population in which the majority is to determine the nation's control should include the back country with which the port is united.

Unless some explanation is given, Italy's insistence will tend to revive the charge that greed was her chief motive in this war. Our entrance into the war was accompanied by a declaration in favor of only just restitution of territory and upon the assumption, often stated, that it was not a war of conquest by the Allies. The terms of the armistice followed these lines.

If the facts are correctly stated, the public opinion of the United States and the disinterested world will sustain the President in resisting Italy's determination to take over Fiume and close Croatian access to the sea. The question is one of Italian politics. Italy has taken possession of Fiume with the strong hand of conqueror against the Croatians. Orlando may lose power in the Italian Parliament if he fails to stand by the Italian claim. Sonnino, his colleague at the conference and his associate as premier, is rigid and uncompromising. He would probably resist Orlando if the latter yielded. The situation is therefore acute. But can Italy afford to break, on such an issue, with the conference? One would think not. The President would seem to be clearly right in maintaining that at least Fiume be made a free port for Croatia as Danzig is to be for Poland. If Italy's wish were to prevail, the settlement, with palpable injustice in it, would create a sense of wrong among the Jugo-Slavs that would return to plague Italy when most inconvenient.

Note

Article in the *Philadelphia Public Ledger,* April 25, 1919.

54

Analysis of the League Covenant as Amended

The amendments to the Covenant of the League of Nations adopted in Paris on Monday will bear careful study, and perhaps it is unwise hastily to express a confident opinion. But several readings suggest the following comment:

In the first place, the language and arrangement of the articles have been greatly improved. The use of different terms to mean the same thing, which tended to prevent an easy reading of the document, has been largely corrected. Provisions having immediate relation to one another have been assembled where they belong, avoiding application of them to subjects or countries which they were not intended to affect. Then names, misleading or clumsy, have been changed. The Executive Council, which was and is not executive but advisory, has become the Council. The Body of Delegates has become the Assembly, a much more suitable term.

Second, rules of construction that ought to have obtained in interpreting the original Covenant are now made express and relieve the real doubts of friends and supporters of the League. The most important of these, perhaps, is the privilege specifically reserved to any member of the League to withdraw from it after two years' notice and after a compliance with its obligation under international law and under the League Covenant incurred before withdrawal. This gives any nation an opportunity to test the operation of the League and its usefulness and to avoid undue and unreasonable danger or burden in the future which actual trial may develop. Moreover, taken with the power of amendment which can be effected by a unanimous vote of the nine countries whose representatives compose the Council and by a majority of the members of the League, there is ample opportunity for such a country as the United States to secure a revision of the Covenant and a reexamination of the status of the states composing the League after peace has stabilized conditions and has shown where changes should be made. We are so important a member of an effective world league, and so indispensable to its successful working, because of our impartial position and world power, that an announcement of our purpose to withdraw unless amendments were made would be most persuasive. In this view Mr. Root's suggestion, that it would be well to reexamine treaty provisions made just after the war in the light of the test of five years or more of peace, can be carried out.

The second change of the same character is the provision that, except where otherwise specifically provided, the action of the Council or the Assembly shall be by unanimous vote. The original covenant, properly interpreted, meant this, but it is of great importance to remove objections of those who did not think so. There are some who believe that such required unanimity will make the League ineffective and that a majority would have sufficed. But progress toward complete international cooperation in a new field like this must be gradual, and must, for the present, leave safeguards to nations against abuse of joint power which, experience may show, can be dispensed with later. The required unanimity in the action of the Council is very important in the answer it gives to the claim that under Articles X and XVI the United States may be required to send expeditionary forces into distant parts of the world to defend the integrity and independence of a country with which we have no relation of interest or to suppress remote wars not affecting us. Such expeditions are to be planned and recommended by the Council, and the plan is to be accepted in the discretion of the countries to whom the recommendation is addressed. The plan would certainly mark the limit of the obligation of the nations to whom it is presented. The United States will have a representative on the Council, whose vote must approve the plan before its presentation. Is it likely, then, that the plan will be unreasonable in proposing an undue share of the League's work to the United States? May we not be sure that what is to be done will be apportioned according to the convenience and natural interest of the members of the League, because it must in effect be by mutual agreement?

It is now made clear that under Article VIII the limit of armament for each country, under a general plan of reduction proposed by the Council, is only to be adopted and made binding as a covenant for each member of the League after its full examination and acceptance by that member. Moreover, there is to be a reexamination of the plan and the limits every ten years, and meantime a specific limit may be increased by consent of the Council.

It is now made an express provision that only nations who choose to accept the duty may be made mandatories of the League. This removes another objection that was strongly pressed. We do not have to take charge of Constantinople or Armenia unless we choose to do so.

One important change made by addition is the result of Mr. Root's constructive criticism. Mr. Root thought, and all who supported the plan of the League to Enforce Peace agreed with him, that the provision for arbitration ought to have required arbitration in justiciable issues, and he defined what he thought was clearly within the meaning of that term. By the present Article XIII the members agree to submit to arbitration any dispute which they recognize as suitable for arbitration. The Covenant then declares disputes of the character described by Mr. Root, and, as the writer recollects, in Mr. Root's language, to be suitable for arbitration. Disputes as to interpretations of treaties, as to international law, as to facts upon which its application turns and damages for its breach are all declared to be arbitrable, or, in other words, justiciable. This imposes on members of the League having a dispute the duty of recognizing such disputes to be arbitrable and to submit them to arbitration. Can this duty be enforced under the League? Practically yes. If a nation declines to arbitrate such an issue, it goes to the Council or Assembly, with interested members excluded. Such body will at once recommend arbitration or will refer the issue to an international court of the League, as it may, to determine whether the issue is arbitrable under the obligations of the Covenant and will doubtless follow the judicial advice thus given. As this machinery thus works out indirectly the result sought for in the plan of the League to Enforce Peace, an amendment to substitute a court of the League to take up and decide such questions directly will doubtless approve itself to the nations.

Mr. Root was anxious that, in addition to the declaration in the preamble, there should be practical recognition of international law as a guiding star of the League, its tribunals and its action. In the addition to Article XIII, which we have been discussing, we find such a recognition in the present Article XIV providing for a permanent international court of justice which is competent to hear and determine any dispute of international character submitted to it and to give an advisory opinion upon any dispute or question referred to it by the Council or Assembly.

The provision for mediation and recommendation of settlement in the first report of the Covenant, which met Mr. Root's unqualified approval, has not been changed, except that the unanimity required for an effective recommendation by the Body of Delegates is now made unanimity by countries represented in the Council and a majority of the Assembly, a change which makes for effectiveness. Another important change is the addition of Article XXI, as follows: "Nothing in this covenant shall be deemed to affect the validity of international engagements, such as treaties of arbitration or regional understandings like the Monroe Doctrine, for securing the maintenance of peace."

This meets two of Mr. Root's criticisms in full. First, it removes all doubt that all present arbitration treaties are to stand and bind the parties to them whether members of the League or not, and relieves those who were concerned lest progress toward peace by arbitration already made might be lost.

Second, it not only enables the United States to maintain the Monroe Doctrine, which was all that friends of that doctrine asked, but it recognizes it as a regional understanding for the securing of international peace.

Never before in our history has the world set its approval upon the doctrine as in this Covenant. It is really a great triumph for the supporters of the doctrine. It is not only a reservation in favor of the United States asserting it, but it is an affirmative declaration of its conventional character and of its value in securing international peace.

The exclusion of immigration and tariff and other internal and domestic questions is secured by the following: "If the dispute between the parties is claimed by one of them and is found by the Council to arise out of a matter which by international law is solely within the jurisdiction of that party, the Council shall so report and shall make no recommendation as to its settlement."

If anything is clearly settled in international law, it is that, except where a nation limits its rights by treaty, it may impose whatever condition it chooses upon the admission of persons or things into its territory. Those who express alarm lest the Council should reach a different conclusion, in spite of international law, can hardly be aware how jealous all countries must and will be of their right to determine methods of raising taxes and protect their industries, and how strenuously many of the nations will insist on the right to exclude persons not desirable as permanent residents. Indeed, Japan has not urged, in the conference, the view that immigration was anything but a domestic question, but only pressed for an express recognition of racial equality in the treatment of foreign persons resident in each country. Even this the conference did not deem it wise to grant.

Finally, we come to Article X, by which the members of the League undertake to respect and preserve against external aggression the territorial integrity and political independence of every member. Mr. Root, as the writer understands, strongly favors this article; but he thinks there should be a reexamination of the arrangements made under the influence of the recent war, after conditions have become stabilized by peace, to remedy the possible mistakes made and to avoid too great rigidity. How this can be brought about indirectly through powers of amendment and withdrawal has already been pointed out.

The arguments against Article X which have been most pressed are those directed to showing that under its obligations the United States can be forced into many wars and burdensome expeditions to protect countries in which it has no legitimate interests. This objection will not bear examination. If Germany were to organize another conspiracy against the world, or if she and her old allies, together with Russia, were to organize a militant campaign for Bolshevism against the world, we should wish to do our share in fighting her, and in doing so quickly. If a stronger nation were to attack a weaker nation, a member of the League, our immediate and selfish interest in the matter would be determined by the question whether it would develop into a world war and so drag us in. But we are interested as a member of the family of nations in maintaining international justice in the interest of international peace everywhere, and we should share the responsibility and burden. It was a mixture of all these motives which carried us into this war and we accepted as a slogan the cry: "The world must be made safe for democracy. We make this war to secure the liberty and independence of nations against the doctrine that 'might makes right.'" This is all that Article X proposes. It is an answer to Germany's assertion of her right of conquest. It organizes the powers of the world to maintain the international commandment, "Thou shalt not steal."

To what extent will it involve us in war? Little, if any. In the first place, the universal boycott, first to be applied, will impose upon most nations such a withering isolation and starvation that in most cases it will be effective. In the second place, we will not be drawn into any war in which it will not be reasonable and convenient for us to render efficient aid, because the plan of the Council must be approved by our representative, as already explained.

In the third place, the threat of the universal boycott and the union of overwhelming forces of the members of the League, if need be, will hold every nation from violating Article X and Articles XII, XIII and XV, unless there is a world conspiracy, as in this war, in which case the earlier we get into the war the better.

The warning effect of such a threat from a combination of nations, like those in the League, is shown conclusively in the maintenance of our Monroe Doctrine. The doctrine was announced in 1823. Its declaration was deprecated by American statesmen because it would involve us in continual friction and war. It was directed against most powerful European nations. Yet we have maintained it inviolate without firing a shot or losing a soldier for now near a century. Article X merely extends the same protection to the weaker nations of the world which we gave to the weaker nations of this hemisphere against the greed of non-American nations. If our declaration accomplished this much, how much more can we count upon the effectiveness of the declaration of a powerful world-league of nations as a restraint upon a would-be bully and robber of a small nation!

Note

Article in the *Philadelphia Public Ledger,* April 30, 1919.

55

Correspondence

The following correspondence is published with the consent of President Wilson.

Washington, Tuesday, March 18, 1919

Personal

Dear Mr. Tumulty:

I enclose a memorandum note to the President that is probably superfluous, but may contain a suggestion. Do with the note as you choose—for the next ten days, the situation in Paris will be crucial and critical.

Sincerely yours,
Wm. H. Taft

Hon. Joseph P. Tumulty,
Secretary to the President,
The White House,
Washington, D.C.

* * *

Washington, D.C.,
931 Southern Building,
March 18, 1919

Mr. President:

If you bring back the treaty with the League of Nations in it, make more specific reservation of the Monroe Doctrine, fix a term for duration of the League and the limit of armament, require expressly unanimity of action in Executive Council and Body of Delegates, and add to Article XV a provision that, where the Executive Council of the Body of Delegates finds the difference to grow out of an exclusively domestic policy, it shall recommend no settlement, the ground will be completely cut from under the opponents of the League in the Senate. Addition to Article XV will answer objection as to Japanese immigration as well as tariffs under Article XXI. Reservation of the Monroe Doctrine might be as follows:

Any American State or States may protect the integrity of American territory and the independence of the government whose territory it is, whether a member of the League or not, and may, in the interests of American peace, object to and prevent the further transfer of American territory or sovereignty to any European or non-American power.

Monroe Doctrine reservation alone would probably carry the treaty but others would make it certain.

Wm. H. Taft

Hon. Woodrow Wilson,
President of the United States,
Paris, France

* * *

Augusta, Georgia,
March 19, 1919

My dear Mr. Tumulty:

Gus Karger has telegraphed me that the President will welcome any suggestions, and the sooner the better. I have thought perhaps it might help more if I was somewhat more specific than I was in the memorandum note I sent you yesterday, and I therefore enclose another memorandum for such action as you deem wise.

Sincerely yours,
Wm. H. Taft

Hon. Joseph P. Tumulty,
Secretary to the President,
Washington, D.C.

Augusta, Georgia,
March 19, 1919

Memorandum for the President:
From William H. Taft

Duration of the Covenant

Add to the Preamble the following:

"from the obligations of which any member of the League may withdraw after July 1, 1929, by two years' notice in writing, duly filed with the Secretary General of the League."

Explanation

I have no doubt that the construction put upon the agreement would be what I understand the President has already said it should be, namely that any nation may withdraw from it upon reasonable notice, which perhaps would be a year. I think, however, it might strengthen the Covenant if there was a fixed duration. It would completely remove the objection that it is perpetual in its operation.

Duration of Armament Limit

Add to the first paragraph of Article VIII, the following:

"At the end of every five years, such limits of armament for the several governments shall be reexamined by the Executive Council, and agreed upon by them as in the first instance."

Explanation

The duration of the obligation to limit armament, which now may only be changed by consent of the Executive Council, has come in for criticism. I should think this might be thus avoided, without in any way injuring the Covenant. Perhaps three years is enough, but I should think five years would be better.

Unanimous Action of the Executive Council or Body of Delegates

Insert in Article IV, after the first paragraph, the following:

"Other action taken or recommendations made by the Executive Council or the Body of Delegates shall be by the unanimous vote of the countries represented by the members or delegates, unless otherwise specifically stated."

Explanation

Great objection is made to the power of the Executive Council by a majority of the members and the Body of Delegates to do the things which they are authorized to do in the Covenant. In view of the specific provision that the Executive Council and the Body of Delegates may act by a majority of its members as to their procedure, I feel confident that, except in cases where otherwise provided, both bodies can only act by unanimous vote of the countries represented. If that be the right construction, then there can be no objection to have it specifically stated, and it will remove emphatic objection already made on this ground. It is a complete safeguard against involving the United States primarily in small distant wars to which the United States has no immediate relation, for the reason that the plan for taking care of such a war, to be recommended or advised by the Executive Council, must be approved by a representative of the United States on the Board.

Add to Article X.

a. "A state or states of America, a member or members of the League and competent to fulfill this obligation in respect to American territory or independence, may, in event of the aggression actual or threatened, expressly assume the obligation and relieve the European or non-American members of the League from it until they shall be advised by such American state or states of the need for their aid."

b. "Any such American state or states may protect the integrity of any American territory and the sovereignty of the government whose territory it is, whether a member of the League or not, and may, in the interest of American peace, object to and prevent the further transfer of American territory or sovereignty to any European or non-American power."

Explanation

Objection has been made that, under Article X, European governments would come to America with force and be concerned in matters from which heretofore the United States has excluded them. This is not true, because Spain fought Chile, in Seward's time, without objection from the United States, and so Germany and England instituted a blockade against Venezuela in Roosevelt's time. This fear could be removed, however, by the first of the above paragraphs.

Paragraph (b) is the Monroe Doctrine pure and simple. I forwarded this in my first memorandum.

It will be observed that Article X only covers the integrity and independence of members of the League. There may be some American countries which are not sufficiently responsible to make it wise to invite them into the League. This second paragraph covers them. The expression "European or non-American" is inserted for the purpose of indicating that Great Britain, though it has American dominion, is not to acquire further territory or sovereignty.

Japanese Immigration and Tariffs

Add to Article XV:

"If the difference between the parties shall be found by this Executive Council or the Body of Delegates to be a question which by international law is solely within the domestic jurisdiction and polity of one of the parties, it shall so report and not recommend a settlement of the dispute."

Explanation

Objection is made to Article XV that under its terms the United States would be bound by unanimous recommendation for settlement of a dispute in respect to any issue foreign or domestic; that it therefore might be affected seriously and unjustly by recommendations against the exclusion of Japanese or Chinese, or by recommendations forbidding tariffs on importations. In my judgment, we could rely on the public opinion of the world, evidenced by the Body of Delegates, not to interfere with our domestic legislation and action. Nor do I think that under the League as it is, we covenant to abide by a unanimous recommendation. But if there is a specific exception made in respect to matters completely within the domestic jurisdiction and legislation of a country, the whole criticism is removed. The Republican Senators are trying to stir up anxiety among Republicans, lest this is to be a limitation upon our tariff. The President has already specifically met the objection as to limitation upon the tariff when the fourteen points were under discussion. Nevertheless, in respect to the present language of the Covenant, it would help much to meet and remove objections, and cut the ground under Senatorial obstruction.

Prospect of Ratification

My impression is that if the one article already sent, on the Monroe Doctrine, be inserted in the treaty, sufficient Republicans who signed the Round Robin would probably retreat from their positions and vote for ratification so that it would carry. If the other suggestions were adopted, I feel confident that all but a few who oppose any League at all would be driven to accept them and to stand for the League.

* * *

Telegram

The White House, Washington, D.C.,
March 22, 1919

Hon. William H. Taft:

Have just received following from the President. "Please thankfully acknowledge to Mr. Taft his message and say that I hope it will be very useful."

J. P. Tumulty

* * *

Telegram

Augusta, Georgia,
March 28, 1919

Hon. Joseph P. Tumulty,
White House,
Washington, D.C.

Venture to suggest to President that failure to reserve Monroe Doctrine more specifically, in face of opposition in conference, will give great weight to objection that League as first reported endangers Doctrine. It will seriously embarrass advocates of League. It will certainly lead to Senate amendments embodying Doctrine and other provisions in form less likely to secure subsequent acquiescence of other nations than proper reservation now. Deem some kind of Monroe Doctrine amendment now to Article Ten vital to acceptance of League in this country. I say this with full realization that complications in conference are many and not clearly understood here. A strong and successful stand now will carry the League.

Wm. H. Taft

* * *

The White House, Washington, D.C.,
March 31, 1919

Hon. Wm. H. Taft,
Dayton, Ohio

The President has asked me to thank you for your cablegram about the Monroe Doctrine.

J. P. Tumulty

*   *   *

New York, N. Y.,
April 10, 1919

My dear Mr. Tumulty:

We are very much troubled over the report that the Monroe Doctrine amendment to the Covenant is being opposed by England and Japan. Will you be good enough to send the enclosed to the President? We had a meeting today of the Executive Committee of the League to Enforce Peace, and Dr. Lowell and I, at the instance of the League, will be glad to have this matter presented directly to the President by cable.

Sincerely yours,
Wm. H. Taft

Hon. Joseph P. Tumulty,
Secretary to the President,
The White House,
Washington, D.C.

*   *   *

New York, N.Y.,
April 10, 1919

The President,
Paris

Friends of Covenant are seriously alarmed over report that no amendment will be made more specifically safeguarding Monroe Doctrine. At full meeting of Executive Committee of League to Enforce Peace, with thirty members from eighteen States present, unanimous opinion that, without such amendment, Republican Senators will certainly defeat ratification of treaty because public opinion will sustain them. With such amendment treaty will be promptly ratified.

William H. Taft
A. Lawrence Lowell

*   *   *

The White House,
Washington,
April 14, 1919

Dear Mr. Taft:

I beg to acknowledge the receipt of your note of the tenth instant, and to say that I have transmitted to the President by cable the message enclosed.

Sincerely yours,
J. P. Tumulty,
Secretary to the President

Hon. William H. Taft,
Washington, D.C.

*   *   *

William H. Taft
Washington, D.C.
May 5, 1919

My dear Mr. Tumulty:

I am very much troubled that this conference at Paris was unable to adopt a provision in favor of religious freedom throughout the world. There is no necessity for such a resolution in respect to the allied countries, because there is now religious freedom there. The acute necessity for it is with respect to Poland, Romania, and those other new States carved out of Russia, Austria and Germany. I would like, therefore, to have you transmit to the President, as coming from me, a cable message of the following purport:

"The Jews of the United States are greatly disturbed over reliable reports coming to them of continued abuses of their co-religionists in Poland, Romania and in the new Slav States created under the auspices of the conference. Is it not possible to impose on these States, as a condition of their recognition and membership in the League, the maintenance of religious freedom under their respective governments? What was done in the Berlin Conference of 1879 ought to be possible in the more favorable atmosphere of this conference, with the additional securities of performance that the League will give."

I understand that unless something of this sort is done, there will be a strong movement among the Jews to attack the League and I do not need to tell you that there are men in the Senate who will seize every opportunity of this kind as an instrument to defeat its ratification.

Sincerely yours,
William H. Taft

Hon. Jos. P. Tumulty,
Secretary to the President,
The White House,
Washington, D.C.

*   *   *

The White House,
Washington,
May 6, 1919

My dear Mr. Taft:

Let me acknowledge the receipt of your letter of the fifth of May quoting a message regarding religious freedom which you wish me to transmit to the President. I am doing so today by cable.

Sincerely yours,
J. P. Tumulty,
Secretary to the President

Hon. William H. Taft,
931 Southern Building,
Washington, D.C.